It all began with a young man who worked at a drug store fountain in Virginia. The owner of the store, a doctor by the name of Pepper, had a beautiful daughter and romance soon blossomed. The young soda fountain attendant mixed countless new concoctions for the approval and delight of the winsome lass.

But, alas, not only did Dr. Pepper not share his daughter's enthusiasm for the experiments at his soda fountain, but he had higher aspirations for his daughter's future, and summarily fired her young suitor, hoping it would remove him from the scene. It did. Heeding the advice of Horace Greeley who said "Go West, young man," the thwarted Romeo didn't stop until he reached Texas where he took up his erstwhile soda-fountain activities at the Old Corner Drug Store in Waco.

Along with his undying devotion to the daughter of Dr. Pepper, the young man brought with him his penchant for concocting new fountain flavors, and as he dreamed of the girl-he-left-behind, he continued experimenting with soft drink ingredients. One day he hit on a combination that he thought was the greatest. It quickly became a favorite at the soda fountain, and having learned of the romance that had bloomed in Virginia, customers teasingly dubbed the new drink *Dr. Pepper*.

Fortunately, the idyll of the genius of the soda fountain and the Virginia belle had a happy ending when the young man returned east and finally won her hand.

—from *Dr. Pepper*

WHY DID THEY NAME IT ...?

by Hannah Campbell

ACE BOOKS

A Division of Charter Communications, Inc.
1120 Avenue of the Americas
New York, N.Y. 10036

The following material appeared, in a different form, in *Cosmopolitan* magazine: Chevrolet, Noxzema, Kodak, Murine, Cook's Tour, Arm & Hammer Baking Soda, Shell Oil, Camel Cigarettes, Dixie Cup, Maxwell House Coffee, Greyhound Bus, Ivory Soap, Log Cabin Syrup.

An Ace STAR Book
by arrangement with Fleet Publishing Corporation

Printed in the U.S.A.

For My Family

Contents

Introduction xi
List of Illustrations xiii

FOOD

General Foods 3
   Post Toasties 3
   Birds Eye 5
   Sanka 9
   Yuban 10
   Minute Tapioca 11
   Jell-O 12
   Log Cabin Syrup 13
   Baker's Chocolate 14
   Maxwell House Coffee 15

General Mills 16
   Bisquick 18
   Betty Crocker 19
   Wheaties 20
   Brown 'n Serve Rolls 21

Potato Chip 22
Pretzel 23
Chewing Gum 25
Dubble Bubble Gum 30
Life Savers 32
Cream of Wheat 35

Quaker Oats 37
Aunt Jemima 40
Morton Salt 42
Heinz 57 Varieties 48
A & P 51
Borden Milk and Elsie the Cow 55
Coca-Cola 63
Dr Pepper 65
Arm & Hammer Baking Soda 66
Lea & Perrins Worcestershire Sauce 68

WHISKEY

Bourbon 76
Old Smuggler Scotch 82
Cutty Sark Scotch 84
I. W. Harper 84
White Horse Scotch 85
Drambuie 86
Benedictine 88
Four Roses 89

CIGARETTES

Camels, Prince Albert 100
Old Gold, Kent, Between the Acts 102
Pall Mall, Lucky Strike 107
Chesterfield 112
Philip Morris 114

HOME REMEDIES

Smith Brothers Cough Drops 119
Noxzema 120
Vaseline Petroleum Jelly 121
Murine 124
Dr. Scholl's Foot Aids 125
Vick's Vaporub 130
20 Mule Team Borax 133

COSMETICS

Avon Products 141
Cutex 144
Prince Matchabelli 146
Charles Nestle and the "Permanent" Wave 149
Ivory Soap 154
Gillete Safety Razor 156
Burma-Shave 159

TRANSPORTATION

Ford 167
Rambler 172
Greyhound 174
Chevrolet 175
Phillips 66 175
Cook's Tour 177
Shell Oil Company 178

POTPOURRI

Community Plate 183
Kodak 188
MGM and Leo the Lion 193
Dixie Cups 195
Talon Zipper 200
Scotch Tape 205

Introduction

A few years ago as I was watching television with my family, someone casually inquired, during a commercial, "Why did they name it *Chevrolet*?"

My father told us that "Chevrolet" was the name of a famous French automobile racing driver, Louis Chevrolet, and that the car was named for him. A discussion of the origin of other familiar brand names followed and Dad entertained us with quite a repertoire of amusing anecdotes and stories about how well-known brand names came into being. I was working for *Cosmopolitan* magazine at the time and he suggested that its readers might also be interested in such lore. My editors promptly concurred and the WHY DID THEY NAME IT . . . column soon appeared as a monthly featurette in *Cosmopolitan*.

The column was confined pretty much to the actual brand name itself but in the course of my research I discovered many wonderful stories about the founders and inventors behind the products— such men of ingenuity, courage and foresight as Gail Borden, King C. Gillette, Clarence Birdseye, and Prince Matchabelli—to name only a few. In addition, I learned about such diverse things as the truly fantastic invention of the zipper; the debut of the All-American potato chip; the fact that the well-loved pretzel boasts an ancient (and authentic) coat-of-arms; and that there really is such a person as Dr. Scholl.

This book is a collection of the stories I have found most interesting—whether about the brand name itself, the product or the man who launched it. There are, of course, many, many others. I regret I could not include them all.

H. C.

List of Illustrations

FOLLOWING PAGE 16:

An early Jello advertisement.

Portrait which became Baker's Chocolate trademark.

One of the earliest Baker's Chocolate advertisements.

One of the Wells Fargo express wagons that hauled Dr Pepper syrup.

An early Heinz pickle-processing factory.

New York City's first electric sign which advertised Heinz' 57 Varieties.

A Gold Medal Flour advertisement.

Soprano Lillian Norton Nordica endorsing Coca-Cola.

The original Log Cabin Syrup container.

The first cardboard Life Savers package.

FOLLOWING PAGE 80:

Delivering Post Toasties soon after their introduction.

An early Minute Tapioca factory.

Coat of Arms of the Viennese pretzel bakers.

The original Morton Salt Girl.

Tavern sign for the White Horse Inn.

Henry McKenna whiskey bottles—1855-1962.

A Lucky Strike advertisement.

The announcement of a color change in the Lucky Strike
package.

Johnny Roventini, whose call became synonymous with Philip
Morris cigarettes.

An advertisement for Star Chewing Tobacco.

FOLLOWING PAGE 112:

One of the Chesterfield advertisements that encouraged "nice
girls" to smoke.

An advertisement that announced Camels cigarettes.

Old Joe, the prototype of the Camels illustration.

The original Ivory Soap package.

An early crew of Ivory Soap salesmen.

One of the first containers for Smith Brothers Cough Drops.

Preparing to distribute Dr. Scholl's products.

Dr. Scholl.

The Charles Nestle permanent waving process.

The first Gillette safety razor.

A package of safety razor blades showing King C. Gillette, the inventor.

Prince Matchabelli.

FOLLOWING PAGE 176:

An early Rambler car and road sign.

An advertisement for 1923 Chevrolet models.

A 1904 Ford advertisement.

An early refinement of the first zipper.

A detailed drawing of the early zipper.

One of the drawings which warned against use of the public drinking cup.

An early railroad Dixie Cup dispenser.

The first "pretty girl" advertising, introduced by Community Plate.

FOOD

General Foods

POST TOASTIES

Until the 19th century, nine out of ten persons in America spent all of their working lives producing and marketing food. This left little time and energy for the production of other goods. Only the very wealthy enjoyed anything but the simplest necessities. Today, only one adult in five is engaged in producing, processing and distributing food. Modern farming methods and new ways of processing and preserving food have left millions of people free to do other kinds of work. Yet food is America's biggest business. The job of providing the American people with the varied diet to which they have grown accustomed requires the facilities of more than 50,000 food processing companies.

Many of these food processors are giant organizations with research facilities that take all the guess-work out of marketing new products. It was not always so. Take for example the experience of C. W. Post who, in 1904, came out with a brand of corn flakes which he overzealously called *Elijah's Manna*. It brought down the wrath of ministers who denounced him from their pulpits for calling upon Elijah and his raven to sell corn flakes, and the British government even went so far as to refuse to register the trademark. The sorely beset Post quickly rechristened *Elijah's Manna* "Post Toasties."

Post had previously spent nine months at "The San," Dr. Kellogg's famous sanitarium in Battle Creek, Michigan. He was suffering from a vague, indefinable illness, and Dr. Kellogg had confined him to a wheelchair. Finally, discouraged and uncured, Post rose from his wheelchair, embraced Christian Science, and proceeded to establish his own institution nearby. He offered to promote a new cereal coffee Dr. Kellogg had concocted, and, miffed when Kellogg refused his services, he ground one of his own which he marketed as a "health food" in 1895 under the name *Postum Cereal Food Coffee*. It was first sold on the streets of Battle Creek in paper bags peddled from a hand cart.

Dr. Kellogg must have rued the day he hadn't thrown in his cereal coffee lot with his former patient, because *Postum* was an instant success and sales reached a quarter of a million dollars the first year. Two years later, Post introduced one of the first ready-to-eat cold cereals. It was made of wheat and malted barley and baked in the form of bread sticks. He called the new cereal *Grape-Nuts*. Though it contained neither grapes nor nuts, he believed that grape-sugar was formed during the baking operation, and the cereal did have a nutty flavor. Like *Postum*, it too was originally sold as a "health food" and in each package he included a copy of his pamphlet, "The Road to Wellville."

From the little white barn in Battle Creek where C. W. Post set up operations in 1895, grew the tremendous organization we know today as General Foods, a giant consolidation of food processors. It was C. W. Post who took the lead in bringing about the huge combine when he merged his own firm with that of *Jell-O* in 1925, retaining the Postum Cereal Company name. The company continued to expand and absorb other companies and products, and in 1929 it changed its name to General Foods Corporation to reflect the diversified nature of its business.

Today, the General Foods Corporation employs 28,000 people, shares ownership with 74,000 stockholders, and markets hundreds of products under 30 major brand names. Some of those earlier brand names—*Jell-O, Minute Tapioca, Walter Baker Chocolate, Log Cabin Syrup, Maxwell House Coffee, Sanka, Birds Eye, Yuban* —are products with a history.

BIRDS EYE

Clarence "Bob" Birdseye, the Father of Frozen Food, was often heard to remark that the credit for quick-freezing should go to the Eskimos, who had been using it for centuries. And we know that in 1626 Francis Bacon was mulling over the idea of preserving flesh by freezing one snowy day as he rode from London to High-gate. Deciding to test his theory then and there, Bacon stopped at a cottage and bought a fowl, killed it and stuffed the carcass with snow. The poor man recorded that the experiment was a success, but he died shortly thereafter from the exposure he had suffered during it. Whoever his predecessors were, however, it was Birdseye who first succeeded in the practical freezing of food on a commercial scale. His discovery of suspended animation through quick-freezing was sold for one of the largest sums—22 million dollars—ever paid for a single process at that time.

Famed as a Yankee from Gloucester, Bob (no one who knew him ever called him Clarence) was actually born in Brooklyn. He had little formal training in technology, yet he was granted more than a hundred patents. In addition to being an inventor, he was also a scientist, an explorer, and an out-and-out adventurer. From his boyhood he sought the unusual, the challenging, the dangerous. Spurning the conventional ways of earning money for an education, Bob trapped black rats and sold them to Columbia University, and frogs which he sold to the Bronx Zoo. One summer vacation was spent hunting birds and mammals in Arizona and New Mexico, and two others in Montana, studying spotted fever and collecting ticks. Never content with only one project underway, he also bought bobcat and coyote skins from Indian traders and sold them at a considerable profit. A 75-mile trap line in Michigan to experiment with ways to trap timber wolves was another side-line.

After several perilous years spent with pack horse and wagon outfits in the deserts of the Southwest where his life was often in jeopardy, Bob went to Labrador when he was 26 years old to sail on the famous hospital ship of Sir Wilfred Grenfell. Deciding to remain in Labrador, he turned to fur trading and embarked on a venture that took him 10,000 miles which he traveled with his own prize team of huge huskies. The trek netted him $6,000, but nearly cost him his life when he narrowly escaped death from freezing.

Romance lured him back to the States in 1915 long enough to marry Miss Eleanor Gannett in Washington, D.C., and then a year later, wife and infant child in tow, he returned to Labrador where he resumed his fur trading and trapping activities. As usual, he took on several other projects at the same time. In addition to conducting a fish and wildlife survey for the United States government, he also bought a schooner and became a professional fisherman.

During the long sojourn in Labrador, Bob and his young family subsisted mainly on fish and local game. The only fresh vegetables were those occasionally brought in by ship. These were greatly treasured, and in order to make them last as long as possible, Bob would put such delicacies as cabbages in a barrel with sea water and then, as they froze, add more water, and then more cabbages, until the barrel was full. In the sub-zero temperature they froze quickly. For months afterward when the Birdseyes wanted fresh cabbage on their menu, Bob would simply go outside, hack one out of the barrel, and let it thaw.

He developed an avid interest in the possibility of preserving food by freezing and discovered that fish and caribou meat frozen in the dry Arctic air were still tender and fresh-flavored when thawed and cooked months later. He knew that the mere freezing of food, as in cold storage, would not preserve its natural flavor and texture, and he concluded that it was due to the rapid freezing in the extremely low temperatures of the Arctic that the meat remained tender and tasty. Convinced that he had unlocked one of Nature's secrets, he returned to the States in 1917 to continue his experiments. When he finally perfected a process for quick-freezing that could be applied commercially he received a patent and in 1923 launched *Birdseye Seafoods, Inc.* on White Street in New York City. For the first time in history, fresh fish could be shipped anywhere, in any weather, without the use of either ice or preservatives.

Quick-freezing is a natural process of preservation. It does not destroy nutrients, as does high heat or radiation; it merely suspends bacterial action. Its secret lies in the fact that the faster a food can be frozen—a rapid reduction in temperature in contrast to the slow freezing of "cold storage" (which damages physical and chemical structure in the freezing process)—the less chance there is of the formation of large ice crystals which tear down the cell walls, let out the natural juices and injure the texture of the food. In quick-freezing, only very tiny ice crystals are formed, which do not injure the food in any way.

But educating the public to these facts was not an easy task, and the investment in equipment and the expense involved in production proved too much; Birdseye's pioneering little company went bankrupt.

Bob remained passionately devoted to his idea, however, and being a "most articulate and persuasive man" soon managed to secure the substantial financial backing that enabled him to open a new company *General Seafoods* in a two-story building on Fort Wharf in Gloucester, Massachusetts. Birdseye's primary concern at this point was research, and though thousands of pounds of frozen fish were packed and sold each year, it was mostly to get consumer reaction. The first floor of the building was devoted to the laboratory and it was in this period that Birdseye developed what is perhaps his best-known mechanical contribution to the frozen food industry: the belt freezer.

Experiments were not limited to fish alone. All kinds of edibles were included. An associate of Birdseye's reminisced: "Bob would eat *anything*. Trawlers would bring in all sorts of unusual catches to the wharf—small whales, sharks, porpoises—once even an alligator—and Bob would freeze and try them all."

Birdseye saw the future of *General Seafoods* in terms of its continued development of patented procedures, methods and equipment which would in turn be licensed for use by frozen-food packing companies. Early licensing efforts were not successful, however, and it was in 1929 that what was then known as the Postum Company together with the Goldman-Sachs Trading Corporation, acquired Birdseye's patents and trademarks for $22,000,-000. Later, the newly named General Foods Corporation took over the entire operation and Birdseye's company became a division of General Foods. His personal share of the sale amounted to almost a million dollars, and in addition, he was made head of the General Foods laboratory in Gloucester.

General Foods retained the *Birds Eye* trademark which is, of course, derived from the Birdseye name. But few people know that the two-word spelling as it appears in the trademark was the original family spelling. The origin of his surname was one of Bob Birdseye's favorite stories. An ancestor of his had been page-in-waiting to an English queen in the days when a person was identified by his accomplishments, some characteristic of his appearance or behavior, or the work he did. It was the duty of Bob's ancestral page-in-waiting to accompany the queen on her hunting trips. One day a hawk circled menacingly overhead and then dived toward the queen. The page shot the hawk through the eye with an arrow, and was thereafter called "Bird's eye" by the grateful queen.

Although quick-frozen foods were packed and sold experimentally by Birdseye's original companies, it took the vast resources of General Foods, its extensive marketing and research organization, to overcome the public's widespread aversion to "cold storage" foods, and launch the modern frozen food industry we know today.

Many leaders in the food industry had early labeled frozen foods "a passing fad," and one famous New York restaurant chain even attached a card to its menu which read:

No frozen food deception here. Your doctor will tell you frozen foods can't give you all the fresh food vitamins.

Shortly thereafter, the American Medical Association publicly announced the inclusion of frozen fruits and vegetables in its list of accepted foods and a shame-faced swank restaurant chain retracted its denouncement with apologies to the industry.

Even though the convenience of frozen foods was early recognized and accepted by restaurants, their use was kept a carefully guarded—and publicly denied—secret. One frozen-food executive, having dinner one evening in a very fine restaurant in Chicago, thought the peas he had been served were a frozen-food product, and questioned the waiter. "Oh no," the waiter hastily assured him, "we never use frozen foods!" But the executive was persistent and further investigation proved him right. The peas, as well as other items on the menu, were frozen. The executive was delighted, and before he left he had convinced the owner of the restaurant that instead of trying to conceal the fact, he should take pride in, and publicize, the progressive thinking behind his use of frozen food.

Resistance came from other quarters too. Butchers wailed that individual frozen meat cuts would take away their livelihood (a cry that has greeted almost every innovation in any field), but actually, quick-frozen meats took meat merchandising out of the cracker-barrel stage and placed it on a par with packaged foods.

Public interest gradually grew in *Birds Eye* frozen foods, although progress was at times slow and discouraging. For several years sizable losses were suffered, but General Foods shared Birdseye's faith in ultimate success, and today it is the world's leading frozen food organization.

As for Bob Birdseye, he saw the industry firmly established after he had provided the idea and the initial impetus, and then characteristically turned his interest and energy to other things. He was a truly great inventor, a many-sided genius whose other achievements were overshadowed by his success in freezing. Even as he had continued to experiment on his frozen food concept in a home laboratory, he carried on work with the United States Housing Administration, in mineral water bottling, and with the United States Fisheries Association. He received several patents for his dehydration of foods process, and an option of $120,000 from one investor alone. He perfected and sold outright a unique and very successful spot light for store window displays, and a harpoon for marking whales which is still in use today.

A contributing cause of his death was an assignment he had been given by a paper company to develop paper out of agave, a Peruvian plant, and it was in Peru that he suffered a heart attack attributed to the high altitudes. He came back to New York City, to his home in Gramercy Square, where he died in October, 1956. He was one of the few men to become a legend in his own lifetime—explorer, scientist, inventor, businessman, adventurer—and individualist.

SANKA

The millions of *Sanka* fans owe their decaffeinated coffee beverage to Dr. Ludwig Roselius—and luck.

Dr. Roselius, head of a large European coffee business, had for years searched for a way to remove caffein from coffee without harming the coffee's flavor and aroma. Then, in 1903, a shipload of coffee consigned to him was deluged with sea water during a storm in passage. Since the cargo was unfit for commercial sale, Dr. Roselius turned it over to his researchers for experimentation purposes.

One important discovery emerged—sea-washed coffee beans reacted differently from the normal coffee beans previously tested. This suggested a new approach to the problem of taking the caffein out of coffee, and a new series of experiments began, from which emerged the forerunner of the process in use today which removes 97% of the caffein without injuring the delicate coffee flavor.

Dr. Roselius named the new product *Sanka*—a contraction of the French phrase *sans caffeine*.

YUBAN COFFEE

At the turn of the century, John Arbuckle a well-known coffee merchant of Brooklyn and a connoisseur of fine coffee, had become quite famous as "Mr. Coffee."

At Christmas time it was Mr. Arbuckle's custom to serve his own special blend of coffee at a dinner party for his friends. The blend was available nowhere else except at the Arbuckle table, or as a gift from Mr. Coffee himself.

Arbuckle referred to the annual holiday dinner as his "Yule-tide Banquet," and the coffee he served was known as *Yu Ban*. This sentimental version of the brand name was shattered only a few years ago when a former employee of Arbuckle Brothers made the following explanation of the origin of *Yuban*: on green coffee shipments, the bags containing the beans for Mr. Arbuckle's special blend were marked

$$A \quad B$$
$$N \quad Y$$

(for Arbuckle Brothers, New York). When a brand name was to be chosen, an effort was made to form a word out of the letters on the bags. Combinations like Bany and Naby were discarded as not euphonious. Yban looked a bit strange, until someone suggested adding the letter "u" to it—and there it was. The fine, round sound of *Yuban*.

MINUTE TAPIOCA

Back in 1894, a sailor was recuperating in the convalescent home of a Boston friend, Susan Stavers. One evening Susan served a tapioca pudding. It was coarse, lumpy, chunky. The sailor looked suspiciously at the pudding and slowly took a bite.

"Is it all right?" Susan asked anxiously.

"I've eaten better," replied the less-than-tactful young man.

Mrs. Stavers was inordinately proud of her reputation as a cook and snapped, "Oh, you have!"

"Aye, ma'am, that I have. This pudding's too lumpy."

"Indeed," said Susan icily. "And I suppose you could make a tapioca pudding without lumps?"

"Why, sure," grinned the sailor. "All you have to do is grind up the tapioca. Run it through your coffee grinder, why don't you?"

Not one to bear grudges, Susan promptly took the young man's advice. She poured tapioca into her coffee grinder, gave it a few turns, and it came out fine and smooth. The pudding she made with it was a sensation not only with the "gourmet" sailor boy, but with her other boarders as well. Word of the delights of her tapioca pudding spread, and, enterprising soul that she was, Susan ground up a sizable quantity of tapioca, packed it in paper bags, and sold it throughout the community.

John Whitman, owner of a newspaper called the *Enterprise & Journal*, heard about Mrs. Stavers' tapioca process. He bought the rights to it and organized the Whitman Grocery Company to sell the new dessert. He bought the tapioca in flake form and ran it through a store-size coffee grinder. At first he called it *Tapioca Superlative* but a year or so later changed the name to *Minute Tapioca* in honor of the famed Minute Men of Revolutionary days, and adopted the picture of the Minute Man as the now well-known trademark.

Although the business was founded on the simple idea of grinding flake tapioca, the manufacturing process has since been changed entirely. Tapioca flour is obtained from the root of the cassava plant, found in Java and South America, and is a staple food source throughout the tropical world. The imported flour, almost as fine as face powder, is partly pre-cooked by highly developed machinery before packaging, and tapioca pudding now requires only a minimum of effort to be served in the home. It has long since taken its place in the line-up of America's favorite desserts.

JELL-O

Jell-O, today's largest selling prepared dessert, had a somewhat less than auspicious beginning. In fact, it seemed for several years it might not begin at all.

Peter Cooper, inventor of the famous locomotive "Tom Thumb" and patron of the arts and sciences, obtained the first patent for a gelatin dessert in 1845. Gelatin itself, however, was discovered long before then. History's first reference to it is in 1682, when a Frenchman named Denis Papin recorded his research on the subject. His experiments resulted in a method of removing the glutinous material from animal bones by boiling. It has no taste, no odor, and, when combined with liquid, no color, but it *is* pure protein. The gourmet-minded French like their foods *en gelee*—and their word for it is *gelatine*. The preferred spelling is without that final *e*, whether you're referring to flavored or unflavored gelata.

Peter Cooper did nothing about his patent for a gelatin dessert, and neither did anyone else until fifty years later when Pearl B. Wait, a cough medicine manufacturer in LeRoy, New York, became bored with the cough medicine business and looked around for a new field. How he happened on Cooper's invention is not known, but in 1897 he started production on an adaptation of Cooper's gelatin dessert. The intriguing name, *Jell-O*, was coined by Wait's wife, Mary, and unfortunately her inspiration for one of the most outstanding brand names in history is unknown.

There is ample opportunity for speculation, of course. It has been suggested that the dessert reminded Mary of jelly, and O was then a popular ending for new food products, as *ine* was one for medical ones (such as *Vaseline*, etc.). Another possibility is that the gelatin dessert had to *jell* before it was ready to eat, and still another good guess is that it was inspired by the similar sound of the main ingredient, gelatin, and maybe Mary didn't know gelatin is spelled with a *g* instead of a *j*.

Inspired as the name was, *Jell-O* didn't set any sales records, and Wait sold the business for $450 two years later to a neighbor, orator Francis Woodward, who had just founded a company for the manufacture of a cereal beverage which he called *Grain-O*. The first year Woodward didn't do any better than Wait had with the new gelatin dessert. In fact, one day as he walked through the plant with his superintendent, A. S. Nico, they stopped in front of a storage section piled high with unsold cases of *Jell-O*. Woodward stood glumly, sourly regarding them. Suddenly, his face brightening, he turned to his companion: "Nico," he said, with a sweeping gesture, "I'll sell you the whole *Jell-O* business for $35." Nico smiled. "No, thanks," he said. "Thanks a lot but no thanks."

Shortly thereafter, Woodward had cause to rejoice, and Nico to weep, because at the turn of the century the long neglected dessert suddenly caught on with the public and made up for lost time. In 1902 sales shot up to $250,000, and four years later soared to just under the million dollar mark. *Grain-O* was dropped altogether, and the facilities of the company devoted entirely to the manufacture of *Jell-O*. Its progress since has been unimpeded, and it is today one of the best known and most popular food products.

LOG CABIN SYRUP

Ever since pioneer days, table syrups have played a very prominent role in satisfying America's sweet tooth.

Our grandfathers contented themselves with syrup made from corn or with molasses made from sugar cane. They bought these syrups from their neighborhood grocer who ladled it out to them from a huge wooden barrel. But there was one man who wasn't satisfied with the taste of the syrup, or with the haphazard, unsanitary way in which it was being sold. He was P. J. Towle, a grocer who lived in St. Paul, Minnesota.

Few people were aware of the delicious flavor of syrup made from the sap of maple trees in our northern forests. Mr. Towle felt sure everyone would prefer it to all others if only it could be made available to them. But the supply of maple syrup was limited, and its cost high. Could he make maple syrup and still keep its price within the customers' means? Towle began experimenting by blending syrup from inexpensive sugar cane with that made from the best Vermont and Canadian maple sugars. Finally, in 1887, he produced the product he sought—an inexpensive blended syrup with maple flavor.

His formula perfected, Towle turned to the problem of marketing it. First, he must have a sealed container for the syrup to insure its cleanliness and purity; and secondly, a name to identify and distinguish it, a name that would inspire public confidence. He thought of his boyhood hero, Abraham Lincoln, but quickly discarded the idea of using the former president's name. Then he hit upon a happy solution: why not name the syrup *Log Cabin* (words that had become practically synonymous with Lincoln) and make the container in the shape of a log cabin?

Towle's flair for showmanship paid off. The tin cabin became as familiar on the American scene as Sunday morning flapjacks. The World War II metal shortage forced the company to substitute glass bottles as containers, but the *Log Cabin* image was by then established in the public mind. Today Towle's brain child remains the most popular blended syrup on the market.

BAKER'S CHOCOLATE

A dozen years before the signing of the Declaration of Independence, and almost a quarter of a century before George Washington became the first president of the United States, a small plant on the banks of the historic Neponset River in Dorchester, Massachusetts, was milling chocolate under the brand name of *Baker's*.

The *Baker* story began in the fall of 1764, when Dr. James Baker befriended a young Irish immigrant named John Hannon. A chocolate maker by trade, Hannon complained that there was no chocolate mill in the New World. The doctor decided to help young Hannon. He leased a mill on the banks of the Neponset River, obtained a run of mill stones and a set of kettles, and supplied the necessary capital.

The new industry prospered, and as early as 1777 John Hannon was advertising his product with a money-back satisfaction guarantee. Then, in 1779, misfortune struck. Hannon started off for the West Indies to buy cocoa beans, but never reached his destination. He was presumed lost at sea, but his actual fate remains a mystery. Dr. Baker continued the business and it was his grandson, Walter Baker, who, in 1824, gave the company the name by which it has since been known.

In keeping with the company's historical background, Walter Baker chose a trademark rich in romance. The origin of *La Belle Chocolatiere* dates back to 1745, when a young Austrian nobleman, Prince Ditrichstein, ventured into one of Vienna's chocolate shops to try the newly discovered beverage from the tropics. A far more important discovery for him was Anna Baltauf, a waitress at the chocolate shop and daughter of an impoverished knight. The prince fell in love with her and later that year they were married.

As a wedding gift, the prince had his bride's portrait drawn in pastel by Jean-Etienne Liotard, a famous Swiss portrait painter. Liotard posed her in the chocolate server's dress she wore the day she met her husband-to-be. Today, the original *La Belle Chocolatiere* hangs in the Dresden Gallery in Germany. It is one of the world's best known portraits and trademarks.

Once a small grist mill operated by a handful of early settlers, the Walter Baker plant today is one of the "Big 3" in a 500 million dollar chocolate industry, satisfying a universal taste for America's favorite flavor.

MAXWELL HOUSE COFFEE

In 1873 Joel Cheek was a traveling salesman with a wholesale grocery firm. Though he sold a variety of grocery products, coffee held a greater interest for him than any of the others from the very beginning. While on the road he often thought about trying his hand at developing his own blend of coffee. He was sure he could improve on the blends he sold if he could only stay put long enough to make a few experiments.

Several years later he got his wish. Promoted to a partnership in the business, he was able to settle down in Nashville. At first he limited his experiments to his spare time, but gradually they demanded more and more of his working day. Finally he realized he had to make a decision beeween his job and his studies. In 1882 he quit the partnership and, after more years of experiments, found the blend of coffee that had fired his imagination.

One of the South's finest hotels at this time was the Maxwell House in Nashville. Its guests included presidents, generals, musicians, diplomats and European nobility. Joel Cheek went to this hotel one day and proudly offered them the new blend of coffee. The management decided to try it and within weeks the guests in the magnificent dining room were talking about the marvelous new coffee. "This Maxwell House coffee, sir," they said, "is superb!"

The famous slogan was born years later when Theodore Roosevelt was an honored guest at the Hermitage in Nashville, the old home of Andrew Jackson. The hostess asked him if he would have another cup of *Maxwell House* coffee. "Will I have another?" he exclaimed. "Delighted! It's good to the last drop!"

When these spontaneous words of the president were adopted as the *Maxwell House* coffee slogan, thousands of wags all over the country immediately wanted to know, "What's wrong with the last drop?" A heated controversy flared over the usage of the word *to* and was only resolved when a well-known professor of English at Columbia University ruled that *to* in this instance was accepted good usage, and included "the last drop."

* * *

General Mills

The history of milling is a story of man's efforts to feed himself. Archaeologists have unearthed milling tools dating back 70,000 years, and very primitive cultivation was practiced in many parts of the eastern hemisphere as early as 10,000 or 15,000 years before the Christian era.

The earliest civilizations of Mesopotamia and Egypt were possible only because the human race learned to cultivate grain as a means of providing food from one harvest season until the next and could abandon its incessant wandering in search of food.

The first attempts at milling were crude: a handful of wild grain

JELL-O

America's
Most Famous Dessert

Jell-O is the dainty dessert that can be made in a minute. It does not require a cook to make it, for there is no cooking to be done. It is made by dissolving the contents of a package of

JELL-O

in a pint of boiling water.

If fruit is to be added to the dessert, you push a little in here and there, to suit yourself. Fruited Jell-O desserts are exquisite.

There are seven Jell-O flavors: Strawberry, Raspberry, Lemon, Orange, Cherry, Peach, Chocolate.

Ten Cents Each, at all Grocers'.

Send to your address and we will send the splendid recipe book, "Dainties of the World," with its beautiful pictures in six colors and gold.

THE GENESEE PURE FOOD CO.
Le Roy, N. Y., and Bridgeburg, Can.

Jell-O was once offered for sale as a business for $35—but there were no takers. Later, at the turn of the century it caught on and is today the largest selling prepared dessert.

The model for "La Belle Chocolatiere" was Anna Baltauf, a waitress at a chocolate shop in Vienna. When she wed an Austrian prince, he had her portrait painted by Jean Etienne Liotard in the dress she had worn when he first saw her. Above: One of the earliest Baker ads.

Dr Pepper flavoring syrup was shipped in 50-gallon wooden barrels at the turn of the century. Wells Fargo express wagons shown above were used to haul the syrup from the original plant in Waco, Texas, which is still in use today.

Opposite page: Women shown processing pickles—one of the products for which Heinz became most famous.

In 1900, New York City's first electric sign—six stories high and ablaze with 1,200 lights—advertised the "57 Varieties."

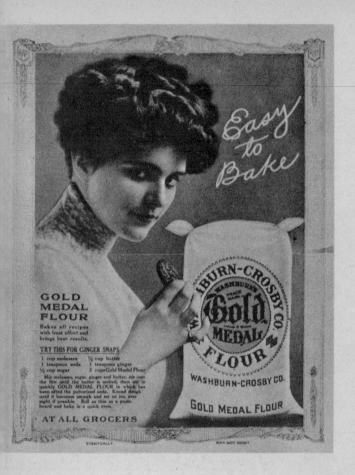

The Washburn-Crosby Company (later absorbed by General Mills) had three entries in the Millers' International Exhibition in 1880, and for each they won an award—gold, silver and bronze medals. To their top grade flour they gave the name it had earned: GOLD MEDAL. Its slogan, "Eventually. Why not now?" became almost as famous as the flour itself.

Early Coca-Cola ads pictured well-known personalities of the era including the famous American soprano, Lillian Norton Nordica (shown above).

The original container for Log Cabin Syrup which was used from 1887 until World War II. Life Savers were introduced in a cardboard package which was quickly discontinued because the mints absorbed the flavor of the glue.

crushed against a flat rock and the bits of hull picked out with the fingers.

Early Egyptians crushed or pounded their grains between stones and with the aid of air currents (wind or fanning)—and later, with the aid of sieves—were able to remove a large part of the chaff and bran. They made from this refined product a relatively white bread which only the rich were privileged to eat.

The arts of both milling and bread-making were markedly improved in the Roman era. From mortar and pestle grinding they progressed to the use of circular mills or querns, slaves or prisoners being used to turn the upper stone about the lower stone. Gradually, large flattened millstones took the place of the circular querns and continued in general use in Europe and this country until about 1870.

Although the use of water power, and later steam power for the turning of the millstones had greatly increased the capacity of flour manufacture, the actual grinding process had changed but little over many centuries.

With the discovery of the steam engine and the harnessing of electric power, however, the first major breakthrough came with the introduction of the steel roller mill which finally replaced the age-old millstone. Roller-crushing made possible a gradual breaking of the grains which released more of the floury kernel unmixed with fine bran and germ. With this process, a very high grade of flour could be produced. Another improvement of great importance was the middling purifier (middling being the medium-sized particles of grain used in the finest flour) which enabled the miller not only to separate the highest grade of middlings from cracked wheat, but also to separate other grades especially suitable for different uses of flour.

These new procedures revolutionized the milling of flour, and today's milling process is a highly complex and efficient operation but the fundamental concept is the same: to provide man with his daily bread.

It might be said that what the steel roller mill did for the grinding of wheat, James F. Bell did for the milling industry. In 1928 while many other American industries had merged—pooling resources, plants and marketing facilities—the small miller still battled his problems as a lone operator, his success or failure determined largely by the whim of the local wheat crop.

As president of the Washburn Crosby Company (whose popular *Gold Medal* flour had been so named from its award of the gold medal in 1880 at the Millers' International Exhibition), miller James Bell sat back and took a long, hard look at the situation. He did not like what he saw. In addition to the unpredictability of wheat crops, he saw glaring inconsistencies among millers in their pricing, shipping and marketing practices which became apparent at the consumer level and proved a detriment to the entire industry.

Against the backdrop of this somewhat dismal picture, Bell presented to the Washburn Crosby board of directors his idea for a solution: a merger of reputable millers, located in strategic wheat-growing and wheat-consuming areas across the country, into a single organization. The idea met with enthusiastic approval and *General Mills* was formed, with Washburn Crosby Company the first to sign. A year later, 1929, the design was complete. Twenty-seven operating companies had been integrated into the new giant that had, in less than a year, become the largest miller in the world.

From the companies absorbed in the *General Mills* organization, and from its own vast program of research and development made possible by the merger, have come many of the ideas and names we take for granted—including the nation's first prepared mix, *Bisquick; Gold Medal Flour; Betty Crocker; Wheaties;* and *Brown 'N Serve Rolls.*

BISQUICK

In 1930, Carl Smith, a sales executive of the Sperry Division of *General Mills,* went into the dining car of a train well past the dinner hour. He had little hope of getting a decent, hot meal at the late hour, but he had boarded the train without having had his dinner and he was hungry enough to take the chance.

Much to his surprise, within minutes he was served a palatable meal, along with a plate of piping hot biscuits! Tentatively, he sampled one of the biscuits. It was delicious.

After the meal, he went into the galley to compliment the chef and to ask him how, at such a late hour, he had been able to produce delicious hot biscuits in a matter of minutes. Pleased at the compliment, the chef smiled broadly. For just such emergencies, he explained, he always kept blended lard, flour, baking powder and salt in the ice chest. Then, when an order came in, he could serve piping hot biscuits in five minutes with no measuring, mixing or sifting necessary.

It was a unique idea and an especially challenging one for a miller. Smith was intrigued and turned the idea over to the research division. The problem was to blend a mixture of flour and shortening that would not go rancid on the grocer's shelves.

The answer turned out to be a little known fat called sesame oil and imported from Italy. It had a peculiar affinity for flour and kept its sweetness intact under most circumstances. It has since been replaced by newer discoveries, but it led to the nation's first prepared mix, *Bisquick,* introduced in 1931.

The name was coined by *General Mills* president D. D. Davis.

BETTY CROCKER

To publicize *Gold Medal* flour, after it became a *General Mills* product a picture puzzle ad was run in a national magazine. When solved, the puzzle was a village scene depicting customers carrying sacks of *Gold Medal* flour out to their trucks. The prize for working the puzzle was a pin cushion in the form of a miniature *Gold Medal* flour sack.

The response half-buried the office force. More than 30,000 people sent in the completed puzzle. Extra personnel was hired to untangle the heaps of mail and a corner of the mill was commandeered for working space.

Unexpectedly, along with the puzzle solution hundreds of women also included chatty little questions:

> *"How do you make a one-crust cherry pie?"*
> *"What's a good recipe for apple dumplings?"*
> *"How long do you knead bread dough?"*

The advertising staff was bewildered but it rose to the occasion. Recipes from laboratory personnel and home economists (and from office personnel and their wives) were collected and each letter received a personal reply:

In answer to your inquiry about a one-crust cherry pie, I suggest you try . . .

Sincerely,

"Sincerely," who? Somehow the letter needed a woman's signature. The Advertising Department again rose to the occasion and came up with a surname: Crocker—the name of the popular secretary-director of the company who had recently retired. Now all they needed was a first name, something cozy and familiar-sounding, like—Betty.

In answer to your inquiry about a one-crust cherry pie, I suggest you try . . .

Sincerely,
Betty Crocker

Today, forty-eight women help maintain the *Betty Crocker* tradition. Five specially trained correspondents answer her personal mail—four to five thousand letters a month—and twenty-three highly trained home economists operate her five kitchens, constantly testing products and creating new recipes.

Betty Crocker's files have grown to include more than 8,000 recipes, and her name appears on over fifty *General Mills* products. The *Betty Crocker* kitchens receive as many as 1,200 guests in a single month, visitors from every state in the Union and many foreign countries.

Betty Crocker is known to almost every woman in the United States—and is truly America's First Lady of Food.

WHEATIES

In 1921 a Minneapolis health clinician devoutly fed bran to his overweight patients every morning. Bran, he eulogized over and over, was a fine bulk food, a perfect "regulator of the digestive tract." It was also, as he served it, an unappetizing gruel.

One morning, perhaps as the patients grumbled about the "fine bulk food," he stirred his potion a little too vigorously and a few drops spattered out on the hot stove. Thin wafers formed and were easily scraped off the stove in flakes. He sampled one as he stirred. It was crisp and tasty. He spattered more gruel onto the stove, and continued sampling as he stirred.

He told James Bell (of the Washburn Crosby Company) about his discovery, and Bell went to work on it. But the bran concoction didn't live up to its promise. Its flat discs, when tumbled about in a package, crumbled to a powder. However, the idea of a flake continued to intrigue the company's head miller, and on a hunch, he decided to try wheat instead of bran. He gathered 36 different varieties of wheat and one of them clicked. The Board of Directors trooped to the mill, sampled the creation, and gave their enthusiastic approbation.

The name was selected as the result of a company contest won by Jane Bausman, the wife of one of the company executives. There was, reasoned Jane, nothing quite so endearing as a nickname —take Theodore Roosevelt, for example, affectionately known as "Teddy," or moving pictures, known universally as "the movies" —so she nicknamed the new wheat flakes *Wheaties*—and America had a new cereal on its breakfast table.

BROWN 'N SERVE ROLLS

Joe Gregor was a small town baker in Avon Park, Florida, who also served as a member of the Volunteer Fire Department. One morning the alarm sounded when his rolls were only half baked. Hurriedly he removed the rolls from the oven and rushed off to the fire station. His civic duty duly performed, Joe returned to his bakery, and the half-baked rolls. He started to throw them out, but instead, "just for the heck of it," slid them back into the oven. The rest is history. The rolls browned in a matter of minutes and were delicious.

An alert *General Mills* salesman heard about the partial baking incident and *General Mills* subsequently perfected the process. When it was thoroughly tested and proved, the company presented it to the baking industry as an act of good will.

*   *   *

POTATO CHIP

The potato chip, the All-American vegetable, was first introduced at a smart spa spot at Saratoga Springs, New York. The year was 1853, and the place was the swank Moon Lake Lodge. One of the guests had recently returned from Paris where French fried potatoes were being served in slimmer versions than in America. The guest sent word to the chef, an Indian chief named George Crum, to cut the potatoes thinner. The Chief reluctantly complied.

Again the word came back: "Thinner!"

Chef Chief Crum served up another batch. Again came back the command:

"Thinner!"

This was more than the badgered chef could tolerate. He sharpened a knife to a razor-like edge, seized a potato and sliced it into paper-thin slices. Then another and another. He plunged the slices into a kettle of boiling fat, quickly dipped them out, frenziedly sprinkled salt on them and marched stoically, albeit triumphantly, into the dining room where, with a flourish, he set the curled and brown potato slices before the startled guest.

The new potato dish was an immediate and sensational success. Moon Lodge capitalized on the Indian chief's creation and featured it on their menu as "Saratoga Chips."

For many years potato chips were called "Saratoga Chips" and it was under that name the following recipe appeared in the White House cook book in 1887:

Peel good-sized potatoes and slice them as evenly as possible. Drop them into ice water. Put a few at a time into a towel, and shake to dry the moisture out of them. Drop them into a kettle of boiling lard. Stir occasionally, and when light brown take them out with a skimmer, and they will be crisp and not greasy. Sprinkle salt over them while hot.

The recipe was simple—in print—but it was decades before the Saratoga Chip came out of the kitchen and saw the light of the market. Potato "chipping" by kettle was a tedious task, and potato peeling was (as it still is) at the bottom of America's favorite hobby list.

It was in the mid-20's that the chip got its first big break—the mechanical potato peeling machine. Enterprising small-business men were quick to see the possibilities and America started to nibble, a practice that has increased yearly. Last year Americans consumed approximately 600 million pounds of potatoes in the form of chips. This is an average of over four pounds per capita, and the industry employs over 25,000 people to keep up with potato-chip-nibbling Americans.

It is not surprising that no one has ever been heard to suggest that we give the potato chip back to the Indians.

PRETZEL

The noble pretzel has its own coat of arms, and a distinguished history. Bakers have been making long, thin rolls of dough into the shape of a pretzel for over fifteen centuries.

Most pretzel historians agree that the delicious twisted oddity was the creation of an Italian monk who gave them to children as a reward for learning prayers. This legend is supported by the Middle Latin translation of *pretiola* which means, "small gift," and by *bracciatello,* meaning "little arms," because the shape of the pretzel suggests a child's arms folded in prayer. *Pretzel* could have easily derived from either of these words, *bracciatello* becoming *bretzel* when it crossed the Alps into Germany, and finally, *pretzel*.

From numerous references in art and literature we know that the pretzel was widely known and liked in the Middle Ages, and it was at the end of that period that the pretzel bakers played a great part in defending Vienna against the Turks, and thereby won for their product a permanent place in heraldry.

Early in the sixteenth century when the Turkish invaders swept into Europe it seemed the whole continent might fall before them.

However, they were stopped at the wall of Vienna in 1510 and although they held the city under long siege, they could not break through its strong defenses. When attack after attack failed, the Turks decided to dig tunnels under the wall, and to avoid detection, they did their digging at night.

But they reckoned without the Viennese pretzel bakers who also did their work at night. From their cellar bakeries they heard the Turks digging and it was the pretzel bakers who spread the alarm and led the assault that turned the enemy back from the underground maneuver. Discouraged, the Turks lifted the siege and all Europe heaved a mighty sigh of relief. The pretzel bakers were honored for their part in the victory with a coat of arms displaying a pretzel, which is still the pretzel bakers' emblem today.

The original pretzels were soft, and the hard form we know today was the result of an accident. A young apprentice baker who had been left to tend the oven fell asleep, and the pretzels were baked to a hard crisp. The irate master baker scolded the unfortunate young man, angrily biting off a piece of the overbaked pretzel he clutched in his hand. To his surprise, he discovered that not only had the flavor been improved by the prolonged baking, but the crunchy texture was a delight in itself. He took the hard pretzels home to his family and they were an instant success. An added advantage was that with nearly all the moisture baked out of them, the pretzels stayed fresh for a much longer time.

The American pretzel, too, has an illustrious ancestry because it came to this country with the earliest colonizers. There is a written reference to pretzels in 1652, in Albany, New York, where a complaint was filed against Jòchem Wessels and his wife, Gertrude, for selling pretzels to Indians. The complaint was not, as would be supposed, against the act of *selling* pretzels to Indians but rather that the baker used his *best* flour for the pretzels, and an inferior grade for the bread he made for the settlers. "The heathen were eating flour while the Christians were eating bran."

Although pretzels were made in home kitchens and small bakeries in many parts of this country, commercial pretzel making had its start in America in the late 1850's in the village of Lititz, Pennsylvania. There, in return for the kind treatment he had received, a traveler gave a recipe for hard pretzels to a baker named Rauch, who in turn gave it to his apprentice, Julius Sturgis. In

1861 Sturgis opened the first commercial pretzel bakery in America. The building still stands in Lititz and in 1961, on the occasion of the industry's centennial celebration, a plaque was mounted on the building, and the year designated as the "Pretzelennial."

Pretzel-making has come a long way since Julius Sturgis opened his modest little bakery in 1861. Today it is a big, nationwide industry, producing over 300 million pounds of pretzels a year—and the demand is constantly increasing.

CHEWING GUM

The person actually responsible for the chewing gum industry is General Antonio Lopez de Santa Anna, the Mexican commander who participated in the War of 1836 against Sam Houston in the Battle of Jacinto. General Houston took the Mexican commander prisoner and Santa Anna was one of the few not executed for his war crimes. Houston himself claimed the safety of the little scoundrel was necessary to insure peace between Mexico and Texas.

At any rate, Santa Anna entered the United States and came to New York. He brought with him a large chunk of chicle, the dried sap of a Mexican jungle tree (sapodilla) which the Aztec Indians used for chewing purposes. Accounts vary as to the exact purpose Santa Anna had in mind in bringing the chicle with him (at the sacrifice of some of his personal belongings, some chewing historians claim). One account states Santa Anna hoped to interest some "Yankee inventor" in it as a substitute for rubber. Others say he just plain liked to chew the stuff. In any event he did meet a genuine Yankee inventor in the person of Thomas Adams of Jersey City. Santa Anna induced Adams to experiment with the chicle as a rubber substitute. The experiments were a total failure and after weeks of futile effort, Adams gave up, and discovered that Santa Anna in the meantime had been granted political amnesty and had returned to Mexico, leaving his Yankee inventor friend to pay expenses and the warehouse bills for storing the chicle.

In the course of his conversations with Santa Anna, Adams noticed that the diminutive General occasionally took a small pinch of chicle from his pocket and chewed it with a great deal of gusto. Adams' own son, Horatio, had also enjoyed chewing the chicle. One afternoon in a Hoboken drugstore Adams saw the druggist sell a piece of paraffin to a little girl, paraffin and spruce being about the only such items available in that day. It reminded Adams of Santa Anna's "chewing" and also Horatio's enjoyment of the exercise. Adams asked the druggist if he'd like a better cud to sell and the druggist assured him he would, and agreed paraffin wasn't really a very good chew.

At home Adams and Horatio went to work on Santa Anna's chicle. (Horatio died in 1956 at the age of 102, although this may be entirely irrelevant to his gum chewing habit.) Father and son mixed the chicle with hot water until it was about the consistency of putty. They rubbed, kneaded and finally rolled it into a couple of hundred little balls, which they presented to the amiable druggist. A day or so later the druggist reported the chews were selling well at a penny apiece.

Adams invested $55 in more chicle (which some say he went directly to his friend Santa Anna for, and others insist he simply ordered from Mexico). He rented a Jersey City factory loft and went to work. The gum was tasteless and was put up in boxes which bore the legend: *Adams' New York Gum—Snapping and Stretching*.

Another Adams son, Thomas, Jr., a traveling salesman, took the gum west as far as Mississippi, and by the time he returned home, orders were flowing in in spite of puritanical outcries of "Vice!" Snuff habituates and pro-tobacco pluggers dismissed it as "sissy." Parents outlawed it, in vain of course, and schoolteachers condemned it bitterly as unfair competition in the class room.

In a more scientific vein, rumors spread that it was really made of horses' hooves and glue. Indigestion was not the worst thing that would result, "they" prophesied gloomily, if a piece were accidentally swallowed. It could cause appendecitis at best and make the intestines "stick together" at worst. Anyone knew "stuck-together" intestines would result in certain death. There must have been hundreds of children who believed their lives were spared in some miraculous fashion as they sat patiently waiting for the Grim Reaper to arrive after swallowing their wad, only to discover he wasn't coming after all. As late as 1932 Nikola Tesla, the electrical genius, solemnly warned: "By exhaustion of the salivary glands, it puts many a foolish victim in the grave!" On the other hand, five years ago, Dr. James H. Doggart told the American Medical Association convention that Jack Dempsey had so strengthened his jaw by his gum-chewing habit that when Georges Carpentier hit him in 1921, Carpentier's thumb was broken instead of Dempsey's jaw, and that was why Dempsey won the fight.

With *Adams' New York Gum—Snapping and Stretching* a success, Adams now turned his efforts toward putting some taste into the stuff. He first tried sassafras, and next licorice. He called the licorice flavor *Black Jack,* and it is the oldest flavored gum on the market today.

The field was by this time becoming crowded; everyone was getting into the act. In 1875, John Colgan, a Louisville druggist, hit the jackpot of popularity when he tried adding aromatic balsam. He called his product "Toulo-flavored Gum." It prospered until 1880 when peppermint flavor was first introduced.

Druggist Edward E. Beeman owed his inspiration to his bookkeeper, Nellie Horton, who suggested he combine a pepsin compound, which he manufactured, with the chicle. Beeman successfully blended the two and chose the picture of a pig for the wrapper. His idea was to convey to the customer that if he chewed Beeman's gum he could eat like a pig.

In spite of the pig on the wrapper, the gum sold well; so well in fact that banker George Worthington from Cleveland offered his services to Beeman in a refinancing and reorganization capacity. Beeman gratefully accepted and Worthington's first act was to get rid of the pig on the wrapper and substitute Beeman's bearded face instead. To Beeman's delight he suddenly found himself a celebrity. He died in 1906, but his picture remained on the product until a few years ago.

Revolution came in the chicle world with the advent of William J. White, a lowly popcorn salesman. The neighborhood grocer received by mistake a barrel of chicle instead of the barrel of nuts he had ordered, and gave it to White to experiment with. White answered inquiries of curious neighbors with the retort: "It's bread. Petrified bread. Found in a baker's oven in the ruins of Pompeii!" White made the discovery that corn syrup blended beautifully with chicle; and he therefore simply put the desired flavor in the corn syrup and blended it with the chicle. Simple. But it made William J. White a millionaire, and in due course, the favored escort of the famous beauty, Anna Held, who publicly chewed gum, and to whom White presented a $120,000 necklace of matched pearls.

White chose peppermint flavor, and the brand name *Yucatan*, inspired by the Yucatan peninsula from whence came much of the chicle of the day. Its success was so tremendous that the *Toulo* companies promptly collapsed. Even today, half of the gum sold is peppermint flavored.

Profits soared and the social-climbing White got himself elected a congressman, built a 52-room mansion and then a large steam yacht which he sailed to England. There, he wangled an invitation to be included in a group who were to be presented to King Edward VII. White startled His Majesty as he had never been startled before by sloughing off protocol and handing the King a box of *Yucatan* chewing gum, along with his best sales pitch. Reminding himself that White *was* an American congressman, the shaken King accepted the gum but firmly declined to chew "right now." It is said King Edward was so unnerved by the episode that he excused himself and cancelled the rest of his appointments for the day.

The elated White, however, cabled American newspapers of the King's "gracious acceptance" of the gum, and the resulting publicity was sensational, and a balm to White's social consciousness since he had been shunned by members of the "upper crust."

Up until World War II the basic ingredient used in most standard brands of chewing gum was chicle. Grown in such jungle areas as Mexico, Central and South America and the Amazon Valley, it is gathered by natives, called *chicleros*, from deep in the jungle and brought to a central camp. The sapodilla tree from which the sap (chicle) comes grows wild and has to be about 70 years old before it can be tapped, and then only once every five years. The syrup flows only during the daylight hours. During the war, because of submarine warfare, Japanese occupation and the lack of shipping facilities, chicle became very difficult to obtain, and most of the gum produced went to the armed forces. It was considered an emergency ration and was also distributed to relieve tension and nervousness and dry throats on long marches. It was even used to patch jeep tires, gas tanks, life rafts and parts of planes. To overcome the chicle shortage, the gum industry spent fortunes in research and came up with synthetic gum bases and plastic resins, similar to tree saps, that could be successfully substituted for chicle and other gums. They found the synthetics easier to control, of uniform quality and perfectly harmless if swallowed. After the war, very few manufacturers went back to the use of chicle, and natural gums continue to be used less and less.

The gum we chew today is mostly *polyvinyl acetate*, a synthetic plastic, supplied almost entirely by Hercules Powder Company—primarily explosive manufacturers. Until recently the chewing gum industry has been rather cagey about publicizing its use of synthetic gum bases because it feels there's more romance in the sap of a jungle tree, gathered by *chicleroes* deep in the mysterious jungle than in a scientist's sterile test tube in an immaculate laboratory.

The growth of the chewing gum industry has resulted in a sideline employment that few people know about: the gum-removal business. Theatres, hotels, churches, restaurants and the like contract for the services of professional gum-removers in much the same manner as they do for exterminators, etc., and many such places have their own full-time "gummers." The New York Central, for instance, has one man whose job it is to service Grand Central Station. He removes a wad totalling seven pounds daily and the weight doubles on a holiday week-end. The late Fiorello LaGuardia publicly chastised the gum industry for the cost of removing gum from the subways. Eager to appease, and cooperate, the larger companies immediately printed on the wrapper of each stick of gum: *Save this Wrapper for Disposal After Use.* It is believed that these are the most publicized—and the most ignored—instructions in the world.

Why do people chew gum? (An average of 168 sticks per person at a total cost of $300 million a year.) For three reasons, say the psychologists. First, to relieve feelings of loneliness and boredom; second, to relieve tension, and third, to provide an outlet for anger and irritation.

And then there are those who just like it.

DUBBLE BUBBLE GUM

For almost 35 years Frank H. Fleer Corporation has been making the largest-selling penny confectionery item in the world—"bubble gum." The company itself, however, is more than a century old, having been in the same family since 1849, when it was founded by Otto Holstein, father-in-law-to-be of Frank Fleer, as a flavor business.

Frank Henry Fleer organized the present corporation in the 1880's and began making gum about 1885. Although he disliked the idea of selling his product in penny vending machines, in a weak moment he one day agreed to an experiment suggested by a never-say-die vending machine salesman. It was the salesman's argument that so great a sales gimmick were the vending machines that people would actually drop a penny in them for nothing. It seemed an excellent way to get rid of the persistent salesman so Mr. Fleer agreed he would buy several machines if the salesman could prove his statement.

The experiment was to be conducted at the old Flatiron Building in New York which was noted for the strong gusts of wind that blew around it unceasingly. It was a popular gathering place for sight-seers and the salesman set up a vending machine at this point, with printed instructions to "drop a penny in the slot and listen to the wind blow."

The salesman got Fleer's order because literally hundreds of people dropped pennies in the slot and continued to do so until the police finally caught on and had the machine hauled away.

An early form of bubble gum was made in the early 1900's by Frank Fleer, which he originally called *Blibber-Blubber* but it was too sticky and did not hold together. In addition, it had a "wet" bubble that usually burst, and stuck to junior's face so stubbornly that only hard scrubbing could remove it. In the meantime, Frank's brother Henry was experimenting with a form of candy coated chicle pellets. Much encouraged with results one day, Henry dashed into Frank's office brandishing a sample of the pellets and exclaimed: "Look, Frank—these little *chiclets* are coming along just fine!"

"That's it," cried Frank. "That's what we'll call them—*Chiclets*!"

Chiclets (later sold to the American Chicle Co.) were an instantaneous success and *Blibber Blubber* was abandoned (to junior's regret and mommy's delight) and did not reappear again until 1928 when Fleer introduced a strong, hardy bubble gum with good surface tension and snap-back. It was dubbed *Dubble Bubble Gum*. *Dubble Bubble* had a "dry" bubble—and wonderful elasticity because of the use of harmless rubberlike tree sap. What's more, it made huge, perfect bubbles. Specifically developed to bring pleasure to children, it was a sensational success and spread over the country like wild-fire. It was the first product of its kind to be nationally recognized as a quality product, and it still dominates the market today, by far the largest selling brand in the world.

Surprising to many people is the fact that chewing bubble gum is prescribed by many dentists for problem gum conditions and before surgery because they feel it is beneficial in strengthening gums and jaw muscles. It has also been used in speech clinics as therapy in building up and exercising mouth and jaw muscles.

Dubble Bubble's fame is world-wide today. GIs introduced *Dubble Bubble* gum to the Eskimos during World War II and the Eskimos now prefer it to their previous favorite—whale blubber. Headhunters in Borneo once kidnapped a diplomatic official and held him for ransom. The price? Quantities of *Dubble Bubble* gum. In darkest Africa two oxen and half a herd of sheep will purchase a wife—but so will a quantity of *Dubble Bubble Gum!* Bubble gum is a great good-will builder with children everywhere in the world.

There are no patents on bubble gum, but each manufacturer has his own carefully guarded secret formula—usually developed and improved over the years by constant testing and experimentation in company laboratories. Last year the Frank H. Fleer Corporation produced over a billion pieces which went to every corner of the globe—including Africa, Japan, Borneo, Alaska, and Pitcairn Island. Laid end to end, that's enough gum to make a belt around the Equator.

Most of this was consumed by bubble gum "connoisseurs" ranging from three to fourteen years. However, many adults chew it too because they find it a better "chew" than regular gum, and they enjoy the flavor—or so they say.

LIFE SAVERS

Edward John Noble was an energetic and ambitious young advertising salesman in 1913 when he happened to see his first package of *Life Savers* in a New York candy store. He was so impressed with the taste, the shape, and the name of the mints, that he went to see the manufacturer, Clarence A. Crane, in Cleveland, Ohio. His purpose was to sell Mr. Crane on the idea of letting him advertise the mints.

"If you'd spend some money advertising," Noble told Crane, "you could pyramid your sales into a fortune."

Unfortunately for Mr. Crane, he was not interested. "My business is chocolates," he said. "The mint idea was just something to fill in during the summer when chocolate sales fall off."

Crane had developed the mints and had them made by a pharmaceutical manufacturer who produced them on his pill machine. The round shape with the hole in the middle was chosen by Crane because he wanted something "different," something that would attract attention. Realizing that the white-circle mints suggested a life saver, and that the public would associate the mint with the name, Crane called them *Life Savers*. He had a label made showing a salty old seaman throwing a life preserver to a young lady swimmer with the copy: "Crane's Peppermint Life Savers—5¢—For That Stormy Breath." The package was about the size of a 12-gauge shotgun shell with slip-on paper caps at both ends.

Ed Noble persisted in trying to sell Crane on the idea of promoting the mints until finally the candy manufacturer asked the question that changed the entire future of the young advertising salesman. "If you think they're so great, why don't you buy the rights and make them yourself?"

Somewhat stunned, Noble managed to gasp, "How much?"

"Five thousand dollars," replied Crane, arbitrarily.

To a young man of Noble's resources the sum might just as well have been five million, but he went back to New York and talked over the idea with a boyhood friend, J. Roy Allen. His enthusiasm was contagious, and together the young men managed to raise $3,800. (The boyhood friend contributed $1,500, and 13 years later sold out for $3,300,000.) For reasons of his own, Crane agreed to lower his price to $2,900, leaving the young entrepreneurs $900 for working capital.

The new partners quickly discovered that the repeat business of $50 a day mentioned in the sale did not materialize. Instead they found there were already hundreds of thousands of rolls on customers' shelves that had gone stale. Disappointment turned to near panic when they found that because of the old-fashioned cardboard package the mints were packed in, they not only quickly lost their flavor, but absorbed the odor of the glued cardboard as well.

Ed Noble's enthusiasm for *Life Savers* had been based on one of those implausible accidents that seem to have been the starting point of more than one fortune: the original package that he bought was only one week old and the flavor was still intact.

Obviously, if they were to salvage their investment, *Life Savers* must have a different package, and quickly. Noble decided to use tin foil to wrap the mints in, with a band label, thereby sealing in the flavor and eliminating the taste of the glue odor. The wrapping had to be done by hand, and Noble developed considerable skill in the operation himself. He could wrap mints faster and better than any of his employees—the employees being six girls whom he paid a weekly salary of $5 each. He met his "payroll" out of the salary he received from his advertising job which he held onto until the *Life Savers* were firmly launched.

Armed with a supply of the bright new packages of fresh mints, Ed set out to sell Crane's former customers—and again met with disappointment. The merchants would not take a chance on adding more of the mints to those already gathering dust on their shelves. The best they would offer was to exchange their stale *Life Savers* for fresh ones.

To the new enterprise, such an exchange would have spelled financial disaster. The only thing to do was to find new customers —fast. Ed called on cigar stores, barber shops, restaurants, and drugstores, persuading each to take a few boxes. The first break came when he talked several saloon owners into putting the five-cent mints on the counter in competition with the free cloves which they provided for their imbibing customers. The mints were a novelty, and they sold.

Later, recalling this phase of the fledgling business, Noble said: "I think those saloon keepers just felt sorry for me. I looked pretty much like a kid in those days, and they thought I was in over my head—which I was!"

The second big break came when he wangled an interview with the head of United Cigar Stores, with the result that *Life Savers* were sold in that organization's 1,200 stores. They were the first item other than smokers' supplies to be carried by United Cigars. Ed told his new customers to "put the mints near the cash register with a big 5-cent price card; then be sure everybody gets a nickel with his change, and see what happens."

What did happen was beyond even Ed Noble's most optimistic hopes and dreams. The two "five cent" ideas hit the jackpot, and within a couple of years his company had made a quarter of a million dollars.

Ed Noble anticipated the trend toward counter merchandising, and designed a *Life Savers* display carton to be placed next to the cash register. It proved so successful that he realized it could not be kept away from competitors, so he designed another display container that would hold not only his own mints, but also other manufacturers' chewing gum, candy bars, and so forth. His own *Life Savers* occupied the center front of the display, and continue to do so in today's familiar modern version of the merchandiser.

From the beginning, Ed Noble believed that the American public, like himself, would need only one taste of his candy to want more. In that first year, the two young partners sat up nights putting samples into glassine bags which were then passed out on streets and in building lobbies by girls appropriately costumed. Ed always considered himself primarily an advertising man and the company's advertising has become famous in the trade.

One celebrated dud occurred more recently when groups of men appeared on the streets encased in metal tubes painted to look like rolls of *Life Savers*. A party of these men trudged up a hill near Columbia University one day and encountered a group of undergraduates. The students, delighted at the unexpected opportunity to liven up a dull day, turned the men on their sides and rolled them down the hill again.

Life Savers, like chewing gum, is an impulse item. The Beech-Nut Company estimates that 75% of *Life Savers* sales are accounted for by people who hadn't thought of buying until they saw the mints on display. Also, flavor preferences in mints are faddish (just as they are in gum) and sampling is used as one way to anticipate a taste trend. Sometimes, however, taste trends are simply inexplicable. For instance, licorice once had a booming sale in St. Louis, but couldn't be given away in Kansas City. Later, it died all over the country and no one could explain why. The popularity of one flavor, however, has never changed—the one that started the whole thing—*Pep-O-Mint*.

Puns and jokes have abounded in *Life Savers* advertising: *hole-some, enjoy-mint, refresh-mint, content-mint*, and, in election years, *the people's candy-date*. One famous comedian scrapped a written commercial for *Life Savers*, and, to the audience's delight, ad-libbed: "You folks are being gypped. Look at the money they save on those millions and millions of holes. You don't think they throw them away, do you?"

Ed Noble believed that if he gave people a quick laugh or smile they would be more apt to buy his product. That he was right is evidenced by the fact that about 90% of all mints and fruit drops sold today are *Life Savers*. He was also right when he told Clarence Crane they could be "pyramided into a fortune." There are over six billion of them produced every year—finding their way to fans in over a million outlets in the United States alone.

CREAM OF WHEAT

The *Cream of Wheat* cereal story begins in the heavy depression that marked the end of the old, self-subsistent economy—the Panic of 1893.

Almost every whistle-stop town along the railroad tracks had a little flour mill like the one that Emery Mapes, George Bull and George Clifford operated in Grand Forks, North Dakota. Flour, when a buyer could be found, sold for $2 a hundred-weight, and during the dark days of that depression it was a desperate struggle for the little mill to stay in business. By the time the Panic was over, there was barely enough capital left to keep operating.

It was against this background that head miller Tom Amidon, who was also a partner in the mill, came up with an idea that not only saved the business but became an American institution. For some time he had been taking middlings—the best part of the wheat berry—home to his wife who made a delicious breakfast porridge from them. The porridge was a great favorite with his family and Amidon suggested to his partners that it could be sold as a breakfast cereal. There was no money available to invest in a new venture of this kind but it was finally agreed that Amidon could pack a few boxes of the cereal and ship it to their New York brokers along with the regular carload of flour.

Amidon painstakingly cut out cardboard cartons by hand for the new cereal and Mapes, who had once been a printer, rummaged around in his stock of old printing plates and found an illustration to "brighten up the package." It was the figure of a colored chef holding a saucepan over his shoulder, and was, Mapes wryly commented, "at least remotely connected with cooking." At this time the purely fanciful name of *Cream of Wheat* was chosen.

A rough picture of the colored chef and the brand name *Cream of Wheat* were printed on ordinary paper and used to wrap Amidon's crudely cut cartons, which were then packed in wooden crates constructed in the mill from waste lumber. Ten cases were made up, and without any advance notice were shipped along with their regular car of flour to the mill's brokers.

No one, not even miller Tom Amidon who had so laboriously and hopefully made up the new cereal, and certainly not his partners, could have anticipated the immediate and popular acceptance of *Cream of Wheat* cereal. Within a short while after the shipment arrived in New York, the brokers telegraphed: "Forget the flour. Send us a *car* of *Cream of Wheat*."

Flour production was promptly abandoned by the mill and its entire facilities turned over to the manufacture of *Cream of Wheat*. Even so, by 1897 the demand had completely outgrown the capacity of the small plant at Grand Forks and the business was moved to Minneapolis, then the best source of raw materials, and a good shipping point to other parts of the country.

The original label was used for several years, but the founders of the company were not entirely satisfied with the picture of the chef. One morning, while having breakfast at Kohlsaats' Restaurant in Chicago, Mr. Mapes noticed a genial and very attractive Negro waiter who went about his work with a smiling competence that drew a friendly response from everyone he served. Mr. Mapes decided that a picture of this man and his engaging smile would be perfect to replace the original chef's picture.

The waiter was delighted to cooperate and was photographed in chef's attire. Since that time his picture has appeared on every package of *Cream of Wheat* cereal. He was paid the sum of $5 to pose, and from the day the picture was made, neither Mr. Mapes nor anyone else in the company ever saw the waiter again. Many Negroes represented themselves as the original chef, but Mr. Mapes was in possession of certain information which made it possible for him to detect impostors.

In 1929, the stock of The Cream of Wheat Corporation was listed on the New York Stock Exchange, and as of August, 1961, there were more than 8,000 stockholders.

Cream of Wheat is today a division of National Biscuit Company's Special Products Division.

QUAKER OATS

Oats made their appearance in New England about 1602 and by 1700 were grown everywhere there were colonists in this country. They provided food for the horses and oxen that were the only means of transportation in early America. They played their part too in adding nearly two inches to the physical stature of Americans.

The tremendous influence of oats on dietary habits in America was started by a German immigrant named Ferdinand Schumacher. Oats had long been a common food in Germany and other European countries when Ferdinand Schumacher came to America in 1850 and set up a grocery store in Akron, Ohio. At that time, many Americans stuffed themselves with ham, sausage, beefsteak, pies and fried potatoes for breakfast. If they did manual labor it helped to alleviate the effects of over-eating, but the less active ones were apt to wind up with gout.

Such oatmeal as was eaten at the time had to be cooked for hours, and few housewives took the trouble to serve it. Ferdinand Schumacher changed all this. He was dismayed that so little oatmeal was eaten by Americans and promptly set about preparing the oatmeal in such a way that it took much less time to cook. He packed it in convenient glass jars and suggested to his customers that they try it with syrup or molasses, and the now current favorites, cream and sugar.

Oatmeal's popularity as a breakfast food soared and before long, Schumacher was selling twenty barrels of it a day. His success inspired others to launch oatmeal companies, and a cut-throat, competitive race for the breakfast food market began. As long as he lived, however, Ferdinand Schumacher was the acknowledged "Oatmeal King of America."

Eventually, the principal oatmeal millers were forced to merge in order to survive and after a series of consolidations of seven of the largest mills, The Quaker Oats Company of today evolved.

Through these "ancestor" companies, the present company dates back well over a century. However, the name *Quaker* was not used until 1877 when The Quaker Mill Company was organized in Ravenna, Ohio. Henry D. Seymour, one of the several founders of the company, conceived the idea for the name and the famous "man in the Quaker garb" trademark. He had combed the dictionary in search of a name for the new company, but failed to find anything that appealed to him. He turned to the encyclopedia, and was intrigued with the story of the Quakers. The parallel between their characteristics—purity, sterling honesty, strength and manliness—and the image he hoped to project of the new company and its product impressed him, and the name "Quaker Mill Company" was adopted. (Incidentally, the name "Quaker" originally came into being in 1650, when a religious sect, headed by George Fox, was founded. The members called themselves "Friends," and, actually, the name "Quaker" was first used in derision by a judge who, when Fox bade him "tremble at the word of the Lord," called Fox a "quaker.")

Henry Seymour's partner, William Heston, also lays claim to the distinction of having chosen the *Quaker* trademark. His story is that while walking through the streets of Cincinnati one day, he saw a picture of William Penn, clothed in Quaker garb. Being of Quaker ancestry himself, Heston immediately decided that "Quaker" was a name that would carry connotations of quality and would make an ideal trademark.

Both men's reasoning for selection of the name seems logical, but the Quaker Oats Company has always been inclined to accept Seymour's version.

At any rate, the trademark was a tremendous success, even though it inspired costly law suits, both here and abroad, and was once even defended against the Society of Friends who petitioned Congress, unsuccessfully, to bar trademarks with any religious connotations.

By 1880, oatmeal was to be found in almost every city, village or farm. It was one of the first commodities to move from the familiar grocery barrel to the separate carton on the grocer's shelves. The guiding force behind this revolutionary concept was Henry Crowell, a progressive-minded man whose thinking amounted almost to prophecy.

Crowell was then president of the American Cereal Company. He was one of the first men in American industry to visualize the unlimited advantages of selling a packaged product, rather than one in bulk, and also to recognize the tremendous possibilities in advertising a product and selling it to the *consumer* rather than to the merchant, which was then the common practice. The miller, the jobber and the retailer did not take kindly to Crowell's new-fangled ideas. They preferred to have their customers simply ask for "oatmeal," which they scooped up from a nondescript barrel and which had been bought indiscriminately from whoever was currently offering the lowest price, regardless of quality. The consumer, however, preferred the standardized weight and price, and also the guarantee of cleanliness of the individually packaged product which the grocer could not provide since his various "barrels" of foodstuffs were intermittently attacked by mice and other vermin.

The American Cereal Company, under Crowell's leadership, adopted Seymour's old Quaker brand (which had come to it through a series of mergers) and packaged their oatmeal in a cardboard container. An advertising campaign such as the world had never seen blossomed across the country. The Quaker—then a full length, stern-featured figure in severe, somber dress—appeared on the broad side of buildings over the length and breadth of the land. Special trains with each car bearing his likeness chugged across the nation, and salesmen lavishly distributed samples. The "Quaker Man" appeared personally at fairs and exhibitions. Newspapers ran editorials extolling the virtue of oats. *Quaker Oats* were carried to the North and South Poles with Peary and Byrd, on African safaris, and into the forbidden land of Tibet by Hedin. International interest was aroused when a gigantic likeness of The Quaker Man was placed on the White Cliffs of Dover. It took an act of Parliament, as a matter of fact, to have the sign removed.

The Quaker Man's first appearance in the 1870's bears little resemblance to the hale and hearty man who represents The Quaker Oats Company and one of America's favorite hot breakfast cereals today. But the ruddy-cheeked and pleasantly smiling Quaker still reflects the qualities for which he was first chosen and he has long since become synonymous with the product that changed the nation's breakfast habits over four generations ago.

AUNT JEMIMA

Of all the familiar trademarks, *Aunt Jemima* is one of the most appealing and expressive. One look at her beaming, good-humored face and thoughts of delicious goodies assail the senses.

The story of *Aunt Jemima Pancake Mix* began in 1889 in St. Joseph, Missouri, famed terminal of the old Pony Express which carried mail all the way west to California. Chris L. Rutt, a local newspaperman, had the idea of a self-rising pancake mix, and with two associates, began experiments with various combinations of ingredients—hard wheat flour and corn flour, phosphate of lime, soda and salt. Within a year they produced the first pancake mix ever made. It was destined to become the world's leader in its field.

The first mix was packaged in plain brown paper sacks, but Mr. Rutt realized that a merchandising plan was essential, and began searching for a name and package design for his unprecedented product. Inspiration came in the fall of 1889 when a vaudeville team known as "Baker and Farrell" came to St. Joseph. Baker's hit number was a song entitled "Aunt Jemima," and soon the whole town was humming it. Rutt immediately decided that *Aunt Jemima* was the name for the new pancake mix since it just naturally made one think of good cooking. However, Rutt and his associates could not raise the necessary capital to promote the product and they subsequently sold their interests to Davis Milling Company. It appeared *Aunt Jemima Pancake Mix* might be headed for oblivion, but instead it catapulted into worldwide prominence when Davis Milling Company executives boldly decided to risk their entire future on it with an all-out promotion at the gigantic World's Columbian Exposition in Chicago in 1893. They constructed the world's largest flour barrel, 12 feet across at the ends, 24 feet long and 16 feet in diameter. Inside the barrel displays were set up where customers were received and entertained. Just outside the huge barrel, "Aunt Jemima" in the person of Nancy Green, a famed Negro cook born in Montgomery County, Kentucky, demonstrated the pancake mix, making and serving a million pancakes by the time the fair closed. Undoubtedly, part of the success of *Aunt Jemima* as a product must go to this remarkable Negro woman who, as Aunt Jemima, became a sensation at the Fair. She had moved from her Kentucky birthplace to Chicago where she was a cook for a judge's family and also acted as nurse for his two sons. Her specialty, coincidentally, had been pancakes.

Nancy Green's inherent talent and friendliness, her ability to project her warm and appealing personality, made her the ideal Aunt Jemima and the living counterpart of the company trademark. She was such a hit that special details of policemen had to be assigned to keep the crowds moving at the Davis Milling Company exhibit. Buyers from all over America, and from foreign countries as well placed over 50,000 orders for *Aunt Jemima Pancake Mix*. At the end of the Fair, Nancy Green was awarded a medal. She continued for many years to represent the Davis Milling Company as Aunt Jemima at expositions all over the country. She died in 1923 at the age of 89, the victim of an automobile accident.

By 1910, the name of *Aunt Jemima* was known in all 48 states, and had attained such a peak of popularity that many persons attempted to infringe on the trademark rights. The *Aunt Jemima* owners instituted suit and were upheld so vigorously by the court that since the last suit in 1917, the name has not been seriously contested.

Until the advent of *Aunt Jemima Pancake Mix*, the flour business had been extremely seasonal, with most sales made in the winter time, but pancake flour immediately enjoyed a 12-months-a-year acceptance. Up to this time, too, pancakes had been strictly a breakfast food, but so great was the appeal and convenience of the *Aunt Jemima* mix that pancakes became standard for lunch, dinner and late supper as well.

The image of *Aunt Jemima* has always been greatly enhanced by her frequent appearances at charity affairs. The Boys Club at Rockford, Illinois, was built, and is operated, solely from funds raised annually by Rockford Kiwanians and *Aunt Jemima*. Within the past five years she has raised over three million dollars for charitable purposes and without compensation for herself or her company.

The Aunt Jemima Mills were purchased by The Quaker Oats Company in 1925 and today *Aunt Jemima Pancake Mix* ranks so far ahead of competition that the only contest is for second place. Over a period of 75 years, *Aunt Jemima* has become a national institution.

MORTON SALT COMPANY

Thousands of years ago, animals wore paths to salt licks, and men followed, seeking game and salt. Their trails became roads and beside the roads settlements grew up. The settlements became cities and nations. The ancient Britons carried their crude salt by pack train from Cheshire to southern England where they were often forced to delay their journey until the high tides of the Thames subsided. There a village known as Westminster grew up, and Westminster became London.

The first written reference to salt is found in the Book of Job, recorded about 2,250 years before Christ. There are 31 other references to salt in the Bible, the most familiar probably being the story of Lot's wife who was turned into a pillar of salt when she disobeyed the angels and looked back at Sodom.

"He is not worth his salt" originated in ancient Greece where salt was traded for slaves.

In Rome soldiers were paid "salt money," *Salarium argentum,* from which we take our English word, "salary."

Salt is vital to existence. Life can be kept in a human or animal body for some period of time when a salt solution is substituted for lost blood. A few races of men have existed without salt but these were the prehistoric creatures who ate liberally of the meat of animals which contained salt in abundance. When salt was crude, impure and hard to get, men opened trade routes and exchanged all manner of goods for a pinch of the precious stuff. It has greatly influenced the political and economic history of the world, and every civilization has its salt lore—fascinating superstitions and legends that have been handed down, sometimes reverently and sometimes with tongue-in-cheek.

In Biblical times, the Jews offered salt to Jehovah with the first fruits of the earth and harvest. Homer calls it divine and the early Greeks worshipped it no less than the sun, and had a saying that no one should trust a man without first eating a peck of salt with him (the moral being that by the time one had shared a peck of salt with a man, he would no longer be a stranger).

The widespread superstition that spilling salt brings bad luck is believed to have originated with the overturned salt cellar in front of Judas Iscariot at the Last Supper.

According to an old Norwegian superstition, a person will shed as many tears as will be necessary to dissolve the salt spilled. An old English belief has it that every grain of salt spilled represents future tears; and in the sixteenth century, a dinner guest seated near spilled salt would refuse to be comforted until the waiter poured wine in his lap. The Germans believe that whoever spills salt arouses enmity, because it is thought to be the direct act of the devil, the peace disturber. Frenchmen throw a little spilled salt behind them in order to hit the devil in the eye, temporarily preventing him from doing further mischief. In America, some people not only toss a pinch of spilled salt over the left shoulder, but crawl under the table and come out on the opposite side.

On the other hand, in certain districts of Russia, no bridal couple will enter their new home without throwing salt in all corners of the house to protect them from evil and encourage happiness and good health. Trusting the powers of salt to a still greater extent, in the Far East it was once the custom to rub all new-born babies with salt to insure their well-being. In remote sections of this country, even today, it is the custom to make young children wear a small bag of salt around their necks to guard them from the "evil eye."

In England salt was considered so important that it was used to determine protocol at meals. A large vessel filled with salt was placed in the middle of the table and all those of noble birth were seated above it. One could easily tell a man's station in life by his position "above or below the salt."

Today, in primitive sections of Africa, salt money is carried in cylindrical cases made of palm leaves. Ten such containers of salt will buy a wife. In other isolated African villages, natives have refused dollars and demanded salt, saying, "We cannot eat dollars." The bars of salt money used there weigh about a pound and are black from handling. When a housewife goes to market, she merely breaks off a piece of salt to pay her bill.

The first patent issued in America—in 1641—was to Samuel Winslow of the Massachusetts Bay Colony to *"furnish the countrey with salt at more easy rates than otherwise can bee had, & to make it by a meanes, & way, wch hiterto hath not bene discovred . . . so it shall not be lawful to any other pson to make salt after the same way . . ."*

America has had her battles for salt. In 1777, Lord Howe made a successful attempt to capture General Washington's stock of salt. Many battles and treaties took place before Western salt licks were free to be used by white men. At the time of the War of 1812 it became very difficult to obtain salt from England, and because of this, commercial salt manufacture was begun at Syracuse, New York. During the Civil War, Syracuse production freed the North of all salt problems, but by 1863, Southerners couldn't buy salt at any price. If the South had been able to protect its salt factories in Virginia and its salt deposits along the Louisiana gulf coast, the Civil War might have ended differently.

The old Erie Canal, which brought Syracuse salt to Chicago at the time the future Morton Salt Company was organized in 1848, was called "the ditch that salt built." Transportation of this bulky, low-priced commodity has always been a major problem.

Actually, table and household uses for salt account for only about four per cent of the total salt produced in the United States. Few people realize that there is salt underfoot in shoe leather, and overhead in the dye of a hat. A single issue of a popular weekly magazine, for instance, requires 114 tons of salt in the production of paper for its pages. Salt used in its pure form and in the many chemicals derived from it, directly affects almost all major industries. Salt manufacturers early learned that they had to offer a low price but uniform quality if they hoped to stay in business. Only men of perseverance and ingenuity survived. Just such a man was Joy Morton.

Joy Morton's is no Horatio Alger story. His father, J. Sterling Morton, was a noted editor and statesman. As a young man, J. Sterling Morton lived in Detroit. He married his college sweetheart, the lovely Caroline Joy, and the young couple immediately set out for new frontiers, eventually settling in Nebraska City where J. Sterling became editor of the *Nebraska City News*. In 1858 President Buchanan appointed him Secretary of the Territory of Nebraska, and he was later acting Governor. Persons of national prominence were often guests in the Morton home, a mansion containing 52 rooms.

Joy was one of four sons born to Caroline and Sterling Morton. He entered the salt business in 1879, investing his entire capital of $10,000 to become a partner in E. I. Wheeler & Company, an outgrowth of a company known as "Alonzo Richmond, Agents for Onondaga Salt" and established in Chicago during the boom year of 1848.

Following the death of Mr. Wheeler in 1885, Joy Morton acquired his late partner's interest and together with his brother Mark formed the small partnership of "Joy Morton & Co." that was to become one of the biggest producers of a vital commodity in the world and the only nationwide salt company.

The office in those early days of over half a century ago was at Illinois Central Pier No. 1, on the site where Chicago's Outer Drive now turns to head north over the Chicago River. There were eight office employees and the office was reached by a long wooden stairway which climbed the west side of a frame warehouse and led to an office decorated in blue and white imitation tile wallpaper.

A large drum heater in the center of the room "cooked the clerks working near the stove and left those near the windows half frozen." Lighting was furnished by individual kerosene lamps of various degrees of efficiency.

The six-day week was accepted practice until Mr. Morton agreed to close the office at one o'clock on Saturday afternoons during July and August, "but only to clerks having their work done." He considered vacations a detriment to both employer and employee because "the clerk spent more money than he could afford and came back all tired out—not much good for a week." But Joy Morton was a man who was close to everyone in his company. The first thing he did on returning from a trip was to greet everyone personally and shake hands. Anyone who wanted to talk to him, including the office boy, simply opened his door and walked in. If a promotion swelled someone's head, Mr. Morton was the first to deflate the expanded ego. He was a wholly democratic man and expected others to be the same.

The turn of the century saw many changes in the salt industry and by 1910 the partnership firm had acquired the properties of several other companies, and Joy Morton & Co. had become the Morton Salt Company.

Efforts to get the country's dealers to buy 3- or 5-pounds of salt (called "pockets") in bags instead of 300-pound barrels met with only lukewarm response. Then, when the Morton brand name, *Seal Salt,* a high-grade table salt packed in a paper-lined bag, failed to gain the popularity that had been expected of it, Joy Morton turned his attention to a new, free-running salt which he packed in a spouted, round package. This time, he insisted, the package would feature the company name rather than a dreamed-up brand name like the disappointing *Seal Salt,* and in 1912, *Morton's Table Salt* was launched in the blue and white asphalt-laminated paper canister with an aluminum pouring spout. Morton Salt pioneered the use of this carton (invented by J. R. Harbeck) that proved so perfect for the product that it was eventually adopted as the standard for the entire salt industry.

About 1912 an unprecedented step was taken by the company to promote *Morton's Salt.* It was decided to advertise, and on a national scale. Until that time no advertising had been done except for a few little souvenir specialties and tradepaper cards. A small number of salesmen were employed, but the bulk of the business came from either post card quotations or from follow-up of inquiries. After considerable deliberation, and after having won the *Good Housekeeping* Seal of Approval, the company contracted to take a series of twelve monthly ads in that magazine. A well-known advertising agency was called in and in due course submitted copy that had been selected by the agency's experts. In addition to the copy for the twelve ads, there were three drawings "on the bench" as possible substitutes, if one of the twelve failed to meet approval.

The birth of the famous "umbrella" girl trademark, and slogan, *When It Rains It Pours* is best told in the words of Joy Morton's son, Sterling II, then president of the company, for it was he who chose the trademark:

"One of the agency men suggested we might look at the three substitutes to see if we liked any of them better than the twelve which the agency considered best. I was immediately struck with one of the three. It showed a little girl standing in the rain with an umbrella over her head; under one arm she had a package of salt tilted backward with the spout open, and the salt running out. Perhaps the fact that my young daughter Suzette was occupying a great deal of my attention at that time had something to do with my interest.

"But, anyway, it struck me that here was the whole story in one picture. The message we wanted to put across—that the salt would run in damp weather—was made beautifully evident. I knew immediately that we could find no better trademark.

"Under the drawing of the little girl was the legend, 'Even in rainy weather it flows freely.' This struck me as being pretty good but rather on the long side. I remember distinctly saying that what we needed was something short and snappy like *Ivory Soap—It Floats*. We worked around with 'Flows freely, runs freely,' but none seemed quite right. Finally, the word 'pours' was suggested. That filled the bill, so 'It Pours' as well as the words 'Free Running' were approved for the new label.

"Then history was made. Someone (and I wish I knew who!) said, 'There is an old proverb, *It never rains but it pours . . .*'" I think everyone in the room realized that we had something there. After a little discussion, I suggested that 'never' and 'but' struck me as poor words to use, that negative connotations should be avoided in a slogan, so we then turned the old proverb around and made it positive instead of negative—*When It Rains It Pours*. We knew that was *it* and our famous trademark and slogan were launched on their triumphant career."

The little "umbrella girl" has undergone several modernizations since its selection in 1911 and is today a sprightly little blonde in modern dress and jaunty pigtails, recognized by young and old alike, and the Morton Salt Company slogan, *When it Rains It Pours* has become a familiar saying.

HEINZ 57 VARIETIES

Henry J. Heinz was born of German parents in Sharpsburg, Pennsylvania, in 1844. He was ear-marked for the ministry, but as the eldest child it fell to him to help his mother in their vegetable garden, and he became an ardent gardener. By the time he was 12 years old, he was already selling the surplus produce at a tidy little profit, and by the time he was 16, had developed a market among Pittsburgh grocers and was employing three or four women.

Henry, however, had not yet decided to make growing and selling produce a career, and when he was 19, he went to Oil City to manage an ice company which his father had entered into as a sideline to his regular livelihood of brickmaking. Unfortunately, Pennsylvania produced a huge ice crop that year, and prices dropped to one cent per pound. Profits evaporated, and Henry, who had set out so confidently, was faced with the prospect of returning home with only his four horses and an empty wagon. Instead, the enterprising young man induced a produce merchant in Oil City to sell him a wagonload of fresh vegetables on credit which he proposed to peddle on his way back to Sharpsburg. When he arrived home, he did have an empty wagon, but he also had a $25 profit.

After several other ventures, Henry became convinced that his future lay in the food business, and in 1869 he formed a partnership with L. C. Noble. One of the first products the young partners marketed was horse-radish. At that time bottled horse-radish was being packed in green bottles to disguise the dishonest practice of using turnip fillers. The only alternative to this unsatisfactory method was for the housewife to buy or grow the roots and then prepare it herself. The partnership of Heinz & Noble began with the cultivation of three-quarters of an acre of horse-radish which they processed and packed in clear bottles, enabling the housewife to see what she was buying.

The partnership prospered, and two years later celery sauce and pickles were added to the line. The original three-quarters of an acre of horse-radish had expanded to 25 acres and, in addition 100 acres of fertile Allegheny River Valley land about a mile above Sharpsburg was being cultivated in other vegetables.

Four years after the founding of the partnership, the disastrous Panic of 1873 struck, spreading its ruin far and wide. Heinz & Noble weathered the Panic but succumbed a couple of years later when banks across the country failed. They had contracted to buy crops which came in far more abundantly than had been anticipated and they were unable to pay for them as obligated. The struggling young partners found themselves bankrupt.

Christmas that year was one Henry J. Heinz never forgot. He wrote in his diary: "No Christmas gifts to exchange. Sallie (his wife) seemed grieved, and cried, yet said it was not about our troubles; only she did not feel well. It is grief. I wish no one such trials. I have no Christmas gifts to make."

Even though he was not legally responsible, Henry took it upon himself as a moral obligation to pay the creditors of the bankrupt partnership, which he managed to do with the financial help of his wife who contributed most of her own family inheritance.

Two months after the bankruptcy, Henry Heinz once again formed a small company to process foods. His brother, John, and a cousin, Frederick, advanced $1600; his wife added the remaining $400 of her inheritance; a neighbor loaned him $1,000; and the owner of the old Heinz home that had been the location of the ill-fated partnership offered the use of the house for several months rent-free. With a total capital of $3000, the business was launched on February 6, 1876, under the name F. and J. Heinz, the initials for the brother and cousin who had contributed capital.

One of the products F. and J. Heinz introduced that first year was ketchup. Making the condiment at home was a tedious task for the housewife. It meant dragging out the old iron kettle to the backyard and gathering enough wood for an all-day fire, or else boiling down the spicy sauce on the kitchen stove and permeating the entire house with its pungent aroma for days. Long hours of stirring was necessary so the pulp wouldn't stick to the cauldron and burn. Everyone in the family took a turn with the wooden paddle, for ketchup-making was a day-long chore.

Ketchup was actually "discovered" in the seventeenth century. English seamen whose ships were anchored in the port of Singapore were introduced to a tangy sauce called *kechap* which the native population ate with their fish and fowl dishes. Back home in Britain, the sailors yearned for the subtle blend of fish brine, herbs and spices, and tried to imitate it, substituting mushrooms, walnuts, cucumbers, and later, tomatoes, for the Far Eastern ingredients they lacked.

How closely they approximated the original "kechap" of the Orientals is not recorded, but *ketchup,* as the English called it—particularly tomato ketchup—became a national favorite. Mrs. Harrison in her *Housekeeper's Pocketbook* of 1748, warned the homemaker never to be without it. Dickens, in *Barnaby Rudge,* smacked his lips over "lamb chops breaded with plenty of ketchup," and even Lord Byron sang the praises of the rich-red sauce in his *Beppo.*

Meanwhile, Maine sea captains, circling the globe for precious cargo, also picked up a taste for the exotic sauce of the Orient, and also for the strange and savory *tomato,* so relished in Mexico and the Spanish West Indies. Before long, Maine families were growing tomatoes in their gardens and making the foreign *kechap* sauce which they used on codfish cakes, baked beans, and meat.

Henry Heinz always insisted on the spelling that is nearer to the original, *ketchup,* although others commonly spell it *catsup. Kechap, catchup,* or *catsup,* it is the best-known condiment in the world, and Heinz' became America's favorite.

Pickles (one of the products for which Heinz became most famous) and other foods were rapidly added to the line. What the founder had lacked in capital, he made up in management. The faith of his family and friends in his ability was justified as the company steadily showed growth and profits, year after year.

Not the least of Henry Heinz's talents was one for advertising and promotion, and it was Henry himself who, in 1896, originated the universally recognized Heinz trademark 57 *Varieties.* Inspiration for the symbol came while Henry was riding in an elevated train in New York City. Among the advertising cards in the train was one extolling the virtues of a brand of shoes that offered "21 styles."

"It set me to thinking," Mr. Heinz said later. "I said to myself, 'we do not have styles of products, but we do have varieties of products.' Counting up how many we had, I counted well beyond 57, but '57' kept coming back into my mind. 'Seven, seven'—there are so many illustrations of the psychological influence of that figure and of its alluring significance to people of all ages. Fifty-eight Varieties, or 59 Varieties did not appeal at all to me—just '57 Varieties.' When I got off the train, I immediately went down to the lithographer's where I designed a street-car ad and had it distributed throughout the United States. I did not realize then, of course, how successful it was going to be."

In 1900, New York City's first electric sign—six stories high and ablaze with 1200 lights—advertised the 57 *Varieties* with the outline of the Heinz pickle at the top.

By the time of Henry Heinz's death in 1918, the company had over 6,500 employees, and the man who could not afford a Christmas gift when the company was founded was a multi-millionaire.

Today, under the guidance of Henry J. Heinz II, the H. J. Heinz Company is one of the world's largest manufacturers and marketers of processed foods. Emphasis is still on the basic research and quality control which was first established in the food industry by the founder. (Henry Heinz played an important role in bringing about the enactment of the Pure Food Law.) There is a feeling, too, that those in control of Heinz today share another view of the founder who, toward the end of his life, was offered a fabulous sum for the company. He refused to sell, and explained his reason in one succinct statement: "I love the business."

A & P

A lot of things happened in the year 1859. John Brown raided Harper's Ferry as the storm clouds of the Civil War gathered; Colonel Edwin Drake drilled the first oil well at Titusville, Pennsylvania, and cleared the way for the Motor Age; the Comstock Lode was uncovered in Nevada; the first hotel passenger elevator was installed in New York's Fifth Avenue Hotel—and George Huntington Hartford opened up a little retail tea store at 31 Vesey Street in New York City.

Like the other events, the opening of that little tea store was destined to effect the lives of most of us, for it became *The Great Atlantic & Pacific Tea Company*, familiarly known as the *A & P*, and from it emerged the concept of lower prices through mass distribution.

Tea was the nation's favorite beverage at that time, and young Hartford decided to try his hand at selling it. He went down to the docks one day and impulsively spent every cent he had to buy a cargo of tea from a clipper ship that had just come into port. He sold the tea from dockside and was amazed to find his profit large enough to permit him to open the small store on Vesey Street. At that time, buying and selling of tea usually went through several hands which greatly increased its cost to the consumer. Young George continued to buy and sell his tea direct and was able to keep his price at about a third of that of other merchants who bought through regular channels. Realizing that he must increase his volume of sales in order to hold to the low price, George advertised extensively and employed promotional techniques and gimmicks that were regarded as nothing short of spectacular, even in that era when P. T. Barnum was at the height of his lapel-grabbing glory.

The Vesey Street store itself was a wonder to behold. Outside, a huge gaslight *T* illuminated the store front of "real Chinese vermilion and flaked gold." Inside, the red and gold scheme was carried over to the huge tea bins which lined the walls. Japanese lanterns and brilliant gaslit chandeliers threw a bright hue over the cashier's cage which was built in the shape of a Chinese pagoda. On Saturday nights a brass band banged out the tunes of the day.

Customers flocked to the store and it soon became the best known and most popular tea house in the city. Hartford advertised his fantastic tea values in such national magazines as *Harper's Weekly*, and invited the public to order his tea by mail. The public did, and ten years after it opened its doors, the original Vesey Street store was abandoned for a larger location next door. Coffee was added to the line, and Wells Fargo wagons delivered George Hartford's tea and coffee all over the country.

In 1869 the driving of the golden spike at Promontory, Utah, symbolically united America's first transcontinental railroad line, linking the Atlantic and Pacific coasts by direct rail service, and opening up a whole new era of transportation. George Hartford, like many other leaders of the time, recognized the industrial and commercial potential behind this engineering feat that had so captured the imagination of the public, and moved swiftly to cash in on it by publicizing the name, *The Great Atlantic & Pacific Tea Company*. It was his dream that *A & P* stores should extend from coast to coast, but it was not until after his death in 1917 that the first *A & P* store was actually opened on the West Coast.

By 1880 there were 95 *A & P* stores scattered from Boston to Milwaukee. Not only was the company recognized as the most efficient coffee and tea business in the world, but more important, it had proven that a single company could operate many stores, and thereby reduce costs, which resulted in lower prices to consumers.

The bustle was still a standard accessory of feminine attire, and horses were still pulling the trolleys when George's oldest son, George L., came into the business at the age of 15. Young George took a great interest in the affairs of the company, and one day happened to mention to a chemist friend that baking powder must contain very expensive ingredients since it cost so much. "Not at all," replied the friend. "It's just alum and bicarbonate of soda." Shortly thereafter, the back section of the company's main New York store was curtained off and a chemist was put to work making baking powder, which the company sold under its own brand name at a fraction of the going price. Not only did this mark the company's first sale of products other than tea, coffee and spices, but it was also the beginning of *A & P*'s manufacture of its own brands.

Another innovation introduced by "Mr. George"—as the younger Hartford became known—was the organization of a huge fleet of traveling "stores" to service vast segments of the population which were cut off from the towns and cities by bad roads. The red and gold *A & P* wagon, whose driver acted as store manager, clerk, cashier and as blacksmith-and-veterinarian to his team of horses, became a familiar sight on literally hundreds of mud-to-the-hubs wagon routes throughout the country.

In 1888 a second son, "Mr. John," joined his brother and father in the business and a few years later, when there were already 200 A & P stores and hundreds of traveling wagon stores, hit upon an idea that became the most important decision ever made in the company's long history.

At that time the A & P stores offered all the services that other merchants gave: they took telephone orders, provided home delivery, gave away premiums and even chalked up charge accounts.

Mr. John proposed to do away with all these services and sell food *only* over the counter and for cash. In this way, he argued, huge savings would result on overhead expenses and prices could be reduced to such an extent that the customers would willingly give up these extra services.

Neither his father nor his brother agreed with him and it was only after many weeks of heated debate that Mr. John persuaded them to at least give him a chance to try out his idea. "All right," his father agreed at last, "open up one store along the lines you describe and let's see what happens."

Mr. John was so confident that he picked the toughest spot in the whole country for his "experimental store"—right around the corner from the company's main outlet in Jersey City, and the biggest money-maker of the chain. He cut corners so closely that he did not even have a sign on the front. But no sign was necessary. In six months the nameless cut-rate "cash-and-carry" store was making more money than any other and the main A & P around the corner was out of business. Another entirely new concept in retailing had been triumphantly launched.

Because their success depended on keeping up with the changing times, the Hartfords were constantly alert for new ideas. When radio was in its infancy, the A & P Gypsies became one of the first programs sponsored by a major national advertiser. When refrigerated railroad cars began to roll on American railroads, they were the first food chain to distribute California oranges, Texas grapefruit and Georgia peaches on a national basis, and to put fresh seafood on the tables of average-income families of the Midwest. When their customers complained about having to wait for service at meat counters, they introduced the first satisfactory system of prepacking meat cuts at a time when the rest of the industry considered it impractical. The establishment of the meat department in 1926 completed the company's efforts to provide the food shopper with all the basic food items under one roof, and thereby gave birth to the "combination store" which led directly to the creation, a few years later, of our modern, one-stop super market.

BORDEN MILK and ELSIE THE COW

Few people have ever heard of the man whose invention did as much perhaps to change our way of life as either Whitney, Howe or Morse. The man was Gail Borden and the invention was the first practical method of condensing milk. Although his name is before the public literally billions of times each year, he is relatively unknown as a personality. However, his life was one of great impact, and although he died almost a hundred years ago, his influence is still felt in the dairy industry.

Gail Borden was born in 1801 in Norwich, New York. His mother, Philadelphia Wheeler, was a great-great-granddaughter of Roger Williams who established Rhode Island and founded the Baptist Church in America. Gail's father was a thrifty Yankee farmer who sought more fertile lands, and with his wife and four boys, made the long wagon trek to Indiana. By his twentieth birthday, Gail, ambitious and imaginative, had finished school and taught for two years. Unusually good at arithmetic, he also became an expert surveyor. But adventure called and Gail and his brother Tom took a flatboat loaded with supplies for settlers down the Mississippi to New Orleans. When they reached New Orleans that summer of 1822, the city was buzzing with the exciting news that the territory of Texas was being opened to Americans for the first time. Gail and Tom met and talked with Stephen F. Austin who was later to become the founder of Texas. Tom joined Austin's famed original 300 families, and went to Texas. Gail, because of ill health, settled in Mississippi where he surveyed in the summer and taught school in winter. One of his students was a beautiful sixteen-year-old girl named Penelope Mercer with whom he fell deeply in love and soon married. Tom wrote glowing letters about Texas until finally Gail could resist no longer and in 1829 he and his young bride set out for the Texas territory. Gail was granted a Spanish league (4428 acres) of land along the Colorado River and began farming and raising cattle. Stephen Austin, head of the little band of Texas settlers, soon asked Gail's help in mapping and laying out the territory, and he took his place alongside his brother Tom as a leader in the community. Gail Borden came to Texas to farm, but the next 15 years plunged him into high adventure in war, journalism and science.

Gail attended the convention that voted to petition for statehood and it was there he met Sam Houston. When the call to arms came, Tom joined Austin's contingent of 300 volunteers and Gail stayed behind to take Austin's place and more importantly, to publish a newspaper that would rally support for the cause. He worked day and night. The first issue of his newspaper—the *Telegraph and Texas Land Register*—came off the press October 10, 1835. It informed its readers:

War is our only recourse. There is no other remedy but to defend our rights, ourselves and our country by force of arms.

Gail wrote the history of Texas as it was being made. On March 2, 1836, he printed Texas' declaration of independence and the headline that became the battle cry of the new republic: *Remember the Alamo!*

Gail and his printer worked until Mexican General Santa Anna neared the outskirts of Harrisburg. Gail escaped to Galveston. The Mexicans burned his print shop and threw his press into the river. On April 21 the Texans met Santa Anna's forces along the Brazos River below Harrisburg. In a quarter of an hour the victory belonged to Texas. Santa Anna was captured the next day and Texas was saved.

President Sam Houston appointed Gail tax collector for the Port of Galveston and a year later he became Secretary and General Agent for the Galveston City Company. For the first time he had a chance to work out ideas that had been in his mind for years.

One of these ideas was to condense food in such a way that it would stay edible for a long period of time. Gail and Penelope had many friends and at a dinner party one evening Gail treated his guests to a most unusual menu: concentrated soups; condensed foods, fruits and extracts. Gail ate heartily and talked of the wonderful flavors he had captured in these dishes. His guests nodded politely, ate gingerly, and courteously but firmly refused a second helping. The meal was not a success. After dinner, they were treated to another Borden invention, the *land schooner*. Against their better judgment, the guests were persuaded to seat themselves in the vehicle. The schooner applied on land the principles used by sailors on the sea. It harnessed the wind. Gail raised the sail. The schooner moved down the beach and gained speed. Five, ten miles an hour, faster and faster. The passengers yelled for Gail to stop. Women screamed and became hysterical when Gail tried in vain to slow the schooner down. In his excitement he swung the rudder the wrong way and the schooner splashed into the waves, turned on its side and slowly skidded to a stop, dumping all the terrified passengers into the water.

The land schooner was not a success, either, but no one was hurt and the young crowd were laughing again by the time they reached the house to dry themselves. In the first flurry of scrambling ashore, someone had inquired, "Where's Gail?" Replied a soaked guest, "Drowned, I do sincerely hope!"

Those early years in Galveston were perhaps the happiest in Gail Borden's life. He adored his lovely wife and their six children. Then, in 1844, tragedy struck, and struck again. Yellow fever swept the city. Gail's four-year-old son died in March and his beloved Penelope in September. Gail helped to dig their graves in the garden. After that he was different. He stayed to himself and turned more and more to his inventions. Two years later he lost another son, and was never again the same.

Gold was discovered in California and a party leaving Galveston asked Gail to help them prepare for the journey. He promised to make them a nutritious meat extract they could use along the trail. The idea wasn't new. The Indians had a concentrated meat they called *pemmican*. They made it by cutting buffalo meat or venison into strips, drying it in the sun, pounding it fine and then mixing it with melted fat. It had a strong, unpleasant taste. Gail succeeded in producing a similar product, with a more palatable taste, in the form of a "meat biscuit." The gold seekers bought 600 pounds of it. Dr. Elisha Kent Kane, the Arctic explorer, used the biscuits on an expedition, and in 1851 it was awarded the Great Council Medal at the International Exhibtion in London. Encouraged, Gail and Tom built a meat biscuit plant in Galveston and Gail optimistically went to Washington to sell the meat biscuit to the army and navy.

They refused even to give his new product a trial. He made effort after effort to market the biscuit commercially, and failed miserably. At the end of five years his resources were completely exhausted and he was heavily in debt. He wrote to a friend in Texas: "Every piece of property I have is mortgaged. I labor 15 hours a day— day-in and day-out."

While Gail was returning from the London Exhibition in 1851 he had witnessed a shipboard tragedy that revived his old interest in inventing a way to preserve milk. Two cows had been on board the ship to provide milk for the children. During the voyage the cows became sick and the cries of hungry babies could be heard all over the ship. One infant died. Gail was deeply impressed by the tragedy. In New York, Washington and other cities he saw much the same scene repeated. A lot of the fresh milk sold was unsafe. People who used it often became sick; some died. And all the milk usually soured in a few hours. Gail kept turning the problem over in his mind, even as he futilely continued to try to market the meat biscuit. In 1852 he went to work on a process to preserve milk. He had preserved meat by condensing it. Why not do the same with milk? He put a gallon of milk in a kettle and boiled off the water until less than a quart was left. He let it cool, then tasted it. It had an unpleasantly strong burnt flavor. No one would buy milk that tasted burned. Was there a way to solve the condensing and flavor problems at the same time?

During a trip to upstate New York Gail had become acquainted with a colony of Shakers, a religious sect at New Lebanon. He knew they used a vacuum pan when they condensed sugar, fruit juices and extracts. It kept out the air; it permitted evaporation with less heat; and it prevented burning and discoloration. Could this be the answer to condensing milk also? Gail hurried to New Lebanon and borrowed one of the pans. For months he worked. Testing, re-testing, checking, re-checking. One day in the spring of 1853 he found a formula that had no burned tinge, and the milk lasted for almost three days before it began to sour. He was elated and hurried off to Washington to file a patent claim.

In Washington his patent application was denied with staggering bluntness. There was "nothing new" in the process, ruled the Patent Commissioner. It was a devastating blow to Gail. He was deeply in debt from the failure of his meat biscuit, and to prove his right to a milk condensing patent would cost money and take time. He had no funds, but he had great faith in the process he had invented. In 1855 he wrote prophetically to a friend: "It [the milk condensing process] is a beautiful article. I do not hesitate to tell you that should I live two years I shall present the world an invention of vast import. Milk will be as common on shipboard as sugar. Remember what I say. I will be recognized as the inventor of this great process."

Two friends, both distinguished scientists, helped him prove his right to a patent. One was Robert McFarlane, discoverer of dyeing processes and editor of the *Scientific American;* the other was Dr. John H. Currie, head of an important laboratory. They offered to test Gail's claims, and their conclusion was that the use of the vacuum pan to keep out air during evaporation was a new and important discovery. The three-year fight with the Patent Office ended and on August 19, 1856, Gail was granted his patent. He was 54 years old.

Two months later the world's first condensed milk factory opened at Wolcottville, Connecticut. Again, it proved to be a financial disaster. New York City customers, accustomed to the watered output of "swill milk dairies"—doctored with chalk for whiteness and molasses for "creaminess"—found Gail Borden's pure condensed milk strange, and rejected it. Gail's two partners were discouraged. One sold his interest and the other bought half of Gail's patent when Gail dejectedly returned to Texas.

In the spring of 1857, Gail Borden returned north to try again. He re-established a working relationship with his former partners and set up business in an abandoned mill at Burrville, Connecticut, under the name "Gail Borden Jr. and Company." This firm was the direct ancestor of the present giant Borden Company.

But Gail's timing was again bad. The new company was formed in the year of the Panic of 1857, and doubtless would not have survived had it not been for a chance meeting on a train between Gail and Jeremiah Milbank, a wholesale grocer and banker. Happening to be seated side by side, the friendly Gail was soon chatting with his companion. Inevitably he told Milbank about his invention for condensing milk, and of the financial obstacles confronting him. Milbank was impressed not only with Gail's invention but with the man himself—his honesty, and forthrightness in describing his financial situation. By the time the two men reached their destinations, they were—solely on the strength of a handshake—partners. Milbank was not one to operate on a shoestring. He settled with Gail's two partners, and in February, 1858, with the financial resources Milbank contributed, the New York Condensed Milk Company came into being, with Gail as president.

The Borden-Milbank partnership was a perfect combination. Gail had the technical knowledge and Milbank had the business acumen needed to make the new product a success. The first samples were carried from house to house. Next, *Borden's Condensed Milk* was ladled out from 40-quart cans pushed through the streets of New York City on a hand-cart. Later, Gail canned the milk, and in cans it kept indefinitely and could be shipped to any part of the world.

Gail Borden never heard of germs. He didn't know that heating killed any harmful bacteria in the milk. Neither did the people who bought the new product; but they soon learned that, while babies and grownups sometimes became sick and died after drinking fresh milk, *Borden's Condensed Milk* was always safe. Gail Borden was "pasteurizing" milk long before Louis Pasteur startled the scientific world with his discovery of microbes.

Gail's timing was more fortunate this time and the new company benefited greatly from a newspaper crusade (conducted by Frank Leslie, editor of *Leslie's Illustrated Newspaper*) against the "swill milk" then in common use. By the end of the year, The New York Condensed Milk Company bought a horse and wagon and started its first route from lower Manhattan to 51st Street.

Less than three years later the first shot was fired at Fort Sumter. The outbreak of the Civil War proved a financial triumph but a personal sorrow for Gail Borden. It marked a turning point for the company when the Government placed an order for 500 pounds of condensed milk, but it set Gail's two sons brother against brother: John Gail joined a New York regiment and Henry Lee, a Texas Cavalry unit.

Gail was in his sixties but he didn't spare himself during the war years. He built several new plants and before the war was over, Union forces were using all the milk Gail could supply. The public wanted it too and demand ran ahead of production. Gail Borden's fortune was made at last.

As *Borden's* success grew, many competitors entered the field, some with inferior products and at least one who actually appropriated the *Borden* trademark name. Outraged, Gail Borden adopted another, more distinctive trademark that was to become almost as well-known as the Borden name: *Eagle Brand.* Some people say he named it nostalgically after the Texas eagle which he had often hunted. Others maintain it was named for Eagle Cove, the home of the Galveston Island Indians. Since the name was adopted in 1866, shortly after the end of the Civil War, it seems more probable that it was inspired by the American Eagle in the wave of postwar patriotism.

Happily, at the end of the war, both his sons returned unharmed and Gail was glad to relinquish many of his duties to them. He was getting old, and he knew it. His health was failing. He talked much of the old days, and of his friends, Stephen Austin and Sam Houston. Gail wanted to go home—to Texas—to spend the rest of his life.

He returned to Texas, but could not remain long idle. The great disappointment of his life had been the meat biscuit, and now he decided to build a small meat biscuit factory. His son, Henry Lee, took charge and the little town that grew up around the plant was called Borden, Texas. Nearby, Gail built a house for himself, and another for Henry Lee.

Texas recognizes Gail Borden as one of her most successful sons. The company he established is a leader in the food industry, and brings milk to more homes than any other firm in the world. Gail Borden did more than invent a process and found a company. He started the modern dairy industry, being the first to use large-scale processing of milk. The original partnership of two has grown to nearly 50,000 who share in the ownership of the business. Employees have increased from the handful who worked in the first tiny factory to over 32,000.

Gail lived in Borden, Texas, until his death January 11, 1874, at the age of 72. His last years were happy. His children were with him. He was in the land he loved. He had often returned to Texas an abject failure, but at last he was back home—a great success. A few years before his death, Gail visited Woodlawn Cemetery, just north of Manhattan, and selected the site where he was to be buried. The simple epitaph on the monument marking his final resting place describes eloquently the story of the man in his own words: "I tried and failed, I tried again and again, and succeeded."

ELSIE THE COW

Many people ask The Borden Company who "invented" their famous trademark, *Elsie the Cow*. The answer is: Nobody—and everybody. The truth is, like Topsy, "she just growed."

Before the New York World's Fair in 1939, *Elsie* was an inanimate trademark used to humanize the company in a minor advertising campaign. To the utter astonishment of the Borden Company, when the *Borden* exhibit opened at the Fair there was an immediate and urgent demand by the public to see the "real" Elsie. A Jersey cow with the improbable name of "You'll Do Lobelia" was hastily pressed into service. From that time on, "You'll Do Lobelia," alias *Elsie the Cow,* was one of the great successes of the Fair, and so much the feature attraction of the *Borden* exhibit that a special boudoir was built for her, Colonial in decor, and complete with four-poster bed. This attracted movie producers and, in the summer of 1940, Elsie was persuaded to travel to Hollywood by streamlined box car to act the role of Buttercup in the picture, *Little Men.* She was met at the Los Angeles Station by famous stars, and parties were given in her honor at the Ambassador and Ciro's—where she was presented with a corsage of orchids which she promptly ate.

The bovine is like no other of her kind. Trained to the role of trouper she travels everywhere, and whenever possible, with her famous boudoir. She knows cameramen by sight and shows her best profile before the pop of the first flash-bulb. In New York, wearied by an MC's overlong introduction on TV, she shouldered him from the microphone, and stole the show with a loud, prolonged moo-ooo-oo. She loves youngsters and is forever visiting children's hospitals, orphanages and schools. She has dozens of hats, embroidered blankets and her own cosmetics—including *Eau de New Mown Hay, Tail Wave Set,* and *Meadow Mud Pack.* During the war she sold millions of dollars of war bonds and there is almost no worthy charity to which she has not given her time in personal appearances.

When she was ten, a very adult age for a lady bovine—there was quite a birthday party for her at New York's Hotel Roosevelt. More than 200 guests came to toast her health. Those admirers who could not attend sent gifts. From Jack Benny came a genuine pin-seal purse, with the price (39¢) still on it. There was an autographed baseball bat from Leo Durocher and bath salts from Lana Turner. Frank Sinatra sent a barrel of molasses and Ray Milland a jar of pickled beets. Ginny Simms presented her with a crepe de chine bed jacket, measured to size, and Pan American Airways gave her a pair of oversize aviator goggles—to affect when traveling incognito.

Today, *Elsie the Cow* is not only *Borden's* trademark character, appearing in company advertising and on most product labels, but surveys show that she is known to eight out of ten Americans, a claim which can be made by only a very few figures of the human variety. Another poll showed that only the president outranked her in recognition.

Elsie is the undisputed Queen of Dairyland.

COCA-COLA

Coca-Cola, one of the best-known trademarks, the most imitated and therefore the most litigated of them all, was originated by Confederate veteran John S. Pemberton, and named by his business associate, Frank M. Robinson. Pemberton, formerly of Wheeler's Cavalry, C.S.A., was also a graduate pharmacist, and was therefore known as both Major and Doctor to his friends. When the Civil War ended, he went into the drug business in Atlanta, at which he was not a conspicuous success. For one thing, he was constantly experimenting and after producing several proprietaries, decided to concentrate all his efforts on a soft drink. After considerable trial and error, he came up with a formula in May, 1886, that satisfied him and he mixed the first batch of the new formula in a three-legged iron pot over a wood fire in the back yard of an ante-bellum red brick house. He had achieved the blend of flavors that he had long sought, but he had no name for it. His friend and bookkeeper, F. M. Robinson, came up with the answer: an alliterative compounding of two of the many ingredients of the new drink—"coca" (the dried leaves of a South American shrub), and "cola" (an extract of the kola nut). Robinson also wrote the name in flowing script, substantially the same as it appears today.

Pemberton talked one of Atlanta's soda fountain owners into dispensing *Coca-Cola* on a trial basis. It caught the public's fancy, and by the year's end Pemberton had sold 25 gallons to the few Atlanta soda fountains existing in 1886. He also spent the sum of $46 for advertising, inaugurating a policy that has been continued by the company ever since. More money has been spent advertising *Coca-Cola* than any other single product in advertising history.

Pemberton died in 1888, and Asa G. Candler, another young Atlanta druggist, acquired complete ownership of *Coca-Cola*—physical assets, trademark, goodwill and all—for the total sum of $2,300. Candler gave up his other business interests to devote full time to *Coca-Cola* and in 1892 organized the Coca-Cola Company. By 1895, he was able to boast that "*Coca-Cola* is now sold in every state of the Union."

Coca-Cola was sold as a soda fountain drink until the turn of the century when a Chattanooga lawyer, Benjamin F. Thomas, got the idea of bottling it. An associate, Joseph B. Whitehead, agreed with Thomas that it could be done, and the two of them went to Atlanta to persuade Asa Candler to let them try it. Reluctantly, Candler agreed. The contract was to bottle the drink only—not to manufacture the syrup from which *Coca-Cola* is prepared. The manufacture of the syrup itself has always been, and remains, the carefully guarded function of the Coca-Cola Company alone.

The two men returned to Chattanooga and with $5,000 opened the first bottling plant. After that, *Coca-Cola* bottling plants sprang up all over the country, each individually owned and operated under their contract with The Coca-Cola Company.

The public is responsible for the nickname *Coke*. At first the company frowned at this practice, fearing loss of identity and substitution, but when customers persisted in asking for *Coke*, the company registered the nickname too (after winning a Supreme Court decision allowing it to do so in 1920) and it is now as zealously guarded as *Coca-Cola*.

The distinctive curved and fluted bottle is registered as a third trademark. Famous designer Raymond Loewy, who had absolutely no connection with it, hails the *Coca-Cola* bottle as "the most perfectly designed package in use today."

Coca-Cola is as American as apple pie and the hot dog. It has woven itself to a remarkable degree into the fabric of the lives of the people of America, and rivals the flag itself in symbolizing the U.S.A. to millions of people all over the world.

DR PEPPER

It all began with a young man who worked at a drug store fountain in Virginia. The owner of the store, a doctor by the name of Pepper, had a beautiful daughter and romance soon blossomed. The young soda fountain attendant mixed countless new concoctions for the approval and delight of the winsome lass.

But, alas, not only did Dr Pepper not share his daughter's enthusiasm for the experiments at his soda fountain, but he had higher aspirations for his daughter's future, and summarily fired her young suitor, hoping it would remove him from the scene. It did. Heeding the advice of Horace Greeley who said "Go West, young man," the thwarted Romeo didn't stop until he reached Texas where he took up his erstwhile soda-fountain activities at the Old Corner Drug Store in Waco.

Along with his undying devotion to the daughter of Dr Pepper, the young man brought with him his penchant for concocting new fountain flavors, and as he dreamed of the girl-he-left-behind, he continued experimenting with soft drink ingredients. One day he hit on a combination that he thought was the greatest. It quickly became a favorite at the soda fountain, and having learned of the romance that had bloomed in Virginia, customers teasingly dubbed the new drink *Dr Pepper*.

Fortunately, the idyll of the genius of the soda fountain and the Virginia belle had a happy ending when the young man returned east and finally won her hand.

Meanwhile, a patron of the Old Corner Drug Store, R. S. Lazenby, had become interested in the *Dr Pepper* flavor. Mr. Lazenby was a beverage chemist and began extensive research on the new soft drink at his Artesian Bottling Works. In 1885, after two years of testing, blending and processing, he put *Dr Pepper* on sale at soda fountains in and around Waco. So perfect was the flavor formula that it has remained basically unchanged through the years.

The drink's popularity spread and by 1910, *Dr Pepper* syrup had become one of the principal freight items hauled from Waco by the Wells Fargo Express.

In 1922, romance again entered the story of *Dr Pepper* when Mr. Lazenby's daughter married J. B. O'Hara, a handsome young army officer from Pennsylvania. O'Hara saw great possibilities in *Dr Pepper* and set up an extensive sales and distribution program for it. The program proved extremely successful and the company soon expanded its quarters and moved to Dallas, Texas. By 1930 the business had grown to such proportions that a modern, three-story syrup plant was constructed. Other plants followed to keep pace with the current sale of over a billion *Dr Peppers* annually in the United States alone.

Dr Pepper has a legitimate claim for its *"At 10, 2 and 4"* slogan. Dr. Walter H. Eddy, a Columbia University professor, was conducting research into the human diet and discovered that three meals a day were not sufficient to provide enough energy to keep an active person at top level efficiency. He pinpointed three in-between-meal times during the day when energy in the human body dropped to its lowest ebb. These were 10:30 in the morning, and 2:30 and 4:30 in the afternoon. Dr. Eddy recommended that people avoid these three let-down periods and restore energy quickly through a pure, healthful soft drink like *Dr Pepper*. The times, "10, 2 and 4" were immediately incorporated into *Dr Pepper's* trademark to remind people to offset these low-energy periods.

Dr Pepper is not a cola. It is a unique blend of many flavors totally unlike any other on the market, and has fully earned its right to the reputation of being the "friendly pepper-upper."

ARM & HAMMER BAKING SODA

The *Arm & Hammer* story dates back to the days when James A. Church ran a mustard and spice business in Brooklyn known as the Vulcan Spice Mill. Over the door of the mill swung a sign depicting the symbol (an arm and hammer) of the mythological Vulcan, hammer-wielding god of fire and metalworking. In 1867 Mr. Church closed his spice factory to go into the baking soda business, and although he foresaw no possible use for it, he took the sign along with him out of sentiment.

The new firm was named Church & Company. Soda was sold by the barrel in those days and along with each barrel went a supply of paper bags in which to package it. The bags were elaborately imprinted with names and pictures to advertise the individual merits of the company's various brands—such as *Lily* (so named for its outstanding purity); *Eagle* (it had the ability to make baked goods rise); and *Tiger* (which symbolized power).

Door to door salesmen played a big part in the success of a product at that time, and Mr. Church engaged the services of the famous Colonel Powell, undoubtedly the most colorful salesman of that era, and probably any other. The Colonel, a 7-foot, 4-inch giant (in his stocking feet), soared to nine feet when he was dressed in his top hat and elevated shoes. This flamboyant man traveled about the countryside in a cart drawn by two huge, plumed horses attired in blankets emblazoned with glowing letters. Crowds collected wherever he went, and he made an imposing figure as he grandiosely swept into a customer's store and with great fanfare and flourish, tacked one of his baking powder signs to the ceiling. Then, turning to his open-mouthed admirers, he extolled at great length the virtues of his product. Inside each package, he told them, they would find a copy of Mrs. Church's own recipe for Gold Cake (made with Church & Company's baking soda, of course) and on his next trip through he would have a brand new recipe for Silver Cake.

But in spite of the Colonel's efforts and Mrs. Church's recipes, sales lagged discouragingly behind competitors. One day Mr. Church sat at his desk, staring wistfully at the old Arm and Hammer sign that now hung in his office. Suddenly the thought struck him that here was the perfect symbol for his baking soda. It took *power* to lift that hammer as it took *power* to leaven baked goods. Mr. Church immediately had a quantity of paper bags printed with the *Arm & Hammer* label and rushed them to all the stores in the area. His hunch proved right. The label was an outstanding success.

Arm & Hammer Saleratus (as baking soda was then called)

quickly became the fastest selling brand on the market. With its introduction in 1867, one of the world's oldest and most widely recognized package designs in the food industry was launched.

LEA & PERRINS WORCESTERSHIRE SAUCE

Over a hundred years ago, a British nobleman, Sir Marcus Sandys, returned to his native England from India where he had served his country for many years as Governor of the Province of Bengal. Sir Sandys was a noted epicure, a *bon vivant*, and he brought back with him a great treasure: a recipe for a rare sauce, a secret blend of spices and seasonings from the Orient that imparted to food a new savor. He had tasted exotic Hindu dishes whose wonderful flavor and piquant tang were based upon the secret recipe, and it was more precious to the old gourmand than all the treasures of the East.

On his return to his country estate in Worcester, England, Sir Sandys immediately sought out the shop of two little chemists on Broad Street, for whom he had great respect, the Messrs. John W. Lea and William Perrins. It was to them he entrusted his precious recipe with orders to make up a small amount for his own use, and for presentation from time to time to esteemed members of the nobility. Sir Sandys entertained frequently and lavishly at his country estate, and tales of the excellence of the dishes which the sauce had been used to season were spread by word of mouth until its reputation was known far beyond the little town of Worcester. The two chemists received permission to sell the sauce to some of their other customers, and soon its production commanded their entire attention. Eventually they permanently acquired the secret recipe from the appreciative old nobleman.

Through the years that followed, travelers to other lands carried its fame abroad, and the demand for it constantly grew. Its flavor was always uniform and neither the heat of the tropics nor the cold of the frigid zone affected its quality and bouquet. It was only natural that it should take its name, *Worcestershire Sauce*, from its birthplace. The town of Worcester is in the Shire of Worcester, "shire" being the British counterpart of our "county." (Incidentally, in England it is known only as *Worcester Sauce*—why the "shire" became a part of the American pronunciation is as a big a mystery as the recipe itself.)

Today there are several *Lea & Perrins* factories. Sir Sandys' secret recipe, which is still carefully guarded, is exactly the same as the day he brought it from India to the small chemists' shop on Broad Street. Now, as then, *Lea & Perrins* are the sole manufacturers of the only *original Worcestershire Sauce*. It has become an institution, found in the world's most famous cafés and hotels—in London, Vienna, Paris, the Orient.

The success of *Lea & Perrins* has attracted many imitators who have sought, always in vain, to duplicate the secret of the flavor which *Lea & Perrins* alone possess. The famous, identifying inscription on their label, "From the recipe of a nobleman in the County," is an honest one, and through it, Sir Sandys might be said to have achieved a measure of immortality that has already survived him by more than a century.

WHISKEY

Introduction

Our primitive ancestors were the first to discover that they derived extra energy and a joyous feeling of well-being from drinking the juices of berries and fruits that had been stored in crocks for a while. Pretty soon they also learned that grain stored in hollowed-out logs while it was wet developed this same mysterious power to enliven them.

Aristotle wrote of the distillation process in the 4th century B.C., and as early as 800 B.C. the natives of the East Indies were making distilled beverages out of sugar cane and rice. Although North American Indians were smart enough to cross two strains of wild grasses and breed a succulent corn that turned out to be one of the best of all grains for making whiskey, they knew nothing about alcohol until early explorers let them in on the secret—trading a quart of the secret for a deer skin and a pint for a doe pelt.

One version of the origin of whiskey is that it was first produced in Ireland. According to this source, the Irish were half-naked cave dwellers until St. Patrick appeared among them in the 5th century and taught them how to make *usquebaugh,* whereupon they proceeded to become the most cultured people in the world. *Usquebaugh* is a shortened form of the Gaelic phrase, *Uisque-beathe*—from the Latin Acqua Vitae, meaning "water of life." *Usquebaugh* was shortened to *oushki* from which our word "whiskey" evolved. It is still an open question who originated Scotch whisky, the Irish or the Scotch.

As to whether or not whiskey should be spelled with an *e*, one authority says that an *e* should be used except when referring to

Scotch whisky. The reason for this is that Scottish printers were as thrifty with their type as with their money, and therefore dropped the *e* from the original spelling on the grounds it was useless and wasteful.

At any rate, the making of liquor had been going on for several hundred years before it came to the attention of the British government. Then, in 1556, alarmed by the quantity of grain being used by Irish distillers, Parliament passed a law imposing the death penalty on anyone in Ireland making whiskey except members of the nobility. The purpose of this law was to save grain, but the result was illicit distilling—an activity that has continued down to the present day and is currently known as "moonshining." The product of American moonshiners is known as "white lightning," and one prominent American distiller, Brown-Forman, produces a corn whiskey called *White Lightning* mainly as a public service to aid the government in combating moonshiners in the southern sections of the Allegheny Mountains who make huge, untaxed profits from their crude product.

Evasion of taxes also gave rise to the word "bootlegger." When excise taxes were imposed, some distillers carefully removed the required government tax stamps after delivering the whiskey to their customers, and used them over and over again. They concealed these stamps in their boots, and whiskey sold with the used stamps came to be known as "bootleg" whiskey.

"Brand name" itself entered the language via the whiskey route. Whiskey was originally shipped in barrels to distributors or tavern keepers. The distillers burned their name, or "brand," on what is known as the "commercial end" or head of each barrel; the other end, known as the "government head," was used for Internal Revenue marks and stamps. The name of the distiller on the barrel was referred to as the whiskey's brand name.

One of the early distillers, E. C. Booze, had a brand called *Old Log Cabin*, and though *Old Log Cabin* itself faded into obscurity, "booze" became a slang word for all whiskey.

In the Colonial days, the popular American beverage was rum, first distilled in 1650 from molasses made in Barbados. Rum was originally *rumbullion* (meaning an uproar or fracas), but soon was shortened to *rum*. "Apple jack," made by allowing fermented cider to freeze, was another popular form of hard liquor.

An entry in George Washington's diary about distilling cider and sowing rye has been taken by some authorities to indicate that he was not only the father of our country, but the founder of this country's whiskey-making industry as well. Whether or not this is true, it is well established that he devoted one of his Virginia farms exclusively to the growing of rye which he converted into whiskey in a still in Mount Vernon. The still is reported to have made a net profit of 83 pounds in 1798, with 155 gallons left in storage. Washington took great pride in the product of his distillery, and proudly served it to distinguished guests, one of which was the Marquis de Lafayette, who is said to have been somewhat startled by the "swift authority" of the "home-made novelty," but was nonetheless unstinting in his approval.

The Revolution had a pronounced effect on the production and popularity of whiskey. As a result of the tight British blockade along the Eastern seaboard, very little molasses or rum got through from the West Indies, and quartermasters in the Continental Army issued rations of whiskey instead of rum to their men. As a consequence, many long-time rum drinkers acquired a taste for whiskey instead, and it remained with them when the war was over and they returned home—in much the same manner as a great number of GI's from the North acquired a taste for Bourbon while taking basic training in the southern states during World War II.

The year of the Revolution, 1776, is also claimed as the year of the first cocktail. Betsy Flanagan, a barmaid at Halls Corners, Elmsford, New York, asserted her femininity and decorated the bar with tail feathers. When an inebriate at the bar called for a glass of those "cocktails," she prepared his drink (a mixed concoction) and stuck in one of the feathers.

After Cornwallis' surrender at Yorktown in 1781, there was a restless movement from settled areas (in one county alone in Pennsylvania there were 500 distilleries), and a number of farmer-distillers took the rugged Wilderness Road from Pennsylvania and Maryland into Kentucky. They settled in the central prairie section, called the Bluegrass Region because of the tiny, dusky blue blossoms that cover the rolling land. For these pioneers Kentucky had everything they needed to make better whiskey than had ever before been made in the Colonies—"The king 'o distillations, known as Bourbon."

BOURBON

Seven of the present counties of Kentucky claim the distinction of having first distilled Bourbon whiskey within their borders. There are claims and counterclaims, and controversies rage at the drop of an opinion. About the origin of the bourbon name itself, however, there is some agreement: Louis XVI of the Bourbon dynasty in France came to the aid of the American colonies in their struggle against Great Britain, and "the Western Country"—an area that comprised all that is now northeastern Kentucky and a part of Virginia—was named Bourbon County in his honor.

Most authorities also agree that the first whiskey possessing the essential characteristics that now distinguish Bourbon whiskey was originally distilled in 1789 by the Reverend Elijah Craig, a Baptist minister, at Georgetown in Scott County (at that time Bourbon County).

There are three factors which have always determined the identity of Bourbon: (1) The water used in making it is entirely free of any trace of metallic substances or other impurities; (2) the principal grain used is corn; and (3) after it is distilled, it is aged in charred kegs made out of white oak. For the early migrating distillers, Kentucky was the Promised Land. It had a great ledge of limestone to cleanse its water and neutralize the acid of the whiskey. The pure limestone water gushed out of the mountain sides and bubbled up in the deep ravines. Thousands of acres of rich meadowland in the blue grass country were ideal for growing the finest corn, and mountain sides were covered with stands of white oak for the storage and aging of kegs. The climate was perfectly suited to the growing of the rare, special strains of yeast that gave each distiller's whiskey its own recognizable individuality.

Many tales are told about the way those pioneers used to slip out at night to their favorite haunts in "the bright of the moon" with a jar of honey, which, when mixed with the wonder-working water from some secret spring, would be used to capture rare types of spores that were then used in breeding a cherished strain. When a distiller found a particular yeast that proved superior, he set about developing a "pedigreed" strain, keeping it closely guarded. Some of the best Bourbon on the market today is produced from these secret yeast "lines" that have been cultivated for a century or more.

A favorite story in Kentucky is about the owner of a family distillery who was far more concerned during Civil War days about preserving his precious yeast strains than he was about saving the ancestral silverware. When a troop of marauding Yankee cavalry swept through his country, he fastened a rope to the yeast jug and lowered it into the well, tying the other end of the rope to the windlass. After taking everything of value while the family stood silently by, a foraging sergeant spotted the line and hauled up the jug. Disgusted when he discovered it contained yeast, he was about to smash it on a rock when every member of the household suddenly attacked him. The master clutched the sergeant's wrists, a servant caught him around the waist, and the mother and daughter wrested the jug away from him. It is possible the sergeant thought the besieged family had gone berserk, but at any rate the jug was saved, and one of the best-known brand names on the market today is still being made with that same ante-bellum yeast strain.

Typical of the protective attitude present-day Bourbon distillers have toward their pedigreed strains of yeast is the "thief-proof" steel refrigerator safe in which the T. W. Samuels Company keeps the yeast culture that has been a prized family possession for four generations. Another example of this esteem is the action taken by the Bernheim Distilling Company, when the gloomy days of Prohibition closed in. Convinced that the country was bound to come to its senses sooner or later, the farsighted men who controlled the company at that time sent the rare I. W. Harper yeast strain to Canada, and kept it there, under close supervision and a considerable expense, until Repeal.

The credit for the discovery of the use of charred oak kegs for aging bourbon is almost as controversial as where Bourbon was made in the first place. The Reverend Craig has his loyal supporters, several generations removed, of course, who maintain that it was the Reverend himself who accidentally happened upon the knowledge that the sharp taste of whiskey is mellowed by aging it in charred kegs. Lending credence to this theory is the fact that shortly after the Reverend set up his still he was turning out good red liquor that most definitely had a special quality.

Another popular legend about the origins of charred kegs is that an unidentified distiller in Pennsylvania saved money by storing his liquor in kegs previously used for the shipment of salt fish. To get rid of the fishy smell, he scorched the inside of the kegs with a blazing pine knot. He soon found that the whiskey kept in the charred kegs had a more pleasing flavor and a delightful ruddy hue.

Still another version is that of the old-time cooper (barrelmaker) who was heating barrel staves at an open fire in order to curve them properly, and carelessly burned a batch of them. Being a thrifty man, he went ahead and delivered a keg made of the charred staves to a customer, without saying anything about it. Months later, when the customer sampled the liquor stored in that keg, he found the flavor far superior to his other liquor, and upon learning the cooper's secret, ordered that all his whiskey kegs be charred in the future.

What goes on in the barrel during the aging of Bourbon is still Nature's secret, but the oldtimers discovered that Bourbon did not really come of age until it had "lived and breathed" through a succession of winters and summers. The mysterious interaction going on in the keg is known to be more pronounced in the summertime, so distillers have come to refer to their Bourbon not as so many years old, but as so many "summers" old. Just how long Bourbon continues to improve in the barrel is yet another source of controversy.

Until the appearance of the celebrated Dr. James Crow in 1835, distilling had never been done by any defined rule, but rather after the manner of the old Kentucky formula—taking a "passel" of meal, a "passel" of malt, "about so much" water, and "biling it down" until it was done. By this process there were frequently days when good whiskey was made, but just as often "the run" failed to produce the hoped-for result. The failure was invariably attributed to a "change in the moon."

Appalled by the carelessness and indifference in many of the small distilleries, Dr. Crow, a meticulous surgeon and chemist who had migrated from Scotland, introduced standardized formulae and procedures, maintained strict sanitation, and produced a whiskey of uniform and recognizable quality. The price of Bourbon soared, and other distillers soon rose to his standards.

Numerous famous men who are known to have been Bourbon drinkers are said to have also been *Old Crow* Bourbon drinkers. A few years ago, an organization was formed to conduct independent research on *Old Crow*, and to coordinate all *Old Crow* research activity. A series of ads were inserted in the *Saturday Review, Harper's* and *Atlantic* magazines, in which an offer of $250 was made for historical facts relating famous nineteenth century Americans to *Old Crow* whiskey. Many amateur historians replied, including a student in Chicago who found an old newspaper article which quoted Andrew Jackson as praising *Old Crow;* a seaman who found a news article stating that Jack London proposed a toast to Martin Eden, "Skaal to *Old Crow*—it's the best"; another scholar who produced a letter dated 1849 from the Governor of Kentucky to the Commissioner of Indian Affairs admonishing him: "Never open your mouth unless it is to swallow a 'leetle' drop of the *Old Crow*."

It has been said that the lenient terms of General Lee's surrender to General Grant were settled over a decanter of *Old Crow*. While there may be some question as to whether General Grant's favorite whiskey was specifically *Old Crow,* there is no doubt that it *was* Bourbon. It is a well-known story of how, at the height of his campaign to bring the war to a successful conclusion, a group of drys called on Lincoln to complain that Grant drank Bourbon. Lincoln's answer was: "Good! Find out what Bourbon it is, gentlemen, so I may give it to some of my other generals, too!"

Dr. Crow's influence was not confined to improving whiskey alone. According to an article in *The New York Times* in 1897, Dr. Crow, a graduate of the Edinburgh College of Medicine and Surgery, was a "philosopher and a brilliant man of letters, and a blue-stocking Presbyterian of the John Knox type." He set an example with his gracious way of life that influenced the whole Bluegrass Region.

The unlettered, homespun farmer-distillers who were getting ahead in the expanding Bourbon industry built themselves bigger houses and began to send their sons to colleges—new colleges that were springing up right in their own state. (A decanter of Bourbon is embedded underneath each of the six Ionic columns of the stately portico of Giddings Hall at Georgetown College.)

The mellowing, old farmer-distillers also picked up the genteel custom, when the day's work was done, of sitting on their spacious verandahs and sipping a Mint Julep.

The lore about the mint julep (the word "julep" comes from the Persian *gulab*—meaning "rose water") is vast, intricate, and, naturally, controversial. Facts are scarce; opinions plentiful. Arguments pro and con have always abounded about how the mint should be treated: crushed, muddled, mangled, squashed, bruised, twisted, or tweaked; whether the ice should be cracked or crushed, and the exact order of procedure for each ingredient. The drink itself is basically uncomplicated. It consists of only four ingredients—sugar, water, sprigs of mint, and bourbon. Jefferson Davis, president of the Confederacy, added what he considered a crowning touch to his mint juleps by lacing them with a tablespoonful of French brandy. Perhaps the most famous, certainly the most lyric, of all mint julep descriptions, is the one written by Judge Soule Smith, a noted Lexington attorney and wit who flourished in the late 19th century.

. . . Who has not tasted it has lived in vain. The honey of Hymettus brought no such solace to the soul; the nectar of the gods is tame beside it. It is the very dream of drinks, the vision of sweet quaffings. . . . Sip it and dream—you cannot dream amiss. . . . No other land can give so sweet solace for your cares; no other liquor soothes you so in melancholy days. Sip it and say there is no solace for the soul, no tonic for the body like old Bourbon whiskey.

Irvin S. Cobb wrote of the mint julep less lyrically but perhaps more to the point: "The first Kentucky julep an alien (Yankee) drinks is a sensation; the second is a rhythmic benefaction; but the third one is a serious error."

Bourbon firmly established itself on the Potomac, and became, if "not actually the fuel of Government, at least its lubricant." Of all the distinguished mid-19th century lawmakers who admittedly required a continuous supply of Bourbon to function efficiently, Daniel Webster was the most noted. He not only made good use of the "best of all whiskies" during the preparation of his great orations, but also fortified himself with Bourbon before delivering on the Senate floor such resounding and history-making phrases as: "Liberty and Union, now and forever, one and inseparable!"

According to one historian, Webster, on the day before he was

In 1904 C. W. Post launched a brand of corn flakes he overzealously called "Elijah's Manna." The outcry from ministers was so great he rechristened his product, "Post Toasties." Below: The interior of one of the first Minute Tapioca factories.

The above coat of arms was awarded to the Viennese pretzel bakers for their part in repulsing the attempt of the Turks to dig under the city walls during the siege of Vienna in 1510. On facing page: The original Morton Salt Girl, illustrating the "When it Rains it Pours" slogan.

THE
WHITE HORSE
CELLAR

Eſtab. 1742

In the early days, whiskey was often known only by the name of the place where it was served. White Horse Scotch was christened by patrons of the historic White Horse Inn, a stagecoach station on the road to Edinburgh and a favorite gathering place for Samuel Johnson and other notables of the period.

1855	1962

Henry McKenna was the first to seed each new batch of sour mash with yeast from the old to keep the taste of his Bourbon distinctive and uniform. Located in Fairfield, Kentucky, the distillery remains unchanged and the output is still only a few barrels a day. Until 1962, when a limited quantity was made available to clubs and dealers, it was sold only in Kentucky. Says a third-generation Henry McKenna: "The only thing that's changed after more than 100 years is the bottle."

AVOID *that future* SHADOW

"COMING EVENTS CAST
THEIR SHADOWS BEFORE"
(Thomas Campbell 1777-1844)

LUCKY STRIKE
"IT'S TOASTED"
CIGARETTES

When Tempted
Reach
for a
LUCKY

"It's toasted"

The American Tobacco Company entered the blended cigarette field in
1916 with Lucky Strike—an old brand name (first used in 1856 on plug
tobacco) but an entirely new blend.

George Washington Hill masterminded the Lucky Strike advertising campaigns and slogans that resulted in a tobacco tour de force. "Lucky Strike Green Has Gone to War!" broke in 1942, simultaneously with the American invasion of North Africa. "Lucky Strike Means Fine Tobacco" became so well known that in 1944 it was shortened to initials: L.S./M.F.T. Below: Johnny ("Call for Phil-ip Mar-ah-riss!") Roventini and friend. Johnny first sang his clarion call in 1933.

It's STAR
tobacco all
the time

Cardinals

STAR
Chewing Tobacco

STAR
Chewing Tobacco

*Embedded in each chew of plug tobacco was an identifying tin tag. Until
1921 plug tobacco sold as well as cigarettes, and Star was the leading brand.*

to deliver his welcome to the Marquis de Lafayette, went fishing and imbibed freely. "As he sat on the bank," wrote the historian, "he suddenly drew from the water a large fish, and in his majestic voice said, 'Welcome, illustrious stranger, to our shores!' The next day, his friends who had gone fishing with him, were electrified to hear him begin his speech to Lafayette with these same words."

Before the Civil War, while whiskey was still being sold in barrels to distributors and saloon or tavern keepers, competition was keen, and it often happened that a whiskey salesman out to drum up trade would slip around unobserved to the storage room where a tavern keeper kept his kegs, and ruin a rival company's liquor by putting a ten-penny nail in the barrel. In some instances, wholly unscrupulous drummers sabotaged a competitor's product in ways that were downright obnoxious—such as dropping a garter snake or some foul substance into the keg. There were many complaints as a result of these vicious practices and doctors who often prescribed whiskey for their patients were hard-pressed to find brands that they were sure were reliable and had not been tampered with.

George Garvin Brown, a young wholesale drug salesman in Louisville, solved the problem and made a fortune for himself and his descendants. After listening one day to his friend, Dr. James Holloway, tell of how difficult it was to find a brand that was always dependable, young George hit on the revolutionary idea af bottling and sealing Bourbon at the distillery. In 1870, in partnership with George M. Forman, Brown bottled the first American whiskey under the brand name *Old Forester*, and wrote the statement that still appears on the label of every bottle: *This whiskey is distilled by us only, and we are responsible for its richness and fine quality. Its elegant flavor is solely due to original fineness developed with care. There is nothing better in the market.*

In the 1880's, Bourbon distillers found themselves with a surplus on hand, and decided to turn salesmen and advertise their liquor for the first time. One of the most illustrious names in Bourbon lore is that of Colonel Edmund H. Taylor.

Edmund Haynes Taylor represented the seventh generation of the Taylor family in America, and in the early stages of the Civil War, Colonel Taylor first engaged in cotton speculation in Frankfort, Kentucky, and then acted as a purchasing agent for the Confederacy. After the war, Colonel Taylor entered the banking business, and through it, the distilling business when his bank had to take over distilleries in financial difficulties. Colonel Taylor produced such brands as *Old Hermitage, Old Oscar Pepper, Carlisle* (named for his ancestral home), *Old Taylor,* and *OFC. OFC* actually stood for *Old Fired Copper,* but at one period when the Colonel was in financial difficulties, wags said OFC stood for "Off for Canada," where the Colonel is supposed to have fled.

Colonel Taylor is known as the "father of the Bottled-in-Bond Act," which, among other benefits, curbed the practice of unscrupulous "rectifiers" who mixed quantities of straight alcohol and prune juice with the Bourbon of prominent distillers.

The Colonel was also a great showman and advertiser, as well as the Beau Brummel of his day. He is said to have owned over a hundred suits and twelve hundred neckties. In the mornings he generally wore a checked suit with a large white felt hat and a red carnation. In the afternoons he donned a Prince Albert coat, light trousers, lemon yellow gloves, and an array of large diamonds. Perhaps his greatest feat of salesmanship was introducing his Bourbon to New York. In St. Louis, where more of it was drunk than anywhere else, he hired some men to gather up empty bottles that still bore the *Old Taylor* label. Three freight car loads were shipped to New York, where another crew of men set them up on bars in private clubs and in the better hotels, taverns, and restaurants. All those empties gave the impression that *Old Taylor* was the rage of New York, and, true-to-form, the natives began to demand it forthwith.

Elevating Bourbon to its present peak of excellence was a gradual achievement. It has been said that you can't fool a dedicated Bourbon drinker. It was tried many times during Prohibition when this theoretically arid land was inundated by a flood of Bourbon imitations hastily concocted in various cities throughout the country.

Bourbon is 100% American. True Bourbon is Kentucky Bourbon. And Kentucky Bourbon is the aristocrat of American whiskies.

OLD SMUGGLER SCOTCH

The story of *Old Smuggler* goes back a long way to the land of wild moors and purple heather, mountain streams, placid lochs, and rolling fields of yellow barley—bonnie, bonnie Scotland.

By the start of the sixteenth century, distilled liquor was being enjoyed fairly extensively in Scotland, although in those days tipping the flagon was pretty much a pastime of the upper classes —hence the phrase, "drunk as a lord." When groups of wealthy Caledonians got together, the host locked the door until the cask in the middle of the room was emptied. In an adjoining room, he provided "shakedowns" (overnight accommodations) for those who became prostrated.

When excise taxes were first imposed in 1643, an acute problem resulting from the high license fees arose, and liquor smuggling soon flourished. In Britain an operator of an unlicensed distillery was called "a smuggler." This illicit trade, encouraged by Scots high and low, reached its peak in 1802. Following the Napoleonic wars, England was left with such a heavy debt that Parliament drastically increased the tax on whisky from 3 to 162 pounds. The thrifty Scots bitterly resented paying so high a price for their traditional drink.

The tax was so high that the only way the legal distiller could stay in business was to maintain a large output, rush through as many gallons as possible, then hustle it off to market. The smuggler, on the other hand, was under no such pressure. He could take his time. Distilling whisky was as much an art to a Scotsman as playing the bagpipe, and he took a conscientious pride in the quality of his product. "Smuggler's" whisky gained the reputation of being far better than that bearing the legal tax. The preference of the public for this whisky was not merely a whim—it *was* superior, and as late as 1820 at least half of the Scotch whisky consumed in Britain was the smuggler's product.

By the time *Old Smuggler* was officially established in 1835, the daring and exciting days of the smugglers had ceased to exist, but the founders of the brand felt that the name would carry on the quality tradition of the smugglers of old, and it was from that 200-

year period of "proud smuggling" that a favorite of all Scotches—
Gaelic Old Smuggler Brand—derives its name.

CUTTY SARK SCOTCH

Over 300 years ago, Berry Bros. & Rudd, Ltd. opened Berry's
Coffee Mill at No. 3 James Street in London, England. The fine
Scotch whisky served there to such patrons as Beau Brummel, Napoleon III and Lord Byron was called simply *Berry Bros. Scotch
Whisky*. Then, at a luncheon in the Old Establishment one day in
the 1870's, it was suggested that the popular whisky be given a
more distinctive name than just that of its maker. Many names
were proposed, some serious, some witty—but one received instant,
unanimous approval.

One of the guests had that day won heavily on the outcome of
the race among clipper ships to reach London with the season's first
cargo of tea. This race was the Kentucky Derby of the shipping
world, and the round-the-globe journey inspired wagers amount-
ing to thousands of pounds. The *Cutty Sark* was the name of the
ship that came in first that season, and the elated winner suggested
the whisky at Berry's Coffee Mill be named in honor of the celebrated clipper ship.

Another guest, an artist, took a sheet of yellow paper from his
waistcoat and sketched the proud ship and her name. The sketch
is still used as the *Cutty Sark* label today, almost unchanged from
the original.

I. W. HARPER

Isaac W. Bernheim, 19, landed in New York from Germany in
1848, with four dollars in American money. He made his way to
Wilkes-Barre, Pennsylvania, where he sold assorted merchandise,
known as "Yankee Notions," to frugal Dutch housewives in the
area. Business for notions was brisk, and young Bernheim soon purchased a horse and wagon. When the horse died, unexpectedly, the
dejected Isaac accepted an offer for a job by his two uncles who

ran a general store in Paducah, Kentucky, a thriving little river town of 5,000 people.

Three months later Isaac became a bookkeeper with a wholesale liquor firm in Paducah and this was his first association with the liquor business. He saved enough money to bring his brother Bernard to the United States and turning over the bookkeeping position to him, Isaac went out on the road to represent the company as a traveling salesman.

Two years later, the brothers Bernheim decided to go into business for themselves, and with the purchase of one barrel of whiskey, set up business in the back room of a wholesale grocery store. One of their salesmen, named Harper, was so well-liked by his customers that they referred to the whiskey he sold as "Mr. Harper's whiskey." In 1872, when the Bernheims wanted a name for their choicest whiskey, they combined the initials of Isaac with the surname of their star salesman, Harper, and the famous *I. W. Harper* brand was born.

WHITE HORSE SCOTCH WHISKY

Although it is open to question just when whisky first became known in Scotland, it is certain that by the fifteenth century the Highland Scots were making the whisky we know as Scotch and its fame was spreading to the Lowlands. Inns and taverns where the best whisky could be had were singled out and the whisky served at such places gained an individual reputation, usually known by the name of the establishment serving it.

In the days of Napoleon, *White Horse* whisky was already known throughout Scotland as the whisky of the famous White Horse Inn in the Cannongate, Edinburgh. The inn was the starting point for the London stage coaches and was the rendezvous of the cavaliers of Prince Charles Edward. Great personalities of the day, among them Dr. Samuel Johnson and the actor-mimic Samuel Foote, gathered to enjoy each other's company.

The legend of the inn's romantic past is featured in the quaint reference to its adventurous stagecoach days that has been incorporated into the label on every bottle of *White Horse* Scotch:

All that are desirous to pass from Edinburgh to London, or any other place on their road, let them repair to the White Horse Cellar in Edinburgh, at which place they may be received in a Stage Coach every Monday and Friday, which performs the whole journey in eight days (if God permits), and sets forth at five in the morning. Allowing each passenger 14 pounds weight and all above 6 pence per pound.

The *White Horse* name itself also has romantic associations. A white horse has always been a symbol of purity and high ideals, and an emblem of power and victory. The Norse gods went forth to war on snow-white horses; the Valkyrie rode white horses; and the horses of many famous generals—from the Saxons Hengist and Horsa to Napoleon—were white.

The Scots become very poetic about the Scotch which has been called *White Horse* since 1742. "Look long into the burn-clear depths," they advise. "Inhale the rich bouquet deeply. And when you drink, sip thoughtfully, for you are tasting something which only the home-grown barley, the clear water of Scottish highland burns, the ancient skills and mysteries known to Scottish craftsmen alone can give you."

DRAMBUIE

Drambuie's story begins when Prince Charles Edward, "Bonnie Prince Charlie" of the ballads, landed on the West Coast of Scotland in the Rebellion of '45. The young pretender's well-loved name of Stuart, together with his gay and gallant manner, brought an impressive rally of the most powerful clans in the Highlands to his standard. They fought gloriously, and often victoriously, until the ill-famed Duke of Cumberland appeared on the scene and disastrously routed the Bonnie Prince and his Highlanders at Culloden.

The Prince fled for his life, and the British government issued a proclamation offering a reward of 30,000 pounds to anyone who could deliver the Prince, dead or alive. But no clansman would betray him, and the Prince contemptuously offered a reward of 30 pounds for the capture of "The Elector of Hanover," alias King George II.

Bonnie Prince Charlie was nevertheless hotly pursued for many months, into the wildest regions of the Highlands, and the remotest reaches of the Islands. But always he found refuge with loyal clansmen who sheltered and concealed him. Finally, Flora MacDonald, a Scotswoman, disguised the Prince as her personal maid and successfully smuggled him onto the Isle of Skye. There one of the Mackinnons of Strathaird took over, and rowed him to a safe hiding place until, in September, 1746, a French ship arrived off the West Coast and, miraculously evading all the British warships, safely transported Prince Charlie to France.

In gratitude, the Prince formally presented to Mackinnon the secret formula for his personal liqueur, *an dram budheach*—Gaelic for "the drink that satisfies"—and far better known today in its contracted form, *Drambuie*.

For nearly a century and a half the Mackinnons kept the treasure to themselves. They made only very small quantities of their liqueur, so precious that only a single cask was used for the annual Gathering of the Clan. A few bottles found their way as special tributes to friends outside the Western Isles, and, occasionally, eighteenth and nineteenth century visitors wrote of it appreciatively in their memoirs, but not until 1906 did the Mackinnon family consent to produce the liqueur on a commercial scale.

Unlike many of his contemporaries of that era, Malcolm Mackinnon, who had been born on the Isle of Skye, emigrated no further than Edinburgh, where he went to work at the age of 17 in an old and established distilling house. At 23 he was made a junior partner. He had already become known as a connoisseur of Scotch whiskies, and his opinion was often sought by blenders more than twice his age. Two years later, the senior partners died, and young Malcolm, or Calum as he was called, found himself in sole command. Immediately he turned to an idea he had been considering for a long time: the possibility of producing the old family *Drambuie* recipe on a commercial scale. He finally persuaded his elders that it could be done, and they entrusted the revered recipe to him with admonitions to guard it closely. Calum agreed and set to work in all secrecy to convert the many and varied ingredients into a commercial formula. It was not an easy task. Calum conducted his experiments alone, in a cellar under Union Street. Jelly bags and copper pans were the only appliances used, and it took a week to make enough of the elixir to fill a dozen bottles, but Calum insisted on performing the ritual exactly as he had seen it done in his boyhood. The final result was a delightful duplication in quantity of the original formula.

Only twelve cases were sold that first year, but the following year orders began to flow in. Scotsmen all over the Empire wanted to sample their homeland's first "commercial" liqueur. In 1916, the cellarman of the House of Lords gave it the seal of his special approbation, and brought it into the front rank of great liqueurs.

Malcolm Mackinnon's insistence on an exact duplicate of the old Skye recipe is still in effect today, and is carried out with modern, scientific equipment. The recipe remains a family secret, however, and is securely locked away. The ingredients that are the essence of the liqueur are still mixed only by a member of the Mackinnon family, and in great secrecy. So potent is this mixture that four small vials are sufficient to create the quintessence of 1200 gallons of *Drambuie*.

BENEDICTINE

Benedictine, the exquisite French liqueur, was first made at the beginning of the sixteenth century by Dom Bernardo Vincelli, a herbalist monk of the Order of St. Benedict. In his desire to relieve human suffering, Dom Vincelli devoted himself to the intensive study of herbs and plants, and their curative properties. The country around the Abbey at Fécamp, that fertile part of the Caux district near the sea, was rich in herbs of all sorts, and Dom Vincelli acquired a thorough knowledge of them all. He used them as a basis for his balms and cordials, among them a special elixir which he called *Elixir Benedictin*. Even in those days the fame of *Elixir Benedictin* spread, and Dom Bernardo carefully transcribed its recipe into a parchment for safe-keeping in the Abbey archives.

Centuries passed, and with them kings and emperors. In the tremendous social upheaval following the Revolution of 1789, Orders were dissolved and monks driven from their monasteries. Many Abbeys were destroyed, and Fécamp itself was burned, but not before the monks had time to entrust some of their jewels, tapestries and archives to certain faithful laymen of the town.

So it was that in 1862 M. Alexandre Le Grand, a merchant whose ancestor had been in charge of lay matters for the ancient Abbey, inherited many of the old manuscripts. Among them, to his great surprise and delight, was the ancient parchment on which three centuries earlier Dom Vincelli had inscribed the 28 ingredients for his *Elixir Benedictin*. The secret of the Benedictine monk was not entirely revealed, however, as many details of the treatment of the plants and their precise mixture were missing.

M. Alexandre Le Grand set to work to find them, searching among the old manuscripts, and experimenting in his laboratory. He worked with great determination to recapture the exact essence of the *Elixir Benedictin*, and in 1863 he announced with pride that his efforts had met with success.

The fame of the liqueur which M. Alexandre Le Grand called *Benedictine* spread rapidly, and by 1876 he had a flourishing business. He had beautiful buildings constructed in the best Renaissance style in which to manufacture the rare old elixir. They are still in use today, a unique blending of Art and Industry. At the end of Abbot's Hall, one of the buildings of spacious proportions, is a stained-glass window commemorating the visit of François the 1st, King of France, to the Abbey of Fécamp in 1534. It was here that the monarch, on tasting Dom Bernardo Vincelli's liqueur, exclaimed, "By my faith, never have I tasted better!"

FOUR ROSES WHISKEY

When the last bugle note died away at the end of the War Between the States in 1865, Paul Jones, a young officer from the Virginia regiment of the Confederate Army, turned homeward to Atlanta and the sad task of rebuilding the family fortune that had been swept away in the holocaust.

With his 66-year-old father, Colonel Paul Jones, young Paul went into the distilling business. It was not an easy task to build a future from the ashes of disaster, but like many other courageous young men of that period, Paul was determined and soon established a reputation for fine whiskey.

The business prospered, and by 1886 had outgrown its facilities.

The Jones family decided to move to Louisville, Kentucky, where top grade grains and a natural supply of pure water were in plentiful supply. It was there *Four Roses* whiskey was born. Its christening is a subject of controversy today, but the following version is vouched for by the late Irvin S. Cobb.

Cobb, who described himself as "by inheritance, nativity and personal conviction" a judge of fine whiskey, recounts that young Paul Jones had sought the heart and hand of a lovely Southern beauty in ante-bellum days. When he declared his love for her and asked her hand in marriage, the young lady told him she would give her answer on the night of the forthcoming cotillion: if her answer was "yes," she would signify it by wearing his corsage of four red roses.

On the night of the cotillion ball, the Southern belle appeared wearing young Paul's four roses, and the couple was married soon after. Years later, when Paul Jones believed he had created an exceptionally fine whiskey, he named it *Four Roses* in honor of his wife and the night she wore his corsage.

Cobb's version of the naming of *Four Roses* has been disputed in Atlanta by J. G. Elliott, manager of the Atlanta Museum. Mr. Elliott claims the brand was named in the very mansion now housing the museum when it was owned by the R. M. Rose family who were in the distilling business. His version is that at a gala gathering at the mansion, four girls arrived dressed alike, and wearing corsages of four red roses. On the spur of the moment, male members of the family dubbed a new whiskey then ready for market *Four Roses*, in honor of the four belles wearing four red roses.

When this account appeared in an Atlanta newspaper, however, a descendant of the Rose family said it wasn't true at all; that the whiskey was actually named for an early ancestor, Rufus Rose, who established the distillery, and his wife and their two children. Before this account grew cold, another Rose descendant of more recent times quarrelled with that earlier version and said *Four Roses* was named for Rufus Rose, his brother Origen, and their sons.

There are only a few real facts in the case of the naming of *Four Roses*. There *was a* distilling family named Rose; they *did* use a rose emblem (but it was only *one* rose); and the Roses *did* subsequently sell out to the Jones family, who *did* move to Kentucky and establish the *Paul Jones* and the *Four Roses* brands.

CIGARETTES

Introduction

When Columbus landed on San Salvador, West Indies tribesmen offered him dried tobacco leaves as a gesture of friendship. Being intent on a new trade route to China, he failed to appreciate the gift as more than a token. He threw the leaves away, which was not only impolite, but shortsighted as well, for tobacco became as good as gold, and inseparable from the history of America itself.

One of Columbus' sailors, Roderigo de Jerez, discovered the real purpose of the gift when he saw the Indians roll the dried tobacco in palm or maize, light one end, and inhale smoke through the other. Between puffs, they blew on the lighted end to keep it glowing, a gesture still common to cigar connoisseurs the world over. When Jerez returned to his native Ayamonte, he lit up the leaf Indian-fashion, and was promptly clapped into prison by the Inquisition. Tobacco was associated with heathen ritual, and God-fearing Christians therefore considered it evil. When poor Jerez was finally released, he found that most of his countrymen had meanwhile taken up smoking.

Natives of the New World were avid tobacco-users, and had been for hundreds of years. Every form of tobacco consumption—pipe, cigar, cigarette, snuff, chew—was well-known to them long before the first Spaniards landed. They even carried a supply of the "green herb" in a gourd around their necks, the forerunner of the modern tobacco pouch.

The Caribs of the West Indies inhaled or snuffed tobacco through a hollow, Y-shaped tube called a *taboca* or *tobago*. The Spanish referred to the leaf itself as *tabaco*, and a cigar in Cuba is still *un tabaco*. The Quiche Mayans word for tobacco was *ziq*, and their word for smoking, *zikar,* which might have prompted the Spanish word, *cigarro.*

As the explorers brought back tales of the miraculous weed, European botanists seized on it as a long-sought wonder drug. Sahahun, a prolific writer and priest who lived with the Mexicans from 1529 to 1590, wrote: "Placed in the mouth, it produces dizziness and stupefies." Perhaps it did, but he also wrote of tobacco's sweet smoking qualities as a kind of ceremonial incense as well as a cure for abcesses, sores, colds, snake bite, chills, convulsions, skin eruptions, and internal disorders. France's ambassador to Lisbon, Jean Nicot, failed in his assignment to marry off Queen Catherine de Medici's daughter to the King of Portugal, but won royal favor all the same when he sent tobacco back to France from Lisbon. Ground into snuff, it made Queen Catherine sneeze so hard that it cleared her sinuses and stopped her incessant headaches. Nicot was duly rewarded by having tobacco's most important ingredient named for him: *nicotine.*

By the late sixteenth century, the Spanish had a monopoly on the markets in England and western Europe. The native tobacco grown by the English settlers at Jamestown was far inferior to the Spanish leaf, and the little colony was near financial collapse in 1611 when John Rolfe came to its rescue. (Rolfe is best remembered for a second, more romantic undertaking in 1614, when he married Pocahontas, daughter of the great chief Powhatan.) Rolfe managed to obtain from the Spanish enemy seeds of their prized tobacco from Trinidad and Caracas. In just what manner he was able to bring off the *coup* is unknown, but it is generally accepted that he bribed sailors on a Dutch trading ship to bring the seeds back to him.

At any rate, in the sandy soil of Virginia, the Spanish tobacco thrived, and in 1613 the first experimental shipment from Virginia arrived in London. It had an excellent aroma, and was an immediate success in the rich London market. Tobacco commerce in America had begun.

The British Crown profited handsomely from taxes on the Virginia leaf, and soon stopped the flow of Spanish tobacco into England by a customs barrier. In Colonial Virginia, tobacco was dubbed the "golden weed," and was worth its weight in wives. A shipload of English maidens, "ninety agreeable persons, young and incorrupt," reached Jamestown in 1619, and eager bachelors paid 120 pounds of tobacco for a bride. Taxes were also paid in tobacco, and "tobacco notes," or "crop notes" began to take the place of leaf itself as Colonial currency.

Tobacco culture in America has been associated with such men as George Washington, Thomas Jefferson, and Patrick Henry. The oldest tobacco company in the world, P. Lorillard, is believed to have begun business with tobacco from the Virginia plantation of George Washington who was even then a big planter.

Tobacco, of course, played a major role in the American Revolution. In 1758, Patrick Henry became Virginia's popular hero when he won a case over the farm price of tobacco. When war came, George Washington appealed to his countrymen: "I say, if you can't send money, send tobacco." The Continental Congress used tobacco to build up credit abroad, and in 1777 Benjamin Franklin was able to draw 2,000,000 *livres* in Paris against a contract to deliver 5,000 hogsheads (casks) of Virginia tobacco.

When the republic was free, but still very young, frontier folk purchased or bartered their tobacco at the post office general store, and it was there that one of the most famous frontiersmen of them all, Daniel Boone, bought " 'baccy" to fill the pipe he is credited with having popularized the corncob. That cheap and handy pipe gained great notoriety when the wives of two presidents, Andrew Jackson and Zachary Taylor, smoked it in the White House.

Although the Indians had long been using tobacco in every form we know today, it was the pipe that led the march of the leaf around the world. Sliced, shredded or crumbled, tobacco was smoked in pipes made of wood, stone, bone, metal, and other substances; often startlingly shaped, carved, and colored. Legend has it that Sir Walter Raleigh was puffing clouds from a pipe when his English servant, thinking he was on fire, poured a pitcher of water (some say it was beer) over him. The popularity of pipe smoking grew rapidly in England, although for a time it was a rich man's pleasure because it was actually worth its weight in silver. Tobacconists balanced it in their counter scales against silver shillings at a rate that would amount to about $3 an ounce today.

Snuff, described by a poet as "the final cause for the human nose," was an everyday commodity in the late 1600's (it was thought to have antiseptic qualities and was prescribed for the Plague), but it did not become really fashionable until the eighteenth century. Devotees of snuff tendered each other a pinch from their boxes with much ceremony and then, sniffing it up their nostrils, sneezed with great satisfaction and *éclat*.

Under Queen Anne, the snuff box became indispensable to the well-turned-out gentleman, while the smoking of pipes was relegated to philosophers and the lower classes. Exquisite inlaid snuff boxes were "worn" like personal jewelry. Some snuffers preferred to "dip"—moistening a stick or twig, dipping it in snuff, and chewing it—while others placed a small amount in their mouths, between gum and cheek, to dissolve. The vogue spread to the American colonies, and in later years Dolly Madison elegantly tendered snuff to guests at the White House.

The United States was growing and prospering when Americans took another tobacco custom from the Indians and began to chew. Clipper ships were carrying our commerce around the world, and their crews found lighted pipes a fire hazard. Eagerly they took to chewing tobacco. It was windy on the plains, and frontiersmen, pushing ever westward, favored chewing tobacco also, though neither snuff nor pipe was abandoned. As its popularity grew, chewing tobacco progressed from being sold in loose-leaf, bulky packages, to long, pressed rectangles called "plug" tobacco.

Plug takes its name from a method of curing tobacco used by family-operated factories in North Carolina around the middle of the last century. These small operators bored auger holes in green maple, poplar, birch, elm and other type logs containing a sweet sap, and then "plugged" the holes with leaf tobacco. The tobacco was tamped in, followed by a blunt-nosed peg that packed it still closer, and, after a month or two, the log was split open and the hunks of sap-sweetened tobacco taken out and stored for the family's chewing, or for the market.

The "swollen" cheek was a familiar sight when the plug chew was in its prime. Charles Dickens deplored the profuse and careless spitting he encountered in the United States, and was moved to remark that he could not understand how Americans had won their reputations as expert riflemen, considering their poor spitting aim. However, even Dickens never saw a better marksman than the cow-boy who lived up to his word when he told a man seated between him and a cuspidor twenty feet away: "Sit still, stranger, I'll clear you."

Early brand names for plug tobacco ranged from the whimsical to the incredible—*Lic Quid, Monkey Wrench Plug, Darling Fanny Pan Cake, Hard Pan, Plank Road, Grit, Old Slug, Jaw Bone, Old Brick, Alligator, Ring Coil Hot Cake, Leatherwood, That*—and one manufacturer became so desperate for a name for one of his numerous brands he called it *Little Worth*. Paradoxically, the more expensive the tobacco the more repulsive the name: *Mule Ear, Lime Kiln Club,* and *It's Naughty But O How Nice*.

Plug slowly faded as the favorite form of tobacco and the ashtray replaced the cuspidor, once an essential item everywhere from the Halls of Congress to the rowdiest frontier saloon. During the Mexican War, when our armies moved south of the Rio Grande, cigarros and cigarrillos took the limelight. Cigar factories were numerous in the United States, since all the work was done by hand. *Paste Segars,* named for the method of fastening the outside wrapper to the filler, was one early New England brand, but the best known was *Windsor Particulars.* "Long nines" were pencil-thin; "short sizes" not so long; and "supers" were finished off with a twist. Short sixes became a fixture in the taverns, and were the earliest "twofers" (two for a cent).

When the country's aspirations veered Westward, shoe string tobacco grown in Pennsylvania was rolled into long, sweetened cigars that teamsters could either smoke or chew, according to their whim. These foot-long cigars jutting out from the faces of drivers headed West came to be known as "stogies" after the name of the town where the covered wagons they drove were made—Conestoga, Pennsylvania. A great favorite was one called *Mayer Rat Tail,* but "stogie" soon came to mean any cheap cigar.

Imported from Cuba, or made in America with Havana fillers, the cigar gained social status and became a symbol of prosperity. The Baroness Dudevant, better known as George Sand, smoked cigars, and Amy Lowell had such a huge supply that many survived her when she died. As a rule, however, cigars were left to the men, who were banished to smoking rooms lest cigar smoke linger in feminine curls or parlor draperies. Queen Victoria forbade the use of tobacco at court, but when her son Edward ascended the throne he set the style after his first royal dinner as King: "Gentlemen, you may smoke!" Mark Twain, a devoted pipe and cigar smoker, declared he smoked only once a day—"all day long"; that he could give up smoking with ease, and had in fact done so "hundreds of times."

Cigars have inspired many famous remarks, but perhaps the most familiar of all is the one made by Thomas R. Marshall, vice-president under Woodrow Wilson. After listening to a Republican senator ramble on at length about the country's needs, Marshall opined: "What this country needs is a really good five-cent cigar."

As the hectic urban rush began, the prolonged pleasure of pipe and cigar gave way to short, convenient cigarettes. In a desperate effort to revive pipe smoking, one manufacturer advertised: "Do pipe smokers live longer?" To which the wits were quick to reply: "No, it only seems longer."

A crude form of the modern cigarette was born when Spanish explorers arrived at Yucatan in 1518. They were welcomed by an old chief who shared with them a Mexican delicacy—the "reed cigarette." The reed, "one and a half hands in length," was filled with native tobaccos and aromatic herbs. When the Spaniards returned home, they simply replaced the reed with a paper wrapper.

Another account of origin is dated 1832. An Egyptian army under Ibrahim laid siege to Acre, an ancient stronghold held by Suleiman Bey and his Turks. A clever Egyptian soldier hit on the idea of rolling the gun powder in hand paper spills. The cannonade attack was speeded up to a remarkable degree and the delighted Ibrahim sent the gun crew a gift of tobacco in appreciation. The cannoneers filled the one pipe they had and passed it from one to the other, each puffing in turn, until a Turkish cannon ball lobbed in and shattered the "community" pipe. The Egyptians were disconsolate until the same enterprising gunner picked up some of his paper spills, rolled tobacco in them instead of gun powder, and passed them out to his fellow artillerymen.

The cigarette industry, however, began when English soldiers had the good luck to capture a train of Russian officers in the Crimea in 1854. The officers were well supplied with Russian mode cigarettes, cigarettes rolled with Turkish tobacco exclusively and made with a cardboard mouthpiece and cotton-plug filter, and the British soldiers, whose clay pipes were often the first casualties of battle, kept the cigarettes when they traded the officers. Returning to London, the British soldiers brought with them a demand for Russian mode cigarettes. Small London tobacconists, among them Philip Morris, Esq., hand-rolled the Turkish cigarettes to order, and inevitably the fad soon spread to New York.

In America, the Russian mode cigarette was at first a specialty item—either an affectation of the upper classes or a custom of the impoverished immigrants from southern Europe who had a great fondness for straight Turkish tobacco. Like cigars, the cigarettes were hand-rolled, and though a few firms began making them, they did so as a sideline to their chewing and smoking tobacco business. Brand names at this stage were most descriptive. Those aimed at high society were called *Opera Puffs, Bon Ton, Fragrant Vanity Fair, Turkish Orientals,* and *Three Kings;* while those aimed at anybody who had a dime bore such names as *Old Rip, Old Judge,* and *Canvas Back.*

Many Americans "rolled their own," and though the deftest rollers could manage in a high wind, the average smoker welcomed the advent of factory or tailor-mades when James Bonsack, a Virginian, invented a cigarette-making machine. Bonsack claimed his machine would reduce manufacturing costs from 80 cents to 30 cents a thousand.

With the perfecting of the Bonsack machine, the cigarette era of plenty arrived. A staggering total of one billion cigarettes was produced in the year 1885 (more than that amount is now smoked *daily*), but it was not until 1921 that cigarettes surpassed all other forms of tobacco consumption.

Over three and a half centuries have passed since the first great American industry began in Virginia with the experimental planting of tobacco by John Rolfe. Among man's fixed customs, tobacco has a long record of world-wide popularity. It never had to overcome class distinctions, for tobacco in some form has always been as familiar in a peasant's hut as in the palace of a king. True, the mighty J. P. Morgan had his mighty Kohinoor cigars—8 inches long and specially rolled for him at $1.25 each—but on the other hand, the Westward-bound frontiersman had his stogies and two-fers.

Pipe, snuff, chewing tobacco, cigar and cigarette—these mark successive eras in American history. One popular vogue overlapped another, and every form of tobacco has its *devotées* now as it had in 1492. But each enjoyed its own heyday, and today, for more than half of the adult population in America, the pattern of living includes the use of tobacco in one form or another.

CAMELS   PRINCE ALBERT

The R. J. Reynolds Tobacco Company was founded in 1875 by Richard Joshua Reynolds. Mr. Reynolds was a lad of 15 working on his father's Virginia tobacco farm when Lee surrendered to Grant at Appomattox only 115 miles away. The South was in the aftermath of reconstruction following the War Between the States when young Reynolds decided to establish his own business. He had been in a tobacco manufacturing partnership with his father in Virginia, but decided to branch out on his own. The eager youth, then 21 years old, traveled by horseback to Winston, North Carolina, and bought a plot of land on Chestnut Street. The small factory he built on that lot was a red frame structure which covered less ground than a tennis court. Winston was only a small village then, with about 800 citizens, and historic neighboring Salem— where George Washington slept not one but two nights—was still a hamlet.

As small as the first Reynolds factory was, its cost of $2,400, including a few crude pieces of equipment, loomed large to young Reynolds. He had saved $7,500 to build the factory and launch his venture, but needed much of that to buy the tobacco for his products. Leaf tobacco auction markets were then, as they still are, operated on a pay-as-you-buy basis.

Like the factory, the Reynolds working force was also small; only two regular assistants and scarcely a dozen seasonal helpers were employed. During the early years of the business, chewing tobaccos were the only products made. A one-horse dray furnished sufficient transportation to cart the products to the depot for shipment.

Nationwide recognition came with the introduction of *Prince Albert* smoking tobacco in 1907, and within a few years it was (and has remained) the top-selling brand. But the year Winston and Salem joined to form Winston-Salem marked a new era of success for R. J. Reynolds for that was the year he entered the cigarette field and launched the world's first blended cigarette. Oriental names were popular with tobacco fanciers of that era, and Reynolds decided that the camel evoked an image of the exotic Orient and suited the Turkish tobaccos the new cigarette would contain.

The new name *Camel* happily coincided with the annual visit of Barnum and Bailey's circus to Winston-Salem. The featured attraction was a stately Arabian dromedary called "Old Joe." Reynolds supplied his stenographer, R. C. Haberkern, with a camera and promptly dispatched him to the circus to take pictures of this magnificent animal. The circus manager took a dim view of the young man with the camera (now retired Chairman of the Executive Committee of Reynolds) and loudly complained he "didn't have time for such foolishness." Whereupon young Haberkern gently reminded him that Reynolds had closed its factory and given its employees a holiday just so they could attend the circus. The manager quickly relented and offered his cooperation.

While the camera was being adjusted, "Old Joe" insisted on turning his head to view the activities. Each time, the manager dutifully straightened the creature's head until finally, irked and insulted by the lack of regard for his curiosity, "Old Joe" shut his eyes, raised his tail, and reared his head in offended dignity. The shutter clicked, and the pose was recorded for posterity.

From this photograph a drawing was made. The artist added the palms and pyramids in the background to enhance the Oriental idea. On October 21, 1913, a gigantic advertising campaign launched *Camel* cigarettes. The campaign took the form of four "teaser ads," each bearing the illustration of "Old Joe" as he appears on the package, but each having different copy. The first appeared a few days before the introduction of *Camels,* bearing the single word "Camels"; the second announced, "The Camels are coming!"; the third predicted, "Tomorrow there'll be more Camels in this town than in all Asia and Africa combined"; and the following day, when the cigarettes were actually on sale, the final ad proclaimed: "*Camel* cigarettes are here."

Some years later, the company came upon one of the best-known slogans in cigarette advertising: "I'd Walk a Mile For a *Camel*."

It originated with an unidentified man who walked up to a sign painter at work on a *Camel* billboard and asked for a cigarette. The sign painter gave him a *Camel*. "Thanks," said the stranger, as he lighted the cigarette and inhaled deeply, "I'd walk a mile for a *Camel*."

Since "Old Joe's" debut in 1913, his image has become one of the most widely-circulated in history, and he has become the world's most pictured animal, appearing on several billion packages of *Camel* cigarettes.

OLD GOLD   KENT   BETWEEN THE ACTS

P. Lorillard, the oldest tobacco company in existence today, was founded in 1760 by Pierre Lorillard, an 18-year-old French immigrant, who opened his little "manufactory" in New York on the High Road to Boston (now Park Row).

Snuff was the young Pierre's specialty, and the foundation for the success of that initial venture into the tobacco business. His closely-guarded recipes for a dozen varieties became celebrated, and competitors tried in vain to guess their ingredients. In an old manuscript, one rival suggests that "by observing what kind of tobacco Lorillard buys at auction or at private sale, the right complexion of the leaf can be come at."

The little manufactory prospered until the tide of the Revolution swept through New York. The patriotic Pierre and his young family fled from the Tory-occupied city to his parents' home outside of town, but it was only a short time until Hessian soldiers took up quarters there also, a fact Pierre bitterly resented. Violence soon flared, and the Hessian soldiers killed Pierre Lorillard, the Huguenot who had come to the New World to find freedom and opportunity.

Pierre's widow struggled heroically—and successfully—to keep the business going until her two small sons would be old enough to take over. The two boys, Peter and George, graduated very quickly from running errands to running the business, and in 1789 they published the first known American advertisement for tobacco. Indian-minded, it shows a tribesman smoking a long clay pipe while he leans against a hogshead marked "Best Virginia," and recommends Lorillard products ranging from cut tobacco plug and snuff to ladies' twist (strips of tobacco leaves woven together.)

Since the Indian was the first to grow and smoke tobacco, and P. Lorillard the first to sell it, the Lorillards have always been inclined to acknowledge tobacco's debt to the red man. Many of their early brand names were Indian in origin, and their trademark depicts two Indians beneath the inscription: "Established 1760." Indians again became allies of the Lorillards and the tobacco industry when their wooden counterparts began to appear in front of the shops where tobacco products were sold. Big as life or bigger, or in miniature, they were painted in vivid colors. Warriors and maidens, proverbially stoic, offered customers tobacco leaves or bundles of cigars. One heroic figure in Chicago, modeled after an Iroquois chieftain and dubbed "Big Chief Me Smoke 'Em" was so highly admired by members of his tribe that they paid regular visits to venerate him as their totem.

As real Indians retreated westward, their wooden images made a stand in the white man's cities and towns, but they too faced battles. Drays or handtrucks ran over some of them; others, not chained to the store-fronts, were carried off into captivity; and some were burned during coal shortages. Citizens who had imbibed too freely either were seized by the spirit of Indian-fighting forebears and ferociously attacked a wooden red man, or draped themselves fondly on his shoulders to tell him troubles that had bored their bartenders. The deadly aim of air rifles or sling shots in the hands of small boys caused many a wooden redskin to rock on his pedestal. Eventually, their stands were equipped with wheels and they were trundled inside for the night, but even so they were doomed and began to disappear in the 1890's, finding safety only in museums and private collections.

The Lorillards prospered, and Pierre's sons moved their factory ten miles north of New York City to the woods of Westchester. They harnessed the Bronx River to turn the wheels of their new snuff mill, and it was one of the earliest and most efficient examples of water-power in America. About 1800, the original wooden mill was replaced by one of native field stone, and it stands today in the New York Botanical Garden in Bronx Park, an ancient mill in a sylvan setting that was, over a century ago, the beginning of a great tobacco empire. A landmark in the tobacco history of America, it has now been restored, and in 1954 was formally dedicated as a monument to the nation's oldest tobacco company.

Peter Lorillard died in 1843, and the event was noted by Mayor Philip Hone of New York in his famous diary:

Died this morning at his seat in Westchester County, Mr. Peter Lorillard . . . in the 80th year of his age. . . . He was a tobacconist, and his memory will be preserved in the annals of New York by the celebrity of Lorillard's Snuff and Tobacco. He led people by the nose for the best part of a century and made his enormous fortune by giving them to chew that which they could not swallow.

As the pipe went westward, the brothers Lorillard hit upon a brilliant idea. They had posters printed listing all their products, and sent them to every postmaster in the United States, and then induced most of them to stock *Lorillard* tobacco. Not only was this a forerunner of direct mail advertising, but it gave impetus to the general store and its cracker-barrel congresses as the postmaster branched out to stock other merchandise.

When the pipe was discarded for the plug chew, the Lorillards quickly established a reputation in the field, and unscrupulous dealers began to sell inferior plugs by slipping them into a *Lorillard* wrapper or box. In 1870, Pierre Lorillard III accidentally found a solution to the problem when he discovered a way for people to identify a genuine *Lorillard* plug. Checking over a day's output of chewing tobacco, he spotted a plug with a piece of tin left in it. Mentally he made a note to fire the person responsible, as visions of a loyal *Lorillard* chewer crunching down on scrap metal made him wince. He returned to his office and the stack of complaints about the continuing sale of inferior plugs fraudulently bearing the *Lorillard* name. The bit of tin he had just seen was still on his mind when the idea occurred to him to use it deliberately as a means of identification. Pierre immediately ordered a supply of tin tags prominently stamped with the *Lorillard* name and had them clamped into each plug.

The first Lorillard plug to wear the novel identification was a brand suitably dubbed *Tin Tag*. Although the device had been patented, other manufacturers seized on it. Staunchly defending his own, Lorillard brought suit in 1885 for infringement of patent but lost when the court ruled that tin tags were not patentable.

Various plug tobacco companies capitalizing on the idea of Pierre Lorillard's popular *Tin Tag* began offering premiums to customers for the tags from their brands. The gimmick backfired for one firm when a group of small boys discovered the company disposed of its redeemed tags by throwing them into an old abandoned well. The ecstatic youngsters gleefully fished 25,000 tags out of the well and before their supply was exhausted had acquired every prize offered in the catalogue.

Premiums reached their peak in 1860 when Lorillard, in honor of its 100th Anniversary, brought out its *Century* brand, a fine-cut tobacco well suited for the hand-made cigarettes of the time. Into one package of each day's production of *Century* tobacco went $100 in currency—sometimes a single note, or fifty $2's, or any combination totalling $100. *Century* was a sensation until the authorities curtailed the practice as being too similar to a lottery.

When cigars replaced plug in the limelight Lorillard responded with such brands as *Sweet Moments, Two Orphans,* and *Old Virginia Cheroots.* Later came *Muriel* and *Van Bibber,* the latter a slender, elegant cigar, named after the debonair hero of stories by Richard Harding Davis. Mr. Van Bibber, a man-about-town and constant theatre goer, often sauntered backstage and into the star's dressing room where he lit a cigar between the wires of the gas burner and then left it half-smoked in the ashtray as he hurried back to his seat to watch the next act. Abandoning a good cigar during the intermission was a great annoyance to theatre patrons, and many a lobby smoker, summoned back by the curtain bell, took his last few puffs so frantically that he resembled a flash fire. A happy solution was reached with *Between the Acts Little Cigars,* packed in a small tin box.

Lorillard later got rid of its regular cigar lines in order to focus its attention on cigarettes. They retained however, the popular *Between the Acts,* and sales increases of this brand in recent years show how well the little cigar anticipated the contemporary mood.

The short, convenient cigarette was welcomed not only for its smoking pleasure, but for its social value. Shy folks lit one in embarrassing moments, and Lorillard took note with its memorable advertising series: "Be Nonchalant—Light a *Murad.*"

In deference to the demand, Lorillard cigarettes started using Turkish tobacco, and brands such as *Egyptian Deities, Helmar,*

Mogul, Turkish Trophies, Gods of the Nile, Harem Beauties, and *Potentates* soon appeared.

When blended cigarettes of domestic and imported tobaccos became popular after the first World War, Lorillard introduced the *Old Gold* brand in 1926. *Old Gold* took its name from the old Southern belt of Virginia where its rich golden tobacco was grown. By the early 1930's *Old Gold* was one of the country's leading domestic brands. With the advent of television, the famous *Old Gold* Dancing Pack became one of the outstanding commercials.

Another dramatic event in the world of tobacco came in the mid-1950's. Just as snuff gave way to the pipe, and as the cigar moved over for the cigarette, and as Turkish tobacco stepped aside for the domestic blend, so in turn did the filtered cigarette appear on the scene and take over the position of eminence it still holds.

Lorillard first took serious note in 1951 of the growing trend in Switzerland and elsewhere toward filtered cigarettes. Despite the fact that they accounted for less than one per cent of all American cigarette sales at that time, Lorillard became convinced that the filtered cigarette was to play a major role in the tobacco industry. Accordingly, in March of 1952, they launched the *Kent Micronite* filtered cigarette, named for Herbert A. Kent, an executive under whom the company had made some of its greatest progress. *Kent* immediately attracted the greatest consumer interest ever accorded a new cigarette up to that time. Lorillard intensified its research program to improve the *Micronite* filter, and the company was in an enviable position in 1957 when *Reader's Digest,* followed by independent research organizations, and echoed by newspapers throughout the country, dramatically reported that the new, improved *Micronite* filter was an advance in filtered smoking, and worthy of special commendation.

Smokers stampeded for the new *Kent,* and sales tripled. The tobacco industry was electrified. In a half-dozen years filter-tip cigarettes rocketed from a tiny fraction of one per cent of the market to half of the national total cigarette sales. P. Lorillard had contributed another historic milestone to the tobacco industry.

Later generations of Lorillards did not limit their contributions to the tobacco industry alone. To Pierre IV the male population owes the Tuxedo which was designed and first worn in 1886 at the opening of the celebrated Tuxedo Park Club, the Lorillards' fabulous game preserve and clubhouse. Pierre IV had decided that something less formal than the tail coat of full-dress was needed, and he ordered a tailless jacket to be tailored on the lines of the "pink" or scarlet coat worn by fox-hunters in riding to hounds. However, at the last moment, Pierre conservatively decided to let the younger generation introduce his new design, and a society columnist protested:

At the Tuxedo Club ball young Griswold Lorillard appeared in a tailless dress coat and waistcoat of scarlet satin, looking for all the world like a royal footman. There were several others of the abbreviated coats worn which suggested to the onlookers that the boys ought to have been put in straitjackets long ago.

Such was the first appearance of the "Tuxedo" as it came to be called, and the society columnist notwithstanding, it was here to stay. Modified to black, the Lorillard dinner jacket became a permanent part of the male wardrobe.

PALL MALL   LUCKY STRIKE

In 1865, Washington Duke, a 45-year-old Confederate veteran and widower, walked back from battlegrounds of the Civil War to his home near Durham, North Carolina. He had fought in the defense of Richmond, been captured and sent to Libby Prison for the duration of the war, was freed after Appomattox, and arrived home with 50 cents. The war had stripped his 300-acre farm bare, and all that was left was a barn half-full of cured tobacco. With the help of his three sons, Brodie, Benjamin and James Buchanan (Buck), Duke set to work grinding and packaging the tobacco. He packed it into muslin bags and labeled it *Pro Bono Publico*. Duke and the three boys loaded the tobacco into a wagon pulled by two blind mules, and hauled it to Raleigh, where they quickly sold it. The proceeds from that first sale were used to buy food for the family.

Duke sold his land to get working capital, and then rented back part of it to grow and sell tobacco. Soon the barn gave way to a frame factory building, and in a few years, the Dukes moved their enterprise to a building on Main Street in Durham.

Meanwhile, another tobacco success story was taking place in Durham. While Washington Duke was a prisoner of war, 50,000 Union troops under Sherman were camped near Durham waiting for the completion of the peace treaty. While they waited, they continued foraging and pillaging, and discovered a supply of bright leaf tobacco in John Ruffin Green's factory near Durham Station. With little else to do, they smoked and chewed constantly.

When Washington Duke returned to his ravaged farm, he found neighbor John Green with his hands full of orders from discharged Yankee soldiers for some of "that fine Durham smoking tobacco." Green quickly abandoned his pre-war brand, *Best Flavored Spanish Smoking Tobacco*, and substituted *Genuine Durham Smoking Tobacco*. The new label was further embellished by the likeness of a Durham bull. (A jar of mustard made in Durham, England, which bore the likeness of a bull's head, had been Green's inspiration.) Although the tobacco is still labeled *Genuine Durham Smoking Tobacco* it has always been called *Bull Durham*.

The career of *Bull Durham* smoking tobacco is a chronicle of spectacular success. After Green's death, a company headed by W. T. Blackwell took over. The Durham Bull was advertised all over America and Europe, and was once even seen on an Egyptian pyramid; celebrities—Lord Tennyson, Rudyard Kipling, Thomas Carlyle, James Russell Lowell, and Will Rogers—endorsed it.

Buck, youngest of the Duke sons, was eight years old when the family hauled that first load of tobacco to Raleigh after his father returned home from the war. His pay was a sack of brown sugar. Sixteen years later, at the age of 24, he was in charge of manufacturing for W. Duke Sons & Company. He had worked hard all his life, and in the process had learned to face facts. And the fact was, reasoned Buck Duke in 1881, that a family business such as the Dukes' simply couldn't compete with the spiraling success of Blackwell's Bull Durham smoking tobacco, a name that had become synonymous with the best of bright leaf tobacco. "Something has to be done," Buck said, "and quick. We're going into the cigarette business."

Duke began operations with a factory manager and 125 skilled immigrant rollers "imported" from New York City. Hand-manufacture of cigarettes was slow and costly, but even so, when Bonsack invented his cigarette-making machine the established cigarette companies refused to use it, claiming smokers wanted their cigarettes rolled by hand; that machine-made goods would never sell, and, furthermore, that the machine didn't work very well, anyway.

Duke ignored the collective opinion of the other companies, and put his own mechanic to work to remedy the machine's defects. By 1884, he was turning out 200 machine-made cigarettes a minute. Carrying cigarettes was also a problem for the smoker, and Duke solved that one by inventing the sliding pasteboard box. With costs lowered by the mechanization, Duke's price was five cents for ten—half the price of competitive cigarettes.

By 1888, W. Duke Sons & Company had a New York factory on Rivington Street, a new plant in Durham, and a skyrocketing sales curve. In addition to the original *Duke of Durham* cigarette Buck had introduced in 1881, the company came out with four other brands in 1884: *Cameo, Cross Cut, Duke's Best,* and *Cyclone.* Among the earlier ones were *Town Talk, Pedro, Velvet Mouthpiece,* and *Pin Head.* All bore the prominent label: "These cigarettes are manufactured on the Bonsack Cigarette Machine." By 1889, Duke accounted for 38 per cent of American cigarette sales.

The quartet of rival cigarette-makers which in 1880 had been called the "Big Four"—Allen & Ginter, Kinney, Kimball and Goodwin—were rapidly becoming the "Little Four." Duke had once approached Lewis Ginter to discuss merging, and was arrogantly told: "You couldn't buy us out to save your neck. You haven't enough money, and you couldn't borrow enough." Ginter discovered he had badly miscalculated, and in 1890 the "Big Four" joined with W. Duke Sons & Company to form a new corporation, The American Tobacco Company. It was the giant of the industry, and its president was James Buchanan Duke.

Subsidiaries were formed, and major companies were absorbed into the combine, including Liggett & Myers, Lorillard, Reynolds, Brown & Williamson, and Phillip Morris.

While the American Tobacco Company's founding was based on Duke's early cigarette success, the cigarette did not move into first place in the tobacco industry until 1921. Meanwhile, before the

Gay Nineties ended, Duke had duplicated his cigarette victory in the chewing tobacco field. The American Tobacco Company founded The American Cigar Company, and acquired such brand names as *Sweet Caporal* (the French word for "corporal," and intended to suggest that the tobacco was a cut above common leaf as a corporal is a cut above a common soldier); *El Roi Tan* (though its name combines the twin attributes of both royalty and Spanishness, the "Roi" was derived from a man named "Roy" and the "Tan" from his partner, a man named Tannebaum); *Cabanas* (oldest known fine cigar); and *La Corona* (the world's best known cigar).

When the rage for Turkish cigarettes flared, The American Tobacco Company introduced *Pall Mall* as a straight Turkish cigarette in a deep purple slide and shell box at a premium price of 25¢ a box. *Pall Mall* was named for a street in London noted for its fashionable address and exclusive clubs. Its choice as a brand name was its association with persons of discriminating taste—"Wherever particular people congregate." The motto on the *Pall Mall* package, *"In hoc signo vinces,"* ("By this sign we are victorious") was meant to further enhance this image.

Cigarette sales climbed, and in 1910 the national total was 8,600,000,000—of which The American Tobacco Company brands accounted for 82 per cent. In 1911 the government declared The American Tobacco Company a monopoly, and under the provisions of the Sherman Anti-Trust Act decreed that Duke's huge tobacco combine be dissolved. When Duke complied, most of today's major tobacco companies emerged, including the "Big Four"—American Tobacco, Liggett & Myers, Lorillard, and R. J. Reynolds.

J. B. Duke retained the name The American Tobacco Company, and in 1916 entered the blended-tobacco field with *Lucky Strike* cigarettes, an old brand name, but an entirely new blend. *Lucky Strike* was the name of one of the first plugs to carry a brand name. It was first made in 1856 by Dr. R. A. Patterson of Richmond, Virginia, who dropped his medical satchel to go into the tobacco business. It was a natural choice in the 1850's, because the California Gold Rush of 1849 had opened the Far West to settlement, and gold was discovered near Denver the following year. The "Pike's Peak or Bust" stampede followed in 1858.

The year 1925 marked the end of an era. The company's founder,

Buck Duke, died in October. He was buried in the chapel on the Duke University campus in North Carolina—the university that bears his name and which he endowed with 40 million dollars in 1924 and another 40 million on his death. His successor as president, Percival S. Hill, died two months later. Taking Hill's place was his son, George Washington Hill, who was to write his own chapter in tobacco annals as the virtuoso of tobacco advertising.

Young Hill, who had grown up in the business and was genuinely fascinated with it, quickly became impatient with the prevailing, unimaginative methods of advertising. *Lucky Strike* had been on the market eight years, but still ranked third nationally; Hill's first move as president was to concentrate all the company's selling and advertising energy on this one brand. The result was a tobacco *tour de force*, a series of strikingly effective campaigns that catapulted *Lucky Strike* into first place in eleven of the next eighteen years. Hill originated such famous slogans as "Reach for a Lucky," and "With Men Who Know Tobacco Best, It's Luckies Two to One."

Supplementing his print campaigns was the radio which had just graduated from the crystal-set-and-earphones stage. Hill was also the mastermind behind the *Lucky Strike* "Hit Parade" program which lasted 25 years, and the well-remembered chant of the tobacco auctioneer, always ending with the classic "Sold, American."

His two last advertising campaigns were among his best. The first of these, in 1942, consisted of just seven words: "*Lucky Strike* Green Has Gone to War." The gold panels on the Lucky Strike package became casualties of the global conflict because the ink base was copper powder, and copper was in short supply. Then chromium, essential to the dark green label, became unavailable. The result was the present white package launched with a dramatic advertising appeal. "Lucky Strike Green Has Gone to War" broke in the fall of 1942, simultaneously with the American invasion of North Africa. In six weeks sales increased 38 percent.

Hill's last advertising campaign consisted of only five words: "Lucky Strike Means Fine Tobacco." By 1944, the phrase was so well known that it was shortened to initials only: "L.S.M.F.T." Hill had them lettered on the bottom of the *Lucky Strike* package, and they have appeared on every package since, just as he wrote them.

In 1946, with *Lucky Strike* on top of the heap, and with his two king-size brands, *Pall Mall* and *Herbert Tareyton*, climbing, Hill died in his Quebec fishing camp. He was no Horatio Alger, but his story is nonetheless an inspiring one: that of a rich man's son who also made good.

CHESTERFIELD

Liggett & Myers Tobacco Company began in 1822, when Christopher Fouls first manufactured snuff in Belleville, Illinois. In 1847, his 18-year-old grandson, John Edmund Liggett, entered the business, and when John Edmund's brother, William, joined the firm in 1858, the name was changed to J. E. Liggett & Brother. In 1873, George S. Myers bought William Liggett's share in the company, and the name Liggett & Myers appeared for the first time.

The company's leading and history-making brand of plug tobacco, *Star,* was first called *New Style,* and, to emphasize its uniqueness, a row of small tin stars was placed across the plug so that each cut would have a star attached to it. This caught the public fancy, and the plug was soon referred to as "the tobacco with the tin star on it," or "tin star tobacco." The promotional value of the tin star was obvious, and the brand name quickly changed to *Star.* By 1885, Liggett & Myers Tobacco Company was the largest producer of plug tobacco in the world, and remained so until its absorption in the American Tobacco Company.

When the American Tobacco Company trust was broken up in 1911, Liggett & Myers emerged with twelve manufacturing branches and some 625 brand names, the top sellers being *Star* and *Horse Shoe* chewing tobacco, *Duke's Mixture* and *Velvet* smoking tobacco, and *Piedmont* and *Fatima* cigarettes. Then, in 1912, Liggett & Myers reintroduced the *Chesterfield* brand of cigarettes.

Cigarettes, in those early days, battled not only one another, but reformers as well. They were condemned not for reasons of health, but on moral grounds. Henry Ford's attacks on the evils of smoking were famous. He said that almost all criminals were inveterate

"Blow some
my way!"

Good tobaccos do surely speak for themselves!

IT stands to reason—the better the tobaccos, the better the taste. And when matched to bring out natural tobacco character—better still!

There's character in Chesterfields—natural character—the natural mildness and good taste of fine tobaccos perfectly blended. How else account for Chesterfield's record—America's fastest-growing cigarette for four consecutive years—how else than through a natural goodness which men find in no other cigarette?

Chesterfield
CIGARETTES

*Such popularity
must be deserved*

LIGGETT & MYERS TOBACCO CO.

Liggett & Meyers was the first tobacco company to use "nice girls" in cigarette advertising.
On following page: top, one of a series of advertisements that introduced Camels; bottom, the model for the trademark, "Old Joe."

Camels

Tomorrow

there'll be more
CAMELS in
this town than
in all Asia and
Africa com-
bined!

The original Ivory Soap wrapper.

A Procter & Gamble crew who helped introduce Ivory Soap by handing out samples. Photographs courtesy of Procter & Gamble.

Left: Smith Brothers originally sold their cough drops from a glass container, but discontinued the practice because of the sometimes unscrupulous substitution of competitive remedies.

Dr. Scholl has been associated with corns, calluses, bunions and fallen arches for the past 58 years. The familiar yellow and blue package has been part of the American scene so long that the name on it is recognized rather than read.

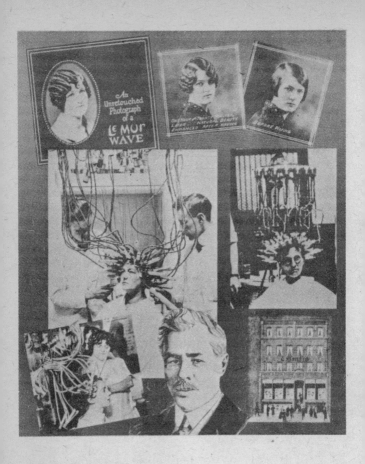

When the inventor of the permanent waving machine, Charles Nestle, advertised the opening of his salon in New York, sixty-two women responded. Sixty-one walked away without the permanent—frightened either by the waving apparatus itself (although it was guaranteed shock-proof) or the price. But one woman stayed and this was the beginning of Nestle's American success. By 1919 a Nestle permanent was part of many women's beauty regimen.

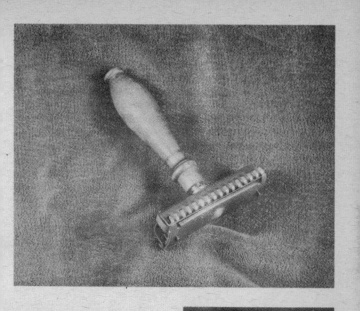

Inventor King C. Gillette said of the safety razor shown above: "Of all the little things that have been invented, it is one of the biggest little things ever issued from the U.S. Patent Office."

Prince Matchabelli, eldest son of a Russian family of nobility, fled to America after the Bolshevik revolution, and turned to making perfume.

smokers, and that he would not hire anyone who smoked cigarettes. Thomas Edison, John Wanamaker, and Connie Mack were among other personalities of the day who allied themselves with Ford against cigarettes. In the early 1900's, a woman was arrested for smoking a cigarette in an automobile on Fifth Avenue, and Irene Castle created a sensation when she was discovered smoking in the Pompeian Room of the Seneca Hotel in Rochester. All the same, many of America's younger set were smoking in the privacy of their homes, and avant garde society ladies affected the habit as evidence of their cosmopolitan sophistication. Women were pictured on the packages of two popular cigarette brands of the day, but they were Oriental women in costume, and therefore no threat to the sacredness of American womanhood.

It was *Chesterfield* that broke the advertising barrier with a poster ad which first appeared in 1926. A man and woman were shown seated on a moonlit river bank. The man was lighting a cigarette, and the girl coaxing: "Blow some my way." It was a daring move, and played an important part in revolutionizing cigarette advertising. It opened the way for a whole new market that could easily double the sale of cigarettes. The expected storm of protest arose against the advertisement, but other companies were quick to follow *Chesterfield's* lead. It meant that women who wanted to smoke no longer had to hide the fact, and could now enjoy openly what had been socially taboo before.

The *Chesterfield* name was one of the brands allocated Liggett & Myers when The American Tobacco Company trust was dissolved. Formerly used by the Drummond Tobacco Company prior to its absorption in the trust, the *Chesterfield* brand name had been the subject of litigation in 1898 when Lichenstein Brothers of New York sued Drummond, maintaining that they (the Lichensteins) originally used the *Chesterfield* name on a cigar. The New York Supreme Court ruled against Lichenstein Brothers on the grounds that "Chesterfield" is a geographical name, as well as that of an actual person. The "actual person," Lord Chesterfield, 4th Earl of Stanhope, had achieved world renown as his name became synonymous with "the gracious way of life," and the supreme enjoyment to be found in the social amenities. The Chesterfield coat, originally Lord Chesterfield's own single-breasted overcoat with concealed buttons, is now a generic term for a classic style in both men's and women's clothing. The same is true of a large, overstuffed sofa which the earl favored, and which style is now referred to as a Chesterfield sofa. His Lordship's impeccable taste set the fashion and the standard of excellence all over the world. Certainly *Chesterfield* was an excellent choice when Liggett & Myers reintroduced it in 1912 for their new blend, because when cigarettes finally came into their own as the favorite form of tobacco in 1921, *Chesterfield* was one of the three brands to "set the fashion and the standard of excellence all over the world."

PHILIP MORRIS

Philip Morris is the oldest name in the cigarette manufacturing field. It traces its ancestry to "Phillip Morris, Esq., Tobacconist and Importer of Fine Seegars," in Victorian London.

Already an established London merchant, with an aristocratic clientele, Morris was quick to take advantage of the demand for "Russian mode" cigarettes initiated by British soldiers returning from war in the Crimea. He soon had a group of expert "rollers" imported from Russia, Turkey and Egypt turning out expensive brands—such as *Philip Morris Cambridge, Oxford Blues,* and *Ovals* —for connoisseurs. The foreign "rollers" were the best available, and in a full ten-hour day, they turned out 3,000 usable cigarettes. Today, machines can turn out a full package of 20 Philip Morris's in one second—170 million perfect cigarettes a day.

The reputation of the Philip Morris brands grew, and demand spread to every outpost of the Empire as well as to America. Gustav Eckmeyer had been the exclusive importer of the Bond Street cigarettes of Philip Morris in New York since 1872, and in 1902 he helped organize the first New York Philip Morris Corporation. *Marlboro* was one of its earliest brands.

American stockholders bought the firm in 1919, and its old and distinguished reputation was one of its greatest assets. The company grew into a major position in the huge and competitive cigarette industry, and is today one of the "big six." One reason for that achievement is undoubtedly the introduction of Johnny, *Philip Morris'* famous page boy, and his clarion "Call for *Philip Morris.*"

Credit for Johnny and his verbal rendition of the *Philip Morris* slogan goes to two advertising men, Milton Biow and Kenneth Goode, who, in 1933, asked a bell-hop at the New Yorker Hotel to page Philip Morris. The bell-hop was John Roventini, a 22-year-old dwarf who stood 43 inches tall and weighed 54 pounds. "Johnny" Roventini, lively, alert, and known for his amiable disposition, looked at the card handed him on which were printed the words, "Call for Philip Morris." Johnny gave the two men a conspiratorial smile and, without an argument, turned on his heel and strode purposefully through the crowded lobby, singing out in the clear voice that was soon to become famous "Call for Philip Mar-a-iss! Call for Philip Mar-a-iss!"

Johnny's lilting voice and unique inflections commanded the attention of everyone in the lobby, and there were responding smiles and murmurings as he made his way through the milling crowds. The two advertising men were delighted. Not only was the slogan a good one, but Johnny himself was perfect. Johnny Roventini became Johnny "Philip Morris," and his "Call for *Philip Morris*" rang out over the airways, and at conventions and ball games, as he traveled about the country in a chauffeur-driven Austin, happily dispensing cigarettes and good-will.

HOME REMEDIES

SMITH BROTHERS COUGH DROPS

The two bearded gentlemen who grace the package of *Smith Brothers Cough Drops* have become a legend—affectionately known to generations as "Trade" and "Mark." Not so well known, however, is the fact that the Smith Brothers actually existed, although their names were William (Trade) and Andrew (Mark).

William and Andrew were sons of James Smith who moved to Poughkeepsie from St. Armand, Quebec, in 1847 to establish a restaurant. James was a fine carpenter by trade, but an even better candy maker and business man. When a journeyman stopped at Smith's Dining Saloon one day and gave James the formula for a palatable and effective cough candy, James foresaw possibilities for such a product in the cold, windswept Hudson Valley and immediately mixed up a batch on his kitchen stove.

The drops were an instant success and demand for the "cough candy" grew fast up and down the river. The Poughkeepsie paper carried an advertisement that "all afflicted with hoarseness, coughs, or colds should test its virtues, which (could) be done without the least risk."

Sons William and Andrew were in on the project from the first. They helped James mix the secret formula and then enthusiastically sold it in the streets of Poughkeepsie. "Hey! The Smith brothers are here!" became a familiar cry when the boys met the New York-Albany stage to peddle their "cough candy." Manufacturing was soon moved from the kitchen of the restaurant to a loft building nearby, and the concoction became known the whole length and breadth of the Hudson Valley. When James died in 1866, the boys continued the business under the name *Smith Brothers*.

With success came a flurry of imitators—*Schmitt Brothers,*

Smythe Sisters, and even other *Smith Brothers* appeared with imitative products. William and Andrew realized they needed a distinctive trademark to unequivocally identify their product, and decided to put their own pictures on the large glass bowls placed on store counters from which the drops were sold, and then put into envelopes for the customer. By pure chance, the word "Trade" appeared under the picture of William and the word "Mark" under Andrew.

The glass bowl container and envelopes had definite limitations —such as the fact no one could be sure it was the genuine *Smith Brothers* product in the bowl or being dropped into the envelopes— and in 1872 the two brothers developed one of the first uniform "factory-filled" packages on the market. They of course transferred their trademark to the new package and with its introduction, production increased from 5 pounds to 5 tons a day.

Now, over a century later, *Smith Brothers* remains a leader in its field. As for Trade and Mark, they hold the world's record for the number of times their likenesses have been reproduced: on each of the millions of packages of *Smith Brothers Cough Drops,* the two *Smith Brothers* factories turn out daily. They have held their own despite the fiercest competition, and would doubtless look with pride on the business they helped to launch with one of the most fortuitous "chance" trademarks in history.

NOXZEMA

Six years after George Avery Bunting became a school principal, he turned his back on the education field and enrolled in the University of Maryland's pharmacy school, from which he graduated in 1899. A few years later he opened a modest little drug store in Baltimore and was soon happily engaged in developing a skin cream formula he had originated. Older residents of Baltimore joke today about the poor store service they received because Dr. Bunting spent most of his time in the back room working on his beloved formula. But his customers liked the genial druggist, and their impatience soon turned to interest. They actually began to enjoy watching him as he mixed, heated and poured the skin cream into little blue jars from a huge coffee pot. More and more of them bought the cream, which was called simply *Dr. Bunting's Sunburn Remedy*, and soon other local druggists were ordering it for their customers.

Encouraged by the growing popularity of his formula, which he had perfected in 1914, George Bunting wanted desperately to devote his full time to it. He had confidence that a good idea always pays off, but could the skin cream in the little blue jars make a place for itself in the fiercely competitive market of the 'twenties? He believed it could—but *not* with a horse and buggy name like *Dr. Bunting's Sunburn Remedy*. He compounded and discarded hundreds of names in the search for one with the necessary force and appeal. Finally, when even the optimistic Dr. Bunting was about to give up, inspiration came from a customer who walked into the store and casually observed, "Doc, you know your sunburn cream sure knocked out my eczema."

From this chance remark, *Dr. Bunting's Sunburn Remedy* ceased to exist, and *Noxzema Skin Cream* was born. Today the little blue jars which the Baltimore druggist once filled from an oversized coffee pot are automatically machine-filled at the rate of 120 per minute—and Doc Bunting's sunburn remedy that "knocks eczema" is a multi-million dollar business.

VASELINE PETROLEUM JELLY

In 1859 all America was excited over reports of Colonel Drake's fabulous oil strike in Pennsylvania. To Robert Augustus Chesebrough, a struggling 22-year-old chemist in Brooklyn, however, it was not very welcome news. Robert had devoted his entire career to learning how to refine cannel oil into kerosene (then a major source of fuel), and the discovery of an abundance of natural petroleum would undoubtedly herald a new era for fuel. There was only one thing to do, decided Robert, and that was to switch over to the petroleum field. And to do that, he'd have to go to the heart of the oil boom country—Titusville, Pennsylvania. Being a young man of action, he invested his entire savings in a round-trip railroad ticket.

Without any idea of what his exact purpose was, Robert strode about the oil fields, sticking his nose into every phase of the complex operations. His curiosity was thoroughly aroused by a substance the workers called "rod-wax," a colorless oil residue that formed around the gigantic pump rods. Young Chesebrough was intrigued to hear the workers curse the stuff when it gummed up their pumps but then bless it when they cut or burned themselves and applied it to soothe their wounds—which were frequent in those early boisterous days of the great oil strikes.

Oil, of course, has been considered a healing balm through the ages, and when Robert had seen enough results of the application of the rod-wax to cuts and burns to convince himself that it really did contain a mysterious healing power, he knew that he had found what he sought in the oil fields. With a quantity of the rod-wax in tow he returned triumphantly to his laboratory in Brooklyn.

Long months of painstaking research followed. He conducted hundreds of experiments in an effort to extract the concentrated residue from crude petroleum, and succeeding in this, to refine and purify the results, which he now called "petroleum jelly" instead of rod-wax. His laboratory overflowed with beakers and trays filled with the colorless substance.

When Robert Augustus Chesebrough finally produced the pure, petroleum jelly he had striven for, he became his own guinea pig to test its healing powers. He inflicted cuts and scratches on himself and burned his hands severely with fire and acids. All his life he carried the scars of his experiments, but each wound had been soothed and healed with the amazing petroleum jelly.

There is a rather sentimental story that Robert chose the name *Vaseline* Petroleum Jelly for his new product because often, when there was no empty beaker in his laboratory, he tossed out the flowers his wife had brought him and filled their vase with petroleum jelly. When he finally perfected the process, there were many vases of petroleum jelly in the laboratory and they inspired the name—the *line* being added because it was the popular ending for medicinal products of the day. However, other sources say that the word was arbitrarily coined by Chesebrough, probably from the German *wasser* (water) and the Greek *elaion* (olive oil) because he believed crude petroleum was formed by the decomposition of water in the earth and the uniting of the hydrogen with carbon.

For whatever reason Chesebrough chose the name *Vaseline* Petroleum Jelly, he registered it for his trademark.

Robert soon managed to raise enough money to set up a plant to manufacture the new preparation. He sent hundreds of free samples to physicians, apothecaries and scientific societies, and then sat back and waited for the orders to start flowing in. They didn't. He received a few requests for more samples and a lot of polite, but negative, responses. Undaunted, he hitched up his horse and buggy and headed for upstate New York, lavishly distributing samples to every person he saw along the way, and stopping at every farm house to leave samples with the lady of the house. Inevitably, the local druggists were obliged to stock up to meet the demand created by Chesebrough's free samples. The trip was such an astounding success that Robert promptly hired several men to hitch up their horses and buggies, and "beat the bushes" in New Jersey and Connecticut.

Within a few years the product was accepted by the medical profession, and the public was soon buying it at the rate of one jar a minute.

Today, over a hundred years after its discovery, Petroleum Jelly has literally a thousand uses, and the company's files continue to grow daily with reports of new ones. Known chiefly as a burn ointment, it is also a valuable aid to the homemaker for it can remove white rings from mahogany furniture, keep rust off garden equipment, polish up patent leather and prevent paint splatters from sticking. It has been used by movie makers to simulate tears and by artists to preserve their paint brushes. Pet lovers find it keeps shampoo out of their pets' eyes, and fishermen use it for trout bait.

It is bought in bulk by cosmetic manufacturers who use it as a base for beauty creams, and by pharmaceutical companies who combine it with wonder drugs in ointments.

There have been times in the company's long history when sales suddenly skyrocketed in certain areas of the world. Such an incident was Sun Yat-sen's liberation of the Chinese people in 1917. Sales in China soared because the coolies were ordered to clip off their queue (pigtails)—which were a mark of subrogation—and discovered that Petroleum Jelly eased the discomfort caused by the bristle of the severed queue. When there was an unexplained buying spree in Russia in 1916, investigation disclosed the Russian peasants had discovered that *Vaseline* added to the oil burned in their holy lamps eliminated the choking smoke fumes.

Of all the myriad uses people have found for *Vaseline* Petroleum Jelly, however, Robert Chesebrough undoubtedly claimed the most unique. So great was his faith in his product that he swallowed a spoonful of it every day of his life, loudly proclaiming it was the secret of his longevity. He died in 1933—an active 96 years old—and significantly, perhaps, no one has ever disputed his proud boast.

MURINE

In 1890 Otis F. Hall, a banker in Spokane, Washington, was chatting with a friend in front of the bank when he noticed that his friend's horse had a broken shoe. As he bent to examine the shoe, the horse's tail struck him in the right eye, cutting the surface of the cornea. A painful ulcer developed, and Mr. Hall was soon on his way to Chicago to seek treatment from Doctors James B. and George W. McFatrich, two brothers who had achieved prominence in ophthalmology.

Under their care, the eye healed completely within a few weeks. In addition, Mr. Hall's young son, who had accompanied him to Chicago, was cured of a minor eye irritation. Part of the treatment the Halls received was a special eye lotion preparation which the Doctors McFatrich compounded themselves and regularly prescribed for their patients. Mr. Hall, impressed with the preparation, felt it should be made available to the public. The McFatrich brothers were reluctant to embark on such a venture. It took Otis Hall several years to convince them that they could perform a far greater service to more people by marketing the product commercially than if they continued to limit its use to their own private practice. When the brothers were finally persuaded to mass-produce their product, the three men formed a company and the first sound eye-drop preparation ever to be launched on a large scale was under way.

What should they call the preparation? The McFatriches felt the name should derive from the chemical formula—muriate of ber-

berine—and by combining the first and last syllables of the formula, the name *Murine* was immediately adopted.

Today, the company that resulted from a horse swishing its tail across a man's face markets its product in more than sixty countries.

DR. SCHOLL'S FOOT AIDS

In a five-story building on Chicago's near north side there is a wondrous machine that would draw a gasp of admiration from Rube Goldberg.

Painted brilliant yellow and azure blue, it is attended by scurrying, white-smocked figures who feed it adhesive, plaster, felt, moleskin and foam rubber. From this diet, the machine produces the means by which millions of persons the world over relieve their aching feet—*Dr. Scholl's* corn, callus and bunion pads.

Americans have associated *Dr. Scholl* with corns, callouses, bunions and fallen arches for the past sixty years, and the yellow and blue package has been a part of the American scene so long that the name on it is recognized rather than read.

Most people assume a puzzled expression when asked, "Who is Dr. Scholl?" They are apt to suggest that "he" is just a trademark, or they ask in turn, "Was there really a Dr. Scholl?"

The name isn't *just* a trademark, and there not only *was* a Dr. Scholl, there *is* a Dr. Scholl. He is an amazing man of eighty years, and for the past sixty of those years he has headed an empire that now employs over 3,000 people in thirteen plants located in the United States and five foreign countries. In addition, there are 423 exclusive retail stores.

William "Billy" Scholl was born and reared on a dairy farm near LaPorte, Indiana, and was one of thirteen children. He found the daily routine of milking cows little to his liking. His interests lay along more creative lines. An exacting thoroughness, which later proved so characteristic of him, evidenced itself at the age of 15 when he designed and sewed a complete set of harness, an awesome task requiring 132,000 stitches. He made his own waxed thread and cut all the straps for the harness from full side leather. The family was much impressed by this achievement and Billy soon found himself serving as unofficial cobbler to the whole family. To put his new-found talent on a paying basis, he became apprenticed to the local shoemaker. The limited horizons of LaPorte did not hold his interest for long and he soon moved to Chicago and a job in a shoe store. He proved to be a fine craftsman in making and fitting shoes to misshapen feet, and was also an exceptionally good salesman.

His work in the shoe store led him to two conclusions: feet were horribly abused by their owners and nothing much was being done about it. With these convictions in mind he confidently set forth on his self-appointed mission to become foot doctor to the world.

To equip himself for this task, he arranged to work at night so he could attend Illinois Medical College (now Loyola) and the Chicago Medical School during the day. He supplemented his regular curriculum by studying every bit of literature available on the subject of feet.

By the time he received his M.D. he had invented and patented his first arch support. He was just 22 years old in 1904 when he slipped his first hand-made arch support into a customer's shoe. The customer stomped around the store and then exclaimed happily: "Say, that's a real foot easer, isn't it?" *Foot-Eazer* it became and has remained. It is still one of the largest-selling items in the company's line of more than a thousand products. It differs from the 1904 model only in refinement of design.

Never in the company's entire history has a product been discontinued. The Doctor personally holds over 300 patents for foot treatments and machines for making foot comfort aids.

The *Foot-Eazer* was an immediate success and the young doctor turned his talents to manufacturing and merchandising it. He rented a store-front cubby hole and with the help of one employee made arch supports for customers who came in for personal fittings. When he was not busy at the store, Dr. Scholl would pack up a supply of *Foot-Eazers* and walk from shoe store to shoe store, introducing and selling them. His most effective sales approach was to walk up to the store manager, calmly remove the skeleton of a human foot from his pocket and toss it on the counter. This would usually mesmerize his customer, and he would then proceed with his lecture that began with the anatomy of the human foot, continued with the various causes of foot trouble, and almost invariably ended with a sale.

By 1907 the *Foot-Eazer* arch support was only one of a constantly increasing line of products which now had nationwide distribution. The line had grown to include pads, remedies and arch supports, and shoes in a tremendous size range—men's sizes from 5½ to 16, AAA to EEEEEEE, and women's sizes from 2½ to 13, AAAAA to EEEEEEEE.

In 1908 Dr. Scholl moved outside the confines of the United States by opening a branch factory at Toronto. This proving successful, he invaded Europe in 1910, opening a factory in London and sales agencies all across the continent.

In 1918 Dr. Scholl literally "put the nation on its feet." Always promotion-minded, he sponsored a series of walking contests. Through his retail stores across the country he sold a device called the pedometer for measuring the distance a person walks. He offered prizes to those who covered the most miles over a given period of time. Competition became so fierce that contestants would rush down to the store, check the latest standings and then walk on, often into the night, trying to outdistance the competition. One man, who went on a European cruise during the contest, spent almost the entire voyage pacing the promenade deck.

Equally successful was the "Cinderella Foot" contest promoted by the Doctor in 1916. Women were invited to come into Dr. Scholl's stores and leave their footprints on the "Pedo-Graph," a device invented by the doctor to measure foot sizes and graphically illustrate foot imbalance or incorrect weight distribution. A panel of qualified judges selected the most perfect foot from the thousands of prints submitted.

This had a terrific impact on the public as they were able to compare their own footprints against the perfect and near-perfect ones prominently displayed in newspapers. The wave of national foot-consciousness resulted in skyrocketing sales for Dr. Scholl's products.

An advocate of the direct approach in everything, Dr. Scholl steadfastly avoids the "artiness" found in many modern advertisements. He shuns subtlety. His ads immediately grab the reader's attention with a one or two word headline in big, black letters: "Corns," "Feet Hurt?" "Calluses" or simply "Foot Relief," but the pattern is unvarying. The bottom of the ad is devoted to the name of the particular foot aid being advertised. Even to the most casual reader, the name of a common foot ailment is indelibly linked with the name, *Dr. Scholl's*. Another permanent feature of the ads is the line drawing of a human foot, usually adorned with the foot aid being featured. The constant appearance of these feet in ads, on billboards, and in full-scale plaster models on the counters of shoe and drug stores has made the human foot almost a *Scholl* trademark.

Many years ago the publisher of one of the nation's largest newspapers took issue with the appearance of a naked foot in the *Scholl* ads. Dr. Scholl won the battle, however, when he pointed to pictures of bathing beauties and ads for swim wear in the newspaper. *Dr. Scholl's* foot, clad only in corn pads, bunion aids, arch supports, or callus pads has regularly appeared ever since.

It is Dr. Scholl's ardent belief that most of the world's foot troubles are caused by improper and improperly-fitted shoes. Tackling the problem in his usual direct way, he undertook an educational campaign among shoe store clerks, and wrote a correspondence course entitled *Elementary Course in Practipedics—practipedics* being a coined word. The course dealt with the structure of the feet, common foot ailments and how they could be corrected on the retail shoe store level. Nine out of ten people have foot troubles of one kind or another, and Dr. Scholl reasoned that if he educated the shoe clerk, the clerk would become more aware and alert to foot troubles, thereby recommending *Dr. Scholl's* products. Dr. Scholl is also the author of a book on feet—*The Human Foot: Anatomy, Deformities and Treatment*—that has wide distribution among shoe fitters.

Another theory of Dr. Scholl's (dear to the hearts of those who sell shoes) is that every person should have a minimum of four or five pairs; that after wearing, shoes should be treed and allowed to rest two or three days to dry out properly; and that, ideally, a person should wear two pairs of shoes a day, changing at noon.

From the beginning, Dr. Scholl has always received letters of praise from users of his products, for who is not grateful to have a corn pacified, a bunion comforted or an aching arch bolstered? Often a note of humor creeps into the letters. One lady, just widowed, wrote that both she and her husband had used *Foot-Eazers* for many years and when her husband died, she had decided it would be only fitting to bury him with the arch supports that had given him such comfort during his lifetime.

Today at 80 years of age, Dr. Scholl runs his business with the enthusiasm of a man just embarking on a new and exciting adventure. Even though he is a very wealthy man he still devotes every waking moment to his business, and adheres to his credo "Early to bed, early to rise, work like hell and advertise." One of the most widely traveled men in the world, he has a number of travel "firsts" to his credit, including the maiden flights of both the Graf Zeppelin and the Hindenburg, and the first international jet flight of the Pan-American Boeing 707. He has, however, never taken a trip for pleasure alone, although he does have one hobby which he often pursues on his travels: he has the world's largest collection of ancient shoes. One of his most popular inventions was created one night in a hotel room and on a recent trip he personally sold $300,000 worth of merchandise. He is possessed of an amazing memory and while some people boast they never forget a face, Dr. Scholl never forgets a foot and has been known to name the correct size (and ailment) of a foot he hasn't seen in 25 years.

If he does find himself with leisure time on his hands while traveling, he is apt to go into a store where his products are sold to see if they are being properly displayed, or he buys quantities of his remedies off the counter without identifying himself and spot checks them for quality. Since he makes this a frequent habit, he estimates that he is one of his own best customers although he has no foot ailments and has never had except for one corn that developed on a recent trip while he was in Singapore. He became separated from his luggage and because he religiously follows his own advice to change shoes regularly, he had a pair made for him within 24 hours. They didn't quite fit and the corn resulted. Undaunted, he applied one of his own *Zino-Pads* and continued briskly—and painlessly—on his way.

The doctor is a bachelor and while he has other residences, his Chicago home is a single room (with the bath down the hall) at the Illinois Athletic Club. He gets up every morning at seven o'clock and has breakfast with a group of friends at the club. He then goes to his office and plunges into the day's work. He attends to his duties with a vigor and at a pace that leaves his co-workers panting. Asked why he continues to work so hard, he replied that he had so many new ideas it just kept him busy trying to get them out of his head. Trim of figure and firm of step, he spends little time at his desk (in fact rarely sits down at all) and strides purposefully about his business like a man on a mission—which he is. Despite the present-day size and scope of the company, its founder still takes personal responsibility for every phase of its activities.

The one concession he has made to success is that he no longer spends all his Sundays at the plant where he used to work in the unheated building with a blanket wrapped around his legs.

The future of *Dr. Scholl's* foot aids seems assured because 90 per cent of the American public walks around on sore feet at least some of the time. "Women are the worst offenders," confides Dr. Scholl, "because they'll go about their work in old, misshapen shoes which offer no support at all and then, to dress up, struggle into a pair of pumps with three-inch heels that neither fit nor conform to the shape of the feet."

Commenting on the incredible amount of punishment to which most people subject their feet, Dr. Scholl said, with a sigh of resignation, but an impish, optimistic grin: "As long as fashion, instead of good common sense continues to dictate the choice of footwear, we'll be in business."

VICK'S VAPORUB

In the Gay Nineties, poultices and plasters for colds were as acceptable as bustles for fashionable ladies or barbershop quartets for musical-minded gentlemen. Unfortunately, however, the poultices and plasters frequently resulted in blisters which of course only added to the woes of an already miserable patient. But the flow of blood in the chest was stimulated by the uncertain plasters, and this did help to relieve congestion, even though the actual medication was of no value since it did not reach affected areas. Vapor lamps, awkward contrivances that allowed for no fresh air whatsoever, were also popular, and while they did at least convey some of the medication to the sufferer's air passages, they were too expensive and complicated for general use. What was sorely needed, decided

Lunsford Richardson, a druggist in the little town of Selma, North Carolina, was an elixir that would combine the virtues of plasters and vapor lamps without their alarming defects. Since colds and congestions were the most common ailments of his customers, Richardson set out to develop such a remedy.

One of the first ingredients he selected was menthol, new to this country at the time, and extremely effective in opening nasal passages. He combined it with other medications in a petroleum base, and the result was *Richardson's Croup and Pneumonia Cure Salve*, a remarkably efficient chest-rub. Vaporized by body heat, the salve soothed and opened the air passage at the same time it stimulated the flow of blood in the chest.

Lunsford organized a wholesale drug firm in Greensboro, North Carolina, to market the new salve and other products. The firm was modestly successful, but in 1905 he sold out and at the age of 55 invested his life's savings in a venture that was to spread from the little North Carolina town all over the world—the manufacture and sale of *Richardson's Home Remedies*. *Richardson's Croup and Pneumonia Cure Salve* was one of the nineteen home cures Richardson had formulated.

Two years later, the business was firmly launched and Lunsford called his son, H. S., home from New York where the young man had gone after graduation from college to seek his fortune. "The summons came at a most propitious time," H. S. Richardson recounted later. "My 'fortune' had been limited to such jobs as street car conductor, clerking at Wanamaker's, and selling blankets." But however modest his various jobs in the city, the one assigned to him now by his father was staggering: the elder Richardson wanted his home remedies to be marketed not only all over America, but abroad as well. And they had never been heard of outside the Greensboro area.

H. S. took over the assignment "unhampered by any sort of previous record to uphold." He began by organizing a small high-pressure sales force and calling on every drug store and general store in the backwoods of North Carolina, traveling by buckboard or horseback over deeply rutted and often muddy roads. It didn't take him long to realize that of all the nineteen remedies he was offering, only the old *Croup and Pneumonia Cure Salve* had any real appeal. He promptly dropped the other 18 products from his line and resolved to find a more marketable name than *Richardson's Croup and Pneumonia Cure Salve* for the remaining one. Lunsford Richardson came up with the answer when he suggested the short and euphonious *Vick's Salve*. His inspiration for the name was his brother-in-law, Dr. Joshua Vick, in whose drug store he had begun his career while studying for his own pharmacist license and where he was working at the time he first developed his formula.

Armed with a brand new name and package for the tried and true salve, H. S. and his men again hit the road. Garrulous storekeepers, accustomed to leisurely perusing a long list of home remedies and supplies while swapping stories with equally garrulous salesmen, were astounded when H. S. or one of his crew made a whirlwind appearance in their isolated and almost inaccessible little communities with but *one* product to sell, particularly since many of their orders were for only one jar of the salve, rarely for more than a dozen.

Progress was made, but very gradually, and young H. S. was in a hurry. He sincerely believed his salve was not only better than the hundreds then on the market, but that it was also different, and he sought an identification that would make these facts clear to everyone. *Vick's VapoRub* was the result of his search. He chose it because "Vapo" suggested his father's original idea of combining the functions of the vapor lamp and the plaster in a single medication, and "Rub" eliminated completely the word "salve" used so extensively by competitors.

Satisfied at last with the name of his product, young Richardson again marshalled his force of skilled drummers and again took to the road. If a merchant had been high-pressured into buying before, he was stampeded into it this time when given the famous "spoon test." It was performed by lighting a match under a tin spoonful of *Vick's VapoRub* and waving it under the startled merchant's nose. The pungent vapor inhaled at such close quarters never failed to convince the dazed prospect that he must order a supply at once.

Progress was rapid this time, and soon the Richardsons invaded the Northern markets, where many besieged merchants must have thought the Confederacy had finally risen again. Salesmen swarmed into the new territory and advertised extensively in the newspapers with coupons that could be redeemed for a free trial jar of *Vick's VapoRub*. Hundreds of people took a coupon to their local merchants and demanded their free jar before the poor fellow had little more than heard of it. By the time a salesman got around to them the merchant had a stack of coupons clutched in his hand and an order all ready in anticipation of repeat business. The company asked for testimonials from these trial users which were widely reprinted in further advertising. The Richardsons were one of the first companies to do large-scale sampling by mail and it was through their efforts that the Post Office Department first allowed samples and direct mail advertising to be addressed to "Boxholder" instead of an individual name.

Sales skyrocketed during the tragic influenza epidemic of World War I and *Vick's VapoRub* gained the national recognition Lunsford Richardson had dreamed of. He died in 1919 but not before he saw his son finish the job he had called him home to do, because in 1918 *Vick's VapoRub* was sold for the first time in Great Britain, marking the beginning of its worldwide distribution.

The name of the company was changed to Vick Chemical Company and continued under this name until it became a division of Richardson-Merrell, Inc. in 1960.

Today the business that was launched with one product, and the help of a small force of energetic drummers has expanded into over 3,000 products which gross over 100 million dollars a year.

20 MULE TEAM BORAX

Hundreds of varied products, from fiberglass and pharmaceuticals to fertilizers and photographic chemicals, contain the same basic ingredient—borax. It is essential to almost every industry and to agriculture. Crude borax occurs in nature as a mineral; it can be refined into a pure chemical compound and always contains four elements: sodium, boron, oxygen and hydrogen.

In its first hundred years, this country's borax industry has grown from a 12-ton output in 1864 to nearly a million tons in 1959. Borax was known to the ancients, and has been used throughout the centuries, but it was not until shortly before the Civil War, when borax crystals were discovered in certain mineral springs, that its great commercial success began. Until then, borax was an unfamiliar, expensive import, limited in use to glass blowing and gold refining. Eight years after the discovery, the Borax Company of California managed to raise the capital necessary to start operations at one of the lake sites.

In 1870, "cottonball" (*ulexite*, one of the borate minerals) was found in quantity on the Nevada desert. It lay in shimmering masses on the ancient, arid lake beds of Columbus Marsh, Nevada, and could be harvested with a shovel and easily processed. This was just what F. M. "Borax" Smith, one of the first great names to emerge in the new industry, did. Smith was a Michigan farm boy who had gone West in an unsuccessful search for gold. When word of the cottonball strikes reached him in 1872, he headed for the Nevada desert, planning to sell firewood to borax manufacturers who needed fuel to process the ore. Once there, however, he quickly recognized the great potentialities in the new industry, and quickly staked out claims on Columbus Marsh and nearby Teel's Marsh. One by one he bought out competitors until he became a powerful figure in the industry.

Another important figure in the borax story is William T. Coleman, who had been a leader of the Vigilante Committees in the 1850's. He was convinced that the future of the West was in borax, as its past had been in gold, and he sent scouts through the desert to find the new mineral. In 1881, he filed claims on the richest fields of cottonball yet discovered—hundreds of glistening, isolated acres in formidable Death Valley. Samples of Death Valley ore had been sent to Coleman by a gold prospector named Aaron Winters, who, with his wife, Rosie, had set up camp near the Valley. Winters had known nothing of borax until one of Coleman's scouts told him how to test ore from the Nevada desert for borax: "Pour sulfuric acid and alcohol on the ore, then light a match to it. If the flame burns green, it's borax."

Winters said nothing to the scout, but he realized that he saw fields of the stuff every day. As soon as the scout left, Aaron hitched up the mules, collected Rosie, and rode off to Death Valley. There he poured sulfuric acid and alcohol over the white crystals and then struck a match. "She burns green, Rosie!" he cried. "We're rich!"

Coleman bought Aaron Winters' Death Valley claims for $20,000 and built the Harmony Borax Works (the rusting remains of which can still be seen). He had to find a way to move the cumbersome product out of Death Valley and across 165 miles of barren California desert to the nearest railroad junction at Mojave.

Wagons pulled by multiple mule teams were used in the desert in those days, and a 12-mule team was the maximum until J. W. S. Perry, Coleman's local superintendent, and a young muleskinner named Ed Stiles, thought of hitching two ten-mule teams together to form a hundred-foot long twenty-mule team. Perry himself designed the massive wagons, which were built in Mojave for $900. They had rear wheels seven feet high, and front wheels five feet high, each with steel tires eight inches wide and one inch thick. The wagon beds were 16 feet long, 4 feet wide, and 6 feet deep. Empty, each wagon weighed 7,800 pounds. Loaded with borax, it weighed 31,800 pounds. Two such loaded wagons, plus the water tank (which held 1,200 gallons and weighed 9,600 pounds) made a total load of 36½ tons which the 20-mule teams pulled.

From 1883 to 1889 the teams hauled borax out of Death Valley, over the steep Panamint Mountains and across the desert to the railroad. Despite the heat—the temperatures often rose to 130—they pulled their heavy loads along the rough trails, traveling 15 to 18 miles a day. It was a 20-day round trip. During the five years that they were in constant use, the 20-mule teams carried 20 million pounds of borax out of the Valley—a considerable tribute to the ingenuity of the designers and to the stamina of the teamsters and the animals.

The 20-mule teams became a world-famous symbol. The borax Coleman hauled out of Death Valley in such a spectacular way was identified by everyone as "20 Mule Team" borax, and Coleman soon adopted the name as a trademark.

Coleman continued to expand his operations until his widespread and complex financial interests led to bankruptcy; and in 1890, "Borax" Smith, who had continued processing cottonball in Nevada, acquired all of Coleman's borax properties. He incorporated his holdings in the Pacific Coast Borax Company.

With the aid of his lively imagination, Smith soon made *20 Mule Team Borax* a household word. He advertised the use of borax for digestion; to keep milk sweet; as a complexion aid ("Don't wash your face in ordinary lake water"); to remove dandruff; and for the bath ("Use half a pound of powdered borax to the ordinary family bath of twelve gallons of water"). It was also "excellent for washing carriages," and useful, he said, in curing epilepsy and bunions.

Like Coleman before him, however, "Borax" Smith finally over-extended and over-diversified his financial affairs, and in 1914 the Pacific Coast Borax Company became a division of a British corporation. Through a transfer of company stock in 1956, the Pacific Coast Borax Company again became an American corporation, and later that year merged with the U.S. Potash Company to form the present corporation, United States Borax and Chemical Corporation.

COSMETICS

Introduction

The origin of cosmetics reaches far back into antiquity—just how far no one really knows. It is probably safest to theorize that Eve introduced them shortly after she bit the apple.

We do know that by the time of the ancient Egyptian pharaohs, beauty shops and perfume stores flourished and make-up was already a highly skilled art. Cleopatra, for instance, painted her eyebrows and lashes "a stark black; her upper lids blue-black; and the lower ones as green as the Nile." Queen Schub-ad had a large supply of colored lip salves which were excavated at Ur and are believed to be between four and five thousand years old.

Beauty and its preservation reached its peak during the time of Julius Caesar. Indeed, one source credits our word "cosmetic" to a man named Cosmis who was the most famous cosmetic dealer in the whole Roman Empire. (Webster does not agree with this version, however, ascribing the origin of the word to the Greek *Kosmetikos,* meaning "skilled in decorating," and the French *kosmos,* meaning "ornament.") At any rate, preoccupation with aids to beauty declined with the fall of the Roman Empire; it was revived in the Middle Ages, and has been increasing ever since.

Strangely enough, cosmetics' misnomer—cold cream—is the oldest cosmetic cream in use today. The formula contains a large quantity of water which evaporates when the mixture comes in contact with the skin, thereby causing the "cool" sensation, and giving rise to the name "cold cream." It was first made by a man named Galen, who lived in the second century A.D. Galen's formula, as recorded in his *Methodus Medini vel de Morbis Curandis,* consisted of one part of white wax melted in three or four parts of olive oil, in which "rose buds had been steeped and as much water as could be blended into the mass." According to a formula published in 1618, the cream also contained rosewater and vinegar.

Lanolin is another very old beauty aid. It was known at the time of Christ as *despyum*. Olive oil, honey, donkey's milk, various resins and gums, and bread dough were other ancient "magic" beauty ingredients. Fragrant herbs and spices and flower oils were of course also known and used.

The fabulous beauty industry as we know it today, however, did not begin until the late 1800's. There were very few beauty products within reach of the average woman 75 years ago. Many women clipped beauty "recipes" from magazines and concocted the strange compounds in their own kitchens. One 19th century volume, *Secrets of a Lady's Toilet,* contained the following little gem purported to ward off wrinkles, and to be the same as used by "the celebrated Madame Vestris":

The white of four eggs boiled in rose water, half an ounce of alum, half an ounce of oil of sweet almonds; beat the whole together till it assumes the consistency of a paste.

A few cosmetics, mostly face powders, were being advertised, but women were, understandably, a bit wary of them. There were, for example, *Turkish Rose Leaves*—it gave "an indelible tint to the face and lips"; *Face Enamel*—a "transparent enamel recommended by physicians and perfectly harmless"; and *Arsenic Complexion Wafers*—to be eaten by ladies who wished to whiten their skin. By the turn of the century, the Victorian attitude that "nice women didn't use cosmetics" was still being felt, but nevertheless, hundreds of Victorian and Edwardian ladies were beating a path to Mrs. Frances Henning's famous Mayfair salon "Cyclax," the first salon in London. They entered by a side door and were served in private. While there, every precaution was taken by Mrs. Henning that they not come in contact with other patrons, whether friend or foe. To prevent such catastrophic and embarrassing meetings, a little Negress in a crisp cap and apron was stationed in a kind of theatre-box construction halfway up the stairs where she could manipulate arrivals and departures so none coincided.

After World War I, however, the pace of life quickened. A four-ounce jar of *Trailing Arbutus,* a vanishing cream, could be bought for 59 cents—a sum that represented almost three hours labor for the poor working girl.

By the mid-twenties, cosmetics ceased to be the theme of moral sermons and were accepted as necessary adjuncts to good grooming and morale. Bobbed hair was no longer considered wicked and lipstick and rouge came out into the open. Make-up became a vital part of life for most women and cosmetics sales spiraled into a multi-billion dollar industry, and are still soaring.

AVON PRODUCTS

The use of perfumes and cosmetics may date back thousands of years, their beginnings vague in the mists of time, but the practice of *Avon Calling* to distribute these products to ladies in the privacy and comfort of their own homes was definitely launched in 1886 by D. H. McConnell.

McConnell began at the age of 16 selling books door-to-door. He soon discovered that books were not exactly in great demand by the housewives of that day, and many times a door was abruptly shut in his face before he even had a chance to go into his sales pitch. He was growing discouraged until he hit upon the idea of giving each prospective customer, as an *entrée,* a small vial of perfume. He made up the perfume himself, with the aid of a druggist friend, and the idea worked like a charm—except that the ladies asked for more of the perfume and remained indifferent to the books. Mr. McConnell didn't realize it then, of course, but this was first hand "market research" at its best. He turned that pioneer market research into a fortune when he abandoned the books and organized The California Perfume Company to make and sell the perfume door-to-door. McConnell named the new company in honor of a friend who had been the first to invest in the company and who lived in California. It was a fortunate coincidence that the name also suggested the perfume-filled air of a state noted for its sunshine and flowers.

The California Perfume Company commenced operations in "a room scarcely larger than an ordinary kitchen pantry," with a staff of two people: D. H. McConnell and his wife. The husband-wife team prospered from the beginning. A small office was soon rented at 126 Chambers Street in New York. "I had one stenographer," Mr. McConnell recalled, "and I myself filled the positions of book-keeper, cashier, correspondent, shipping clerk, office boy and manufacturing chemist."

In his book-selling days, Mr. McConnell had gone into homes in all parts of the country and had been genuinely touched by the struggle so many women were having to make ends meet. They had little or no chance to earn the extra money that could add much to the pleasure and comfort of their lives and that of their families. He believed wholeheartedly in the direct-selling method, and from his own experience knew it to be a satisfying and stimulating way to earn money. He was convinced it would be a dignified and pleasant way for women to contribute to their family incomes.

Mrs. P. F. A. Albee was hired as the first representative of the company, and is regarded as the first *Avon* Lady. She, in turn, engaged a number of others, and they set out with hope in their hearts and a *Little Dot* set of four perfumes in their hands. They encountered a friendly welcome and customers were soon asking, "Do you have any other products?"

A few years later, the McConnell family moved to Suffern, New York, in Rockland County, and brought their manufacturing facilities with them—to the harness room of their stable. The New York office was retained but was moved into larger quarters at Park Place.

The company continued to prosper, and in 1894, with great pride and faith in the future, Mr. McConnell again expanded his facilities. He constructed a small wooden factory with living quarters on the second floor for an employee. This momentous event was heralded in the local Rockland County newspaper:

Suffern, N.Y.—The contract has been given out for the erection of a large factory at this place. The new industry will employ quite a number of hands and it promises to be very beneficial to the interest of the village.

Three years later the company had twelve employees in its plant and produced perfumes in 18 fragrances. (*White Rose, Heliotrope, Carnation, Violet,* and *Jockey Club* were great favorites.) In addition, a varied line of household products was manufactured, such as baking powder and olive oil, and flavoring extracts that included peppermint, celery and onion.

Another interesting item in the line was *Tooth Tablet*, the forerunner of tooth paste. The tablet was hard and packaged in a jar. One simply wet his toothbrush and rubbed it over the tooth tablet until he worked up sufficient lather to clean his teeth.

Bay Rum was the principal hair tonic produced during those early years, and shampoo, talcum powder, face powder, rouge, *eau de cologne* and witch hazel cream rounded out the line.

The products made in Suffern were carried by horse-drawn vans to the New York headquarters and shipped from there to their destinations. The system that had been put into operation by Mrs. Albee was now used for a constantly increasing number of representatives all over the country.

"Possibilities grow greater and greater every day," Mr. McConnell told his employees at the turn of the century and it was a prophetic statement. His products and method of distribution won customers from the first and attracted many intelligent, industrious women eager for the earning opportunity opened to them. When he introduced a line of pure, high-quality beauty aids, women responded with a surge of enthusiasm that soon found 8,000 women distributing the products and 35 people employed in the Suffern factory. The entire line of perfumes, toilet articles and household products was awarded a Gold Medal for quality and beauty of packaging at the famed Panama Exposition in 1915.

By the middle 'twenties, two concrete and steel buildings dwarfed the earlier frame ones, and capacity had been increased 200 per cent. Liquid filling was just becoming mechanized in 1927. Until then, most of the cream filling operations were done by hand: filling and smoothing, capping, labeling and cartoning. Assembly for shipping was done by girls with hand trucks. They made the rounds to itemized bins for each article on their lists. Orders were checked along a ledge and then pushed off to the packers' benches for final packing and shipping. The output of a whole department was about 9,000 bottles. Today, one assembly line alone turns out many times that number.

During its 50th Anniversary Year, in 1936, the name of the company was changed to encompass all the items in the line. Mr. McConnell himself chose the name *Avon* because of his great love for Shakespeare, and for the village of Suffern. "Suffern-on-the-Ramapo" reminded him of Shakespeare's "Stratford-on-Avon."

National advertising of *Avon* products also made its debut in 1936 in *Good Housekeeping* magazine, and that same year executive offices were moved to their present location at 30 Rockefeller Plaza in Radio City.

Avon products are still sold exclusively to the customer by its 125,000 sales representatives. Although many women have made it a full time career, most *Avon* representatives are housewives who devote only a part of their spare time to it. These representatives are independent and are not direct employees of the company. They are, in D. H. McConnell's favorite phrase, "in business for themselves."

Today there are four major *Avon* manufacturing laboratories in America, and foreign ones are in progress. The production facilities in the home plant at Suffern are unequalled and people in the industry come from all over the world to study its filling and finishing lines. In addition, 15,000 visitors tour the plant annually.

The plant at Suffern that proudly began operations with twelve hands in a small, two-story frame building in 1894, now employs over 800 people who are a part of *Avon Calling*—the world's greatest house-to-house sales organization.

CUTEX

Manicuring is one of the oldest of the beauty professions. Excavations at the royal tombs at Ur of the Chaldees in southern Babylonia yielded a beautiful, solid gold manicure set used by some fastidious Babylonian in the year 3200 B.C., or over five thousand years ago. The *kohl*, a powder-like preparation used with the set to color the nails and eyelids, is in a remarkable state of preservation. Great Babylonian and Roman warriors of the day spent several hours before going into battle having their hair lacquered and curled, and their nails painted the same shade as their lips—a vogue that has been recently revived.

Queen Nefertiti, wife of the famed heretic king, Ikhnaton, and one of history's most beautiful women, painted her finger and toe nails a rich, ruby red, while Cleopatra favored a deep rusty shade. The use of color on the nails was governed by a strict social order and woe to her who toned her nails above her station! Persons of low rank were permitted only the palest of hues. Shades grew deeper as one gained social status, but absolutely no one dared to flaunt colors as brilliant as those of the Queen. Apparently these ancient ladies used color much more lavishly.

Mesdames Pompadour and Bovary, and Iseult of the White Hands are said to have owed a great deal of their charm and power to lovely and expressive hands. For centuries women of the upper classes in Spain have used color on their nails but it took a man named Northam Warren to revive the ancient custom in America by making women hand-conscious, and giving them a simple and economical way to manicure their nails.

Born in 1879, Northam Warren was the son of a Congregational minister. He graduated from the University of Kansas, and then studied at the Detroit College of Pharmacy. He scanned the career opportunities in several fields, tried a few of them, and then made his fortune from an idea which he originated and developed—liquid cuticle remover.

The introduction of his new product in 1911 revolutionized the art of manicuring. Until then, the cutting of the cuticle had been a tedious and awkward affair and few people even attempted the process at home. Of all the many steps involved in a manicure, including the time-consuming task of buffing powder or paste to produce the desired "shine," cuticle removal and trimming was the most difficult. Scissors were the only known method of dealing with the problem and only a few skilled manicurists were able to employ it without cutting into the "quick," a painful mishap that often resulted in infection.

Advertised as a way to "make manicuring easier," *Cuticle Remover* was an instant success. A professional manicure that had formerly required from one to two hours could now be done in less than half an hour, and with far more satisfactory results. *Vogue* magazine, *Harper's Bazaar* and others heralded the new concept in manicuring and by 1912 it had been adopted by most professional manicurists and by hundreds of thousands of American women who were delighted to be able to manicure their own nails. No toilet preparation in modern times has enjoyed a more spectacular acceptance.

Northam Warren was not a man to rest on his laurels, however. In 1916 he introduced the first liquid nail polish in this country. He coined the name *Cutex*, taking the first syllable from his *Cuticle Remover*, and adding *ex*, a popular suffix of the times. The polish was completely colorless, and its appeal was that it lasted longer and was easier to apply than either the powder or the paste then in use. An extensive advertising campaign soon had women from coast to coast looking at their hands and trying out the new-fangled product that would shine their nails so easily and quickly. A year later, 1917, the first tinted nail polish made its appearance in the rose-colored shade that Madame DuBarry is said to have worn.

During the Depression years of the '30's, when many industries were cutting back, Northam Warren instituted a bold advertising campaign to introduce deeper and darker shades of nail polish. It proved to be a well-timed and strategic innovation, and it also marked the beginning of our current fashion of brightly colored nails.

When *Cuticle Remover* was introduced in 1911, less than one-fourth of the women in the United States used any manicuring products at all, either at home or in beauty shops. Today, 74.2 per cent use a manicure preparation of one kind or another. The former Northam Warren Corporation is the oldest manufacturer of manicure preparations in the world and *Cutex* is the largest-selling brand. It is so well-known that one foreign manufacturer duplicated the name and packaging of *Cutex*, and defended himself in court on the grounds that *cutex* is a generic term for nail polish. He lost.

PRINCE MATCHABELLI

Georges Matchabelli, a handsome and charming young prince, was the eldest son of a Russian family of the nobility. He was educated in keeping with his position in life: at the Royal Academy in Berlin he learned mining engineering in preparation for the day when he would take over the management of his family's vast estates in the south of Russia; and he studied languages in preparation for the role of ambassador for his country.

The prince learned his lessons well, and when he became ambassador his personal charm soon made him a great favorite in all the glittering capitals of Europe. His marriage to the reigning beauty of the day, the famous actress Maria Carmi, was internationally acclaimed, and it seemed the young couple were destined to live happily ever after.

And so they might have, except for the Bolshevik revolution in 1919. Family holdings and estates that had been in the Matchabelli family since the ninth century were seized. The young prince never saw his home again, and if he had not been in Europe at the time of the uprising, he too would have been caught up in the maelstrom that enveloped his family and life-long friends.

The plight of the prince and his glamorous princess in Europe was desperate when the great impresario, Morris Gest, decided to bring his famed religious spectacle, *The Miracle,* to America. The Princess Matchabelli had played the part of the original Madonna and Morris Gest asked her to repeat the role on Broadway. Maria accepted, and the prince accompanied her to New York, where the play—and the princess—were an immediate success.

Prince Matchabelli, however, had no intention of being known only as the husband of Maria Carmi. In spite of the luxury and elegance of the life into which he had been born, the prince was not happy in idleness and he looked around for a way to use his energy and abilities. He found it in a little antique shop which he opened on Madison Avenue and which he called *Le Rouge et le Noir*. His personal magnetism plus his royal title proved an irresistible combination to wealthy socialites and theatrical celebrities, and the shop quickly became a mecca for them.

The prince further endeared himself to the ladies by blending for them individual, personal perfumes to match their personalities —a hobby he had picked up while he was still in college. So popular was this practice that perfume bottles soon crowded out the antiques and bric-a-brac. The prince finally abandoned the antiques entirely and turned to making perfume. He became perfume-chemist, manufacturer, merchandiser and advertising director all at the same time. He performed admirably in all the tasks, but it was in the inspired and brilliant design of the perfume bottle that he achieved his greatest success.

The *Prince Matchabelli* perfume bottle (only slightly altered today) is in the shape of a regal crown which the prince adapted from the one appearing at the top of his own family coat-of-arms. It was decorated in gold, and made of porcelain imported from Germany. It has since been adapted by an American company into glass and is considered one of the finest examples of handmade, commercial glass container today. It is manufactured by a semi-automatic process but the gold decoration and antiquing is still applied separately by hand, as is the *baudruche* (the almost invisible seal between bottle neck and ground-glass stopper) and the golden cord wound around the neck of the bottle.

Prince Matchabelli's first employees, all personal friends, were charming, sophisticated royal refugees like himself. The group included princes, counts and barons—and their female counterparts. One of them, Baron Paul Wrangell, was the first man to appear in the *Hathaway* shirt ads with the now-famous patch over one eye.

These royal personages worked at various and sundry jobs in the manufacture and sale of the perfume and cosmetics, as did Prince Matchabelli himself. They hand-operated the machines one minute, filled perfume bottles or ground sachet powder the next, and then, a few moments later, often stepped jauntily into the Avenue with hat, cane, spats, and gloves to deliver a rush order to a fashionable account. The princesses, countesses and baronesses exercised their creative talents on the magnificently wrapped packages.

Within three years after the formation of the perfume company, the prince's perfume blends were being distributed from coast to coast. While he could no longer, of course, create an exclusive blend for each woman (except in rare instances), he did create a fragrance for individual types of personalities which he named after great ladies: *Duchess of York, Catherine the Great, Princess Marie,* and *Ave Maria* for his wife for her portrayal of the Madonna that had brought them to America.

The Prince's suave, urbane friends acted as his representatives all over the country, but the prince himself was undoubtedly his own best publicist. He talked easily and charmingly, and women listened, whether at social gatherings, in press interviews, or on personal visits to fashionable stores. He had many theories about perfume, one of which was that every woman is a creature of many moods, and that she should always choose a perfume to suit her particular mood—whether it be that of the great lady or gay sophisticate; the witty companion or mysterious woman of intrigue. This idea is still interpreted today in such modern and diverse fragrances as *Wind Song, Stradivari,* and *Prophecy.*

Spurred on by spiraling success, the Prince added new items to the line, including the still very popular bath oil, *Abano,* which he named for the word "bath" in his native tongue. Plans were made to move into elegant new showrooms and offices on Fifth Avenue which were to be completed in June of 1935. The most outstanding decorators of the day were engaged. Cecil Beaton, the famous English artist and photographer, acted as consultant, and Pavel Tchelitchew did a portrait of the Prince dressed in full regalia which was to be on display. Tragically, however, following a Western sales trip the Prince died in March, 1935. In June, the Princess Matchabelli had the gala opening as planned, and as the Prince would have wished. The elegance and splendor of the magnificent showroom was a tribute to the man who in ten years had not only made a million dollar business out of his hobby, but had also picked up the pieces of his shattered life and made of them a successful, happy and productive human being.

CHARLES NESTLE AND THE
"PERMANENT" WAVE

The desire for curly hair has resulted in some rather weird and frightening contraptions for curling it but, nevertheless, through the ages curls have been somehow achieved by those not so blessed by nature.

Two thousand years before the Christian era, heated irons were used on royal beards and wigs in Egypt. At about the same time, kings and warriors of Assyria were having their abundant locks and flowing whiskers put into ringlets and waves by slaves who used a heated device resembling a carpenter's plane. The Greeks used cylindrical irons and terra cotta rollers.

In Rome, aristocrats had their ringlets waved with a *calamin-*

strum, a hollow tube about which the hair was twisted. It was then heated by the insertion of a hot rod. The results are much in evidence today on classic statues.

During the Dark Ages, hair fashions disappeared, to emerge in the Renaissance when "crisping irons" (somewhat resembling our modern waffle irons) were introduced at the Italian Court and became a tremendous success. In sixteenth century Spain, ingenious pins and twisters were contrived, probably by the same artisans who made armor and swords.

By 1700 ringlets were out, and solid rows of waves were in. Wigs called "perukes" were curled on heated pipe-clay rollers. Perukes are, incidentally, still sported by English barristers and judges.

Hairdressers came into their own during the reign of Louis XIV, and his successor, Louis XV. Ladies held *levées* (morning receptions) while their hair was being dressed with quantities of false hair, padding, and monstrous decoration, sometimes so bizarre as to include a live bird in a cage. These exaggerated fashions went out with the reign of Marie Antoinette.

At the dawn of the nineteenth century there was a "classic" revival. During the Regency in England, the Directoire and First Empire in France, ladies wore ringlets over their ears and Psyche knots (a conical coil at the back of the head). Curls were even more desirable when the Empress Eugenie arrived with a profusion of massed ringlets visible under her tilted hats.

England under Victoria went in for a different vogue. Her Majesty's smooth, primly parted hair with its loops above the ears and "waterfall" of cascading curls in back brought a demand for macassar oil and brilliantine. This fashion spread to the United States, and American curls disappeared until the Gay Nineties, when Lillian Russell and other famous beauties revived them. While these beauties had their hair "done" by professionals, the average woman wound her hair on rags, or used devices of kid and wire, known as "kid curlers." Others wielded curling tongs on themselves with many frizzed heads and burned fingers as a result.

But the time was near when curls would be within every woman's reach. By the beginning of the twentieth century, Marcel in Paris had become famous for his method of hair waving, and Charles Nestle, inventor of the permanent wave machine, had begun active experiments with his "Scientific Everlasting Wave."

Charles Nestle was born Karl Ludwig Nessler in a small village in the Bavarian Alps. He possessed an inquisitive mind that early caused him to wonder why all the curl came out of his sister's hair when it rained, while the wool on the lambs he tended curled tighter and tighter.

Karl was the youngest of his family and generally ignored by his older sisters and brothers but he amused himself by reading the biology books his brothers and sisters studied, and looking at the pictures. It was an illustration in one of the books, showing that straight hair is round and curly hair elliptical, that started Karl on his search for knowledge about hair.

Karl's father was a shoemaker, and it was the custom then that sons should follow the trade of their fathers. However, it soon became painfully apparent to the elder Nessler that son Karl lacked aptitude for the cobbler's bench, and because of Karl's interest in hair, the father apprenticed him to the town barber.

In those days the barber in a small town was also apt to be the doctor, dentist, and surgeon, and in his apprenticeship Karl learned the basic rudiments of chemistry. But the opportunity was limited and Karl was ambitious. He envisioned better things and decided to go to Switzerland, just across the border.

In Switzerland he found work in a watch-parts factory. At first the work fascinated him but he soon tired of it and returned to barbering and the study of hair. He moved from one city to another, and always to larger and better shops. Finally he found the opportunity he sought in an apprenticeship to a large shop where only hairdressing was done. As he learned hairdressing he continued his own study and research: What is hair? What is it made of? How and why does it react to certain chemicals? How can it be made to stay curled?

Karl heard about the *Marcel Wave* that was the rage of Paris and promptly set out to see for himself what the new method was all about. Paris proved to be a mecca for Karl with its lovely, fashion-conscious women who continuously demanded more and more curls. He became a hairdresser in an elegant Parisian salon where he mastered the *Marcel Wave* but he continued work and research on a "permanent" wave of his own—a wave that would, through a combination of mechanical and chemical means, last longer than anyone had ever dreamed.

Two pretty girls, Yvonne and Katharina, worked in the salon with Karl. Both were notable in the life of the young man because he gave the first permanent wave to one and married the other. Yvonne received the first distinction—all the hair on her head was "baked" off with the exception of one lonely strand that retained a beautiful curl. Karl was delighted with the lone curl that survived and it convinced him that he was on the right track. All he needed was more experience in administering the wave he had long dreamed about and laboriously created. His reputation as a proficient *Marcel* operator grew and provided him with the money he needed to buy equipment and continue his experiments. When his proficiency as a *Marcel* operator came to the attention of a socially prominent English lady, she persuaded him to come to London and open his own shop.

When Karl Nessler opened his salon in London he anglicized his name to Charles Nestle, and displayed a sign in front of his shop that took advantage of his well-traveled past:

CHARLES NESTLE
Hairspecialist
Operating in Basel, Geneva,
Milan, Paris and London
Coiffeur for Men and Women

Katharina Laible joined him in England and became Mrs. Charles Nestle.

Karl, now Charles Nestle, advertised his theories on permanent waving, lectured extensively, used diagrams and quoted scientific authorities, but found few listeners for the subject closest to his heart. Meanwhile, his reputation as a hairdresser grew, and he achieved note as a manufacturer of false eyebrows and eyelashes. A reporter for the *London Daily Mirror* listened politely to Nestle's lengthy explanation of his permanent wave theory, and then wrote for his paper: "This man Nestle makes wonderfully real eyebrows, eyelashes and moustaches for his select clientele," and didn't mention the permanent wave. However, the response to the story was terrific, and business boomed. The profits were used to further the development of the permanent wave machine.

By 1905 Nestle was able to find a few customers for his permanent wave, but only because of his fine reputation. In 1906 he rented a hall to demonstrate the machine to the hairdressers of London. Their reaction was unfavorable, and most of them expressed the fear that the permanent wave would mean the end of the hairdressing business. Actually, of course, it was the permanent wave machine that made a business out of hairdressing.

But Charles Nestle was not discouraged. He continued to make improvements on his machine, and through extensive advertising in magazines and newspapers, the Nestle name grew in prestige and the popularity of his permanent wave method increased proportionately. His system involved winding the hair, spiral fashion, on a rod, applying a covering of alkaline paste, and covering all with an asbestos tube and a heated iron of gas-pipe size with tong handles, which was held in place until the hair had been sufficiently steamed. Hair three feet long was considered desirable, and it was waved only around the hairline. The process took at least six hours.

In 1909 electricity replaced the gas-pipe, and was communicated directly to the heaters by overhead wires, much like the machines that were in use for years afterward. Just prior to 1914, at his beautiful salon at 245 Oxford Circus, Charles Nestle proudly unveiled a door plaque that proclaimed "Under Royal Patronage." This brought even more, and wealthier, clients to the Nestle establishment, where only his own "Scientific Ever-Lasting Wave" and "Art Eye-Lashes and Brows" were available.

Things were going well for Charles Nestle when the first guns of World War I sounded. He had never become a British subject, and was therefore required to leave the country as an alien. He came to New York in January, 1915, and was amazed to find over 600 imitations of his patented process of permanent waving. Although for the most part the machines were inferior and their operators incompetent, there was little he could do to protect himself. With most of his assets gone, he sublet space in a shop to give permanent waves of the type and quality he was famous for in Europe. He used the remainder of his funds for an advertising program. The first advertisement announced his opening, and the superiority of the permanent wave he alone could give. Sixty-two women responded to the ad, and sixty-one walked away without the permanent—frightened either by the waving apparatus itself (although it was guaranteed shock-proof) or the price, which was much higher than that charged by any other shop in New York.

But one woman stayed to get a "permanent," and this was the beginning of Nestle's American success and the rebuilding of his fortune. Because of the excellence of his work, the Nestle clientele grew steadily. By 1919 a *Nestle* permanent was a part of many women's beauty regimen at the magnificent Nestle Salon on Fifth Avenue.

In 1920 a *Nestle* representative toured the world with the eight-heater machine then in use to wave the hair of the most prominent women in every country, including ladies of the Japanese royal family.

In 1927 Charles Nestle opened the largest beauty salon in the world at Broadway and 51st Street in New York. Here all the great stars of stage and screen, society ladies and debutantes proudly came for permanents. The Nestle appointment book recorded such names as Ethel Barrymore, Helen Menken, Lillian Gish and Norma Shearer.

Charles Nestle, American citizen, had come a long way from the little shepherd boy named Karl Ludwig Nessler who had grown up in the Bavarian Alps and who had been apprenticed to the village barber. He was a fabulous figure in the business world of the turbulent 'twenties—wealthy and world-renowned.

When the Nestle Company was later merged with the LeMur Company of Cleveland, Charles Nestle, although many times over a millionaire, continued to travel extensively and to lecture to scientific groups on the subject of hair, and to students of beauty culture all over the world.

The Nestle-LeMur Company continues to carry on the work begun by Charles Nestle, and today furnishes the beauty salon trade with products for permanent waving, as well as supplies for every phase of modern hair care and styling. In addition, they are the manufacturers of the world's largest-selling temporary hair coloring—*Nestle Colorinse* and *Nestle Colortint*.

IVORY SOAP

In 1878 the Cincinnati firm of Procter & Gamble perfected a formula for a revolutionary new hard soap. It was white and pure (qualities then found only in imported, expensive castiles) and it floated. The company had devoted years of research and thousands of dollars to make their new soap white and pure, but its unique "floating" ability was the result of an accident. A careless workman took an extra long lunch hour one day, and left a batch of the new soap stirring vigorously in a *cutcher* (vat). When this somewhat less-than-diligent fellow returned, he nonchalantly shipped the batch out anyway in the hope his negligence would go undetected. It did—until the surprised company was suddenly deluged with orders for more of "that soap that floats." Apparently the prolonged stirring had beaten air into the mixture and the formula was hurriedly revised and modified until "floating soap" was produced every time.

A bit on the conservative side, Procter & Gamble called its new product *The White Soap*. This was, declared young Harley Procter, too simple a name even for those relatively uncomplicated times and he persuaded his father, a partner in the firm, to let him launch a campaign to really put *The White Soap* on the market. It was just the opportunity the eager young man had been waiting for to try his own progressive ideas in advertising and marketing.

First, decided Harley, the new product must have an identity, a name that would capture the fancy of the public. "To be white, to be pure, and to float." These were magic words to Harley, as he began his search for a name with the necessary force and appeal. His imagination worked overtime as he considered and discarded hundreds of possibilities. After weeks of desperate, intense absorption in his quest, inspiration came one Sunday morning as he sat in church. Though he struggled to follow the minister's sermon, his mind wandered constantly to the problem of his still nameless soap. Suddenly he became aware of the words the minister was reading from Psalms 45:8:

All thy garments smell of myrrh, and aloes, and cassia, out of the ivory palaces, whereby they have made thee glad.

The new *White Soap* was successfully christened *Ivory*, and Harley now sought scientific backing for its claim of purity. Samples were sent to chemistry professors at Yale, Michigan and Princeton for analyses and the result became one of the most famous slogans in advertising history: "99 and 44/100 % pure."

GILLETTE SAFETY RAZOR AND BLADE

Of all the little things that have been invented, it is one of the biggest little things ever issued from the U. S. Patent Office . . .   King C. Gillette

Changing the face of man in the space of a few years is a pretty broad claim to make, but when King C. Gillette invented the first safety razor, man's shaving habits were revolutionized the world over.

The hirsute growth on the face of man and how he has dealt with it has been, down through the ages, an important factor in the lives of king and peasant, soldier and tradesman. A clean-shaven face was a status symbol with the ancient Egyptians and bronze razors of ingenious design have been found in their tombs. The American Indian stoically pulled his beard out with clam shells used as tweezers. Alexander the Great ordered his soldiers to shave to prevent the enemy from grasping them by the beard. Peter the Great of Russia strove to make his barbaric nobles more civilized by having them shave. William the Conqueror and his Normans were also beardless—but on the other hand, the war-like Norsemen clung to their fierce, flowing beards as evidence of strength and manhood, as did a harassed young man in a recent Broadway comedy as he defended his hard-won beard: "Please!" he cried. "It's my virility symbol!"

George Washington had a fine set of straight razors (wielded by his faithful servant). Napoleon's face was also barren of whiskers, even though he was terrified of shaving. But thumb through the albums of our Civil War days—and the succeeding seventies, eighties, and the 'nineties—and you will find most men gazing at you from behind luxurious crops of hair foliage. The young man of 25 could hardly be distinguished from his grandfather of 75.

By the turn of the nineteenth century, the bronze instrument of the Egyptians had changed but little. The method and principle were practically the same. Only the rich man could afford a daily shave by his barber. The man-in-the-street courageously struggled through the beard-slaying operation once or twice a week armed only with a hook-type, straight-edge razor.

And so the battle raged: to shave in fear and trembling, or not to shave. It was resolved, once and for all, by a traveling salesman-inventor named King C. Gillette.

King Gillette was born in Fond du Lac, Wisconsin, in 1855, and from the time he was seventeen years old, when his father lost everything in the great Chicago fire, he was on his own. At 21 he was earning his living as a traveling salesman, but his real interest lay in inventions. He was awarded several patents but had neither the time nor the money to commercialize them. In 1891 he was persuaded by a friend, William Painter, to join his sales force at the Baltimore Seal Company. The company made rubber bottle stoppers for beer and carbonated beverages. Later, William Painter invented the Crown Cork—the tin cap with the cork lining which is still extensively used—and the name of the company was changed to Crown Cork & Seal Company. Painter and young King engaged in many long conversations about their mutual interest in inventions, and in the course of one of these discussions, Painter made a remark the essence of which became an obsession with King.

"King," Painter said, "you are always inventing *something*. Why don't you concentrate on just one thing—something like the Crown Cork—that people use once and throw away?"

From that moment on, the stage was set for the near-visionary manner in which the safety razor and blade came into being. Every waking moment King was alert for an inspiration for something —*anything*—people would use once and throw away. He went through the alphabet and listed every material need he could think of, but to no avail. Then, in the summer of 1895, it happened. In King Gillette's own words:

"It was born as naturally as though its embryonic form had matured in thought and only waited its appropriate time of birth. One morning when I started to shave, I found my razor dull, and it was not only dull but it was beyond the point of successful stropping. It needed honing which meant it would have to be taken to a barber or cutler. 'A razor is only a sharp edge,' I said to myself, 'and all back of it is just support. Why do they go to all the expense and trouble of fashioning a backing that has nothing to do with shaving? And why do they forge a great piece of steel and then spend so much labor in hollow grinding it when they could get the same result by putting an edge on a piece of steel only thick enough to hold an edge?'

Gillette Safety Razor and Blade 157

"As I stood there with the razor in my hand, my eyes resting on it as lightly as a bird settling down on its nest, the Gillette razor was born—more with the rapidity of a dream than by a process of reasoning. In that moment I saw it all: the way the blade could be held in a holder; the idea of sharpening the two opposite edges on the thin piece of steel; the clamping plates for the blade, with a handle half-way between the two edges of the blade.

"All this came more in pictures than in conscious thought as though the razor were already a finished thing and held before my eyes. I stood there before that mirror in a trance of joy. My wife was visiting in Ohio and I hurriedly wrote to her: 'I've got it! Our fortune is made!' Fool that I was, I knew little about razors and nothing about steel, and I could not foresee the trials and tribulations I was to pass through before the razor was a success. But I believed in it with my whole heart."

After the sudden inspiration, King rushed out to a hardware store and bought some pieces of brass, steel ribbon used for clock springs, a small band vise, and some files. With these materials, he made the first razor. He also made endless sketches, which have since been used extensively in patent matters.

To his great disappointment, King could not interest any financial backers in his invention. The razor was looked on as a joke by all of his friends who usually greeted him with, "Well, Gillette, how's the razor?"

For six years King Gillette tried in vain to find financial backing. During this time he continued his experiments with steel blades. He had discovered that the steel used had to be of a particular quality and that it would cost many times what he had originally supposed. (Later, the Gillette Company was to spend over a quarter of a million dollars in laboratory tests alone before the question of steel quality would be decided.) The "experts" whom King consulted invariably advised him to forget it; that he would never succeed in putting an edge on sheet steel that would shave.

"But I didn't know enough to quit," recalled Gillette. "If I had been technically trained, I would have given up, or probably would never have begun. I was a dreamer, and in search of the gold at the foot of the rainbow. I dared where wise ones feared to tread.

"I tried every cutler and machine shop in Boston and some in New York and Newark in an effort to find someone who knew something about hardening and tempering thin steel so it would keep its flatness and not be warped by strains. Even the Massachusetts Institute of Technology experimented and failed absolutely in securing satisfactory results."

Finally, in 1901, King persuaded some friends to raise the sum of $5,000 to form a company, and start manufacturing. The "plant" was in Boston over a fish store and next to a wharf where garbage was dumped into scows. There a young graduate from the Massachusetts Institute of Technology, William E. Nickerson, refined Gillette's original safety razor, and developed processes for hardening and sharpening sheet steel. King Gillette said of Nickerson: "He was the only man in the world who could have perfected the razor."

Experimentation and research soon absorbed the $5,000 and the company was $12,000 in debt. It was rescued by a shrewd Boston investor, John Joyce, who recognized the possibilities of the razor and advanced the funds necessary to put the company on its feet and properly launch the razor. The first year the Gillette razor was marketed, 1903, a total of 51 razors and 168 blades were sold. But, it was a start, and in 1904, sales leaped to an unbelievable 90,844 razors and 123,648 blades. One man who had paid $250 for a block of 500 shares of the original $5,000 investment was bought out by Gillette four years later for the sum of $62,500.

In the sixty years since the first Gillette razor went on sale, the company has produced over a *half billion* razors and over *fifty billion* blades in its plants throughout the world, freeing an astronomical number of men from whisker bondage.

The Gillette trademark—King C. Gillette's face and signature—is one of the world's best known portraits and signatures. It has been reproduced over 100 billion times—which suggests something of the scope and intensity of the conquest of the beard by King C. Gillette and the company he founded.

BURMA-SHAVE

Alexander Woollcott said it was harder to pass up a Burma-Shave jingle than to eat just one peanut and one bard of the road went so far as to write, "T'would be more fun/ To go by air/ If we could put/ These signs up there."

The Burma-Shave jingle signs were originated by Allan Odell, son of the founder of the company, in 1926. Allan's father, Clinton Odell, had built up a very successful sales organization for an insurance company when he was forced to retire because of his health. Financially, he was well able to devote his life to fishing in any of Minnesota's 10,000 lakes, but retirement did not agree with him. The early 20's found Clint Odell engaged in the process of manufacturing a liniment, the formula for which was supposed to have come from an old sea captain—as did all liniment formulae in those days. The essential oils in the liniment did come from Burma and Malay, however, and Clint combined the word "Burma" with the Latin word *vita* (meaning life or vigor) for the name of his new company.

Another son, Leonard C. Odell, now vice-president of the company, recalls that "although our liniment was a good, hot product, it was also an odorous one, and applying it did not only cure your ailment, but often notified your neighbors of your whereabouts." At any rate, it made a lot of friends, but not enough to keep the business going.

Meanwhile, the elder Odell, who was a seasoned traveling man, had discovered an English brushless shaving cream called *Lloyd's Euxesis*, with which he was much taken because it eliminated the shaving brush which often became mildewed and ill-smelling during weeks of travel. From *Lloyd's Euxesis* came the idea of a brushless shaving cream for Americans, and since the company was already *Burma-Vita*, *Burma-Shave* just "fell into line naturally."

Getting the American male to accept the revolutionary brushless shaving cream, however, did not fall into line so easily.

Young Allan, fresh out of college, had been eagerly looking for new worlds to conquer, but even he was growing discouraged at the conspicuous lack of success in getting the conservative male population to buy the new brushless shaving cream. He was mulling over the situation one day as he drove along a country highway and saw a series of signs extolling the virtues of a filling station a short distance down the road. Allan brightened up immediately. But would his father gamble enough money to advertise *Burma-Shave* on roadside signs?

The advertising experts said it wouldn't work, of course. You had to sell shaving cream with statistics, they argued, with testimonials and smiling, well-shaven faces. At that critical juncture in the company's life, however, Clint decided anything was worth a try, and agreed to spend $200 for the first set of road signs. They appeared in September, 1926, on U.S. Highway 65 near Lakeville, Minnesota. Allan wrote the first jingle which he said he had mumbled to himself when he saw the filling station signs: "Cheer Up/ Face/ The War/ Is/ Over."

To Allan and his younger brother, Leonard, fell the job of installing the signs. Leonard drove a truck loaded with freshly-painted signs and the necessary tools for setting them up while Allan raced ahead in a car to find a likely spot and an amiable farmer willing to rent the space. By the time Leonard arrived, Allan had talked the farmer into the deal, and the brothers went to work. "I dug every hole for a sign in the whole Midwest," Leonard said, recalling the blisters of that year. "You might say I learned the business from three feet under the ground up."

The $200 gamble paid off. Sales jumped spectacularly from almost zero to $68,000 in one year. *Burma-Shave* was on the road at last—figuratively as well as literally.

"Are your whiskers/ When you wake/ Tougher than/ A two-bit steak?"/ startled motorists read. Or, "A peach/ Looks good/ With lots of fuzz/ But man's no peach/ And never was."

Soon people were reading the *Burma-Shave* jingles all over the Midwest. Drivers slowed down to read, "Henry the Eighth/ Prince of Friskers/ Lost five wives/ But kept/ His whiskers." Wives chuckled too, and slyly called their husbands' attention to such jingles as: "He played/ A sax/ Had no B.O./ But his whiskers scratched/ So she let him go." Farther down the road, the husband had his turn, and read aloud: "Soon shaving brushes/ Will be trimmin'/ Those screwy hats/ We see/ On women."

Sales continued to climb, even during the depths of the depression. The merry little jingles provided a bright spot wherever they appeared, and the public's response was reflected in the company's soaring sales figures.

Fred Allen did one of his best radio shows on "The Murder of the *Burma-Shave* Poet," and safety experts got into the act when they pointed out that the signs helped to slow down drivers.

Burma-Shave took the hint, and such jingles as "Don't take a curve/ At 60 per/ We hate to lose/ A customer," and "Past school-houses/ Take it slow/ Let the little/ Shavers/ Grow" appeared.

The Odells didn't realize just how seriously some people took their jingles until one series of signs suggested: "Rip a fender/ Off your car/ Send it in/ For a half-pound jar." Dozens of tiny fenders from toy cars poured into the Minneapolis office, and jars of *Burma-Shave* were duly dispatched. But the big surprise came when they began to receive crates containing real, ripped-off fenders! "It was incredible," recalls Leonard Odell. "We were stunned, but never-theless, we mailed out the half-pound jars—and in a hurry."

Another literal-minded motorist responded to "Free, free/ A trip/ To Mars/ For 900 empty jars" with a letter advising that he had 898 jars saved up and would report any day now for his free trip. The Odells hastily replaced the signs with: "If a trip to Mars/ You'd earn/ Remember, friend/ There's no return."

Today there are over 7,000 sets of *Burma-Shave* signs dotting highways all over the country. Each set consists of six signs spaced about 100 feet apart, and bolted to fence-high iron or wooden posts. Souvenir hunters used to carry off entire sets of jingles, so now, in order to discourage this flattering but costly practice, the bolts holding the signs are securely counter-sunk in place.

Sites for all the *Burma-Shave* signs are leased from farmers at an annual cash rental. The farmers all show a genuine loyalty to-ward the signs. They protect them from farm animals, guard them against souvenir hunters, and repair broken ones. "The *Burma-Shave* 'crop'," they explain, "doesn't have to be planted, irrigated, cultivated, or harvested."

Jingles are selected annually from contests open to both profes-sionals and amateurs, and though "Sunday afternoon jinglesmiths and backyard poets become bards of the open road," several well-known poets have also won *Burma-Shave* jingle money. Of course, the primary purpose of the signs is to sell shaving cream, and the sound principle behind the *Burma-Shave* jingles, one of the most imaginative advertising campaigns ever conceived, is that the easiest way to make sales is to make friends. That is why the jingles are always catchy or humorous. Jingles in poor taste are never ac-cepted. Though many of those submitted annually would undoubt-edly amuse many motorists, others might be offended. Below are some of the jingles that were "censored"—that you will *not* see by the roadside, but which the Odells, father and sons, have enjoyed:

> *If wifie shuns*
> *Your fond embrace*
> *Don't shoot*
> *The iceman*
> *Feel your face*
>   Burma-Shave

> *Listen, birds*
> *Those signs cost*
> *Money*
> *So roost a while but*
> *Don't get funny*
>   Burma-Shave

> *My man*
> *Won't shave*
> *Sez Hazel Huz*
> *But I should worry*
> *Dora's does*
>   Burma-Shave

> *After*
> *4 drinks*
> *The British sing*
> *God shave*
> *The king!*
>   Burma-Shave

The signs are completely changed once a year. A new batch of jingles appears during the spring in northern and eastern United States, and during the fall and winter in other sections. They have become a national institution.

And what is the favorite of the original "jinglesmith," Allan Odell?

"Within this vale/ Of toil and sin/ Your head grows bald/ But not your chin/ *Burma-Shave*."

TRANSPORTATION

HENRY FORD AND HIS FABULOUS
MODEL "T"

The "Tin Lizzie" was not only an automobile (notwithstanding what *some* people called it) but it was also an American institution. It is credited with the dubious achievement of having put America on wheels. No other automobile, and no other personality, had more impact on the American way of life than the "Tin Lizzie" and its parent, Henry Ford—one of America's original "rugged individualists."

Henry's career began with several brilliant failures. He abandoned a career in power engineering in 1899 to become chief engineer of the brand new Detroit Automobile Company. A year and a half later, the firm was in bankruptcy, having sold less than six of its automobiles. After the company failed, Henry was hired as an experimental engineer by the men who had purchased the bankrupt company's assets.

In 1901, "because racing was supposed to tell something about the merits of an automobile," he accepted a challenge by Alexander Winton, then the king of American racing. When the race resulted in victory for Ford and his car design, several of the former Detroit Automobile Company stockholders formed the Henry Ford Company. Henry was named chief engineer and received one-sixth of the stock in exchange for his car design. Friction developed almost immediately between Henry and the stockholders and he soon left the company.

Although he was gaining fame through his racing cars, his dream was a company of his own. But it was difficult to interest investors. Finally, mostly through the efforts of a Detroit coal dealer, Alexander Y. Malcomson, $28,000 was raised and the Ford Motor Company incorporated in 1903. There were twelve original stockholders, including the famous Dodge brothers. Henry was made chief engineer and vice-president, and given 255 shares of stock in exchange for his automobile design and 17 patents on its mechanism.

Most of the stockholders wanted to build big, heavy and expensive automobiles, with the market confined to a limited number of wealthy people, but farsighted Henry would not agree. "I'm going to build a *car for the masses*," he stubbornly insisted. Production was started in a converted wagon factory on Mack Avenue, Detroit, in July, 1903. The first car was the early *Model A*. Manufacturing consisted mainly of assembling, since the running gear—engines, frames, transmissions and axles—as well as wheels, tires and bodies, were made by outside suppliers. The early *Model A* had a 72-inch wheelbase and an over-all length of 99 inches. It weighed 1,000 pounds. The engine was under the seat and the starting crank and steering wheel were on the right side of the car. The *tonneau* (back seat) was detachable and slipped on and off from the rear. Entrance to the *tonneau* was through a rear door. The price was $750 for the runabout and buyers who wanted a *tonneau* paid $100 extra. A leather top could be bought for $50, or a rubber-lined canvas top could be had for $30.

Seven other models followed, identified by alphabetical letters, and it is to be assumed that the missing letters represented duds. The *Model K* for instance was known to be a colossal failure—it was too expensive to build, the selling price too high and the market too limited. While these models were being marketed, however, Henry was hard at work on another four-cylinder car that was a considerable improvement over anything the company had yet produced. In 1908 he introduced the *Model T* (so called simply because it followed *Model S*) and it became the most famous of any automobile before or since.

The *Model T* was an immediate success, and the demand for it soared to such staggering proportions that the company was forced at intervals to stop accepting orders until the backlog could be reduced. From the time of its introduction until production was finally halted on May 31, 1927, a total of 15,007,033 *Model T*'s were produced and sold.

The name "Tin Lizzie" originated with the *Model T*. In those years a great many families employed a domestic who was a maid of all work during the week but come Sunday she strutted off to church in great dignity. These domestics were frequently named or referred to as "Liz" or "Lizzie." Like Lizzie, the *Model T* was also a "maid of all work"—sometimes being used to grind fodder, churn butter, saw wood, or pull a plow in the fields—but come Sunday, she was prettied up to take the family regally to church. Everyone already referred to the *Model T* as a "tin car," so "Tin Lizzie" was a natural. (Actually, far from being tin, the *Model T* bodies and fenders were of heavier gauge sheet metal than is used on most modern automobiles).

Henry Ford had what he had always wanted in the Tin Lizzie—a car for the masses. "Let them have any color they want," he said in 1914 (in the interest of speeding up production), "so long as it's black." This decree was greeted incredulously by Henry's production chief, and three days later the man quit, convinced Ford's decision would bankrupt the company.

Stories and jokes about the *Model T* flourished throughout its long reign and for many years afterward. Examples:

"What shock absorbers do you use on your Ford?"
"The passengers."

A little boy watching a man cranking his Ford, impudently asked: "Why don't she play, mister?"

Henry Ford encouraged them, apparently on the premise that any publicity was good publicity. His attitude was not shared by one officer of the company who huffily cancelled all *Ford* advertising in a newspaper that had printed some of the *Model T* jokes. Henry promptly re-instated the advertising, remarking that the officer in question "had no sense of humor."

From the beginning, the very life of the Ford Motor Company had been threatened by the famous Selden patent. In 1895 George B. Selden had obtained a patent on a "road locomotive" to be run by a "liquid hydrocarbon engine of the compression type." Theoretically, this was to cover every conceivable type of operable vehicle powered by hydrocarbon fuel. In other words, no manufacturer of automobiles could produce and sell cars without paying royalties to Selden, and the Association of Licensed Automobile Manufacturers had been formed as an agency to grant licenses under the Selden patent and to enforce payment of the royalties. Henry Ford refused to become a member of the A.L.A.M. and refused to pay tribute to the Selden interests. "The Selden patent is a freak among alleged inventions," said the fiercely individualistic Henry, "and is worthless as a device." He was entangled in legal actions thereafter for a period of 8 years, suffering defeat in the lower court in 1909, but winning a hard-fought victory when in 1911 it was held that Ford had not infringed on the so-called Selden patent. The entire automotive industry benefited from his victory.

Production of the *Model T* had never been able to keep up with demand. Automobiles were still being built much as carpenters build a house: all materials were assembled in piles, the frames were placed on saw horses, and the entire car assembled in one spot. Many men have claimed credit for the moving assembly line, but it is most probable that the idea evolved as a result of several men's thinking and experimenting. At any rate, the first attempt at a moving assembly line in the *Ford* company was in 1913, and by 1914 the *Model T*—from bare frame to completed automobile— could be produced in 93 minutes.

After another serious disagreement with stockholders (including the Dodge brothers) which wound up in a law suit which he lost, Ford vowed never again to be dictated to by stockholders, and thereupon, in 1919, using his entire capital and some borrowed money, Henry Ford bought out all other stockholders and the gigantic corporation came under the control of one man. The cost of buying all outstanding stock was $105,568,858. This amounted to a return of approximately $12,500,000 for each original $5,000 investment.

Model T production reached fantastic levels during the 'twenties. In 1923, a total of 2,011,125 *Model T* passenger cars and trucks were built—a record that was to stand for 32 years, until 1955.

Basically, although some mechanical improvements had been added, the design of the *Model T* had not changed in nineteen years. But time had finally run out for the *Model T* and Henry reluctantly had to admit a new and better car must be built. *Ford* plants closed down for six months and re-tooled for what became the new *Model A*. This was a highly improved car in all respects, and it is estimated that one-fourth of the people in America saw the car during the first week it was released and exhibited. *Model A* production continued through 1931, but once more, time ran out on the *Ford* car. Competition was crowding, and a new and better model was again called for.

The "new and better car" was the V-8. It was a turning point for Ford Motor Company, and an example of the strange genius of Henry Ford. The four-cylinder car was efficient, and the V-8 was nothing more than two four-cylinder engines aligned together at an angle, and using a short, rigid crankshaft. Henry Ford knew that if he was to turn out *Ford* automobiles with the same speed he had turned out the *Model T* and *Model A,* the cylinder block would have to be cast *en bloc* (2 banks of 4 cylinders set at right angles to each other in one massive piece) just as his four-cylinder *Model T* had been. Experienced engineers and foundrymen insisted it could not be done. Henry Ford insisted it could. The day came when the problems were solved, and Henry Ford Company was the first automobile manufacturer in history to successfully mass produce such an engine. It was many years before competitors attempted V-8 production.

Henry Ford was a leader in every sense of the word. Ford Motor Company built the first all-metal, tri-motor airplane ever used commercially in the United States; instituted the first commercial mail flight; perfected the first radio beam for guiding planes and then donated it to the nation. Henry Ford and his son Edsel established the Ford Foundation in 1936, and it is now the wealthiest philanthropic organization of its kind in America.

Edsel Ford, Henry's only son, who had been president of the company since 1919, died in 1943 in the midst of the war effort. His father, then 80 years old, resumed the presidency until his grandson, Henry Ford II, was released from the Navy and returned home to take his place.

Henry Ford died at his Fair Lane estate in Dearborn, only a mile from where he had been born on April 7, 1947, at the age of 83. A hard-working man of simple tastes, he never lost his enthusiasm for square dancing and practical jokes. He remained active to the last day of his life, and although he never "left his home town," he became one of our most famous pioneering Americans.

RAMBLER

The *Rambler* automobile is a mere sixty years old, but the name itself is one of the oldest in transportation. Thomas B. Jeffery, the English-born inventor of the *Rambler* automobile, was for many years a very successful manufacturer of bicycles which he sold under the *Rambler* name. Though he built his fortune in the bicycle and automobile business, he is best known for his invention and manufacture of the clincher tire in the 1880s.

Jeffery sold his bicycle business, and at America's first automobile race in 1895 he saw the new mode of transportation for the first time. With the proceeds from the sale of his prosperous bicycle company, he bought a vacant plant in Kenosha, Wisconsin, and happily began experimenting with the new "horseless carriage." By the fall of 1900, Jeffery had developed two new "gasoline vehicles" —a "runabout" (completely open) and a "stanhope" (with top). These first experimental cars were "radical" in design, with the engine mounted in the front and a steering wheel mechanism on the left. However, in a shrewd gauge of public opinion, when Jeffery introduced the car for sale two years later, the engine was rearmounted and the car steered by a tiller from the right-hand side.

These *Rambler* "carriages" (Jeffery had retained the trade name) were one-cylinder, 12-horsepower cars. The runabout sold for $750, and the stanhope for $825. They were an instant success. In 1902, when only 23,000 motor cars were registered in the United States, Jeffery turned out 1,500 vehicles to become the world's second mass-producer of automobiles. (A year after *Oldsmobile* and a year ahead of *Ford*.)

"Customer relations" might also be said to have been in its infancy as evidenced by a priceless 1902 *Rambler* Instruction Manual which bluntly states:

The easiest way of avoiding trouble is to learn the carriage (automobile) thoroughly and understandingly; it is an incontrovertible fact that fully nine-tenths of the troubles experienced by the operators of motor cars are caused by the ignorance of the former, and not by the defects of the latter.

Early owners were also charged with heavy maintenance responsibilities for keeping their "carriages" in good operating condition: "Every point of lubrication should be carefully gone over each morning before commencing the day's work."

Mysteries of the carburetor were explained in detail, and step-by-step instructions provided for adjusting the poppet valve if the one-cylinder engine should begin to smoke or misfire. No claims for gasoline economy were made. In fact, the manufacturer frankly admitted that "ordinarily a great waste occurs."

Nevertheless, most '02 *Rambler* owners were pleased with their vehicles, but one dissenting voice came from Elmira, New York: "It seems to us that this machine is geared to run at too high a speed for our roads. In fact, we know this is the case, unless there is some way of making it run slower than we have yet found out." (Top speed of the 12-horsepower engine was 25 m.p.h.)

Jeffery's success was due not only to sound engineering, but also to imaginative promotion. His advertising manager, Ned Jordan, covered the countryside with more than 5,000 road signs which indicated the distance to the nearest town or city, and in which direction it lay. This was a master stroke, since the only way to get from one town to another was by asking the nearest farmer for directions. Each sign was, of course, prominently inscribed with the word, *Rambler*.

Thomas B. Jeffery died in 1910, and the purchaser of his company was Charles W. Nash, who had resigned as president of General Motors to found a new company, and build a car under his own name. In 1918 the first *Nash* car, powered by a six-cylinder valve-in-head engine, made its bow.

In 1937, *Nash* merged with the Kelvinator Corporation under the leadership of George Mason who had been Chrysler's works manager at the age of 30. He promptly put *Nash* engineers to work on a new, economical, lightweight car which appeared in 1940 as the *Nash* "600"—so named because it could go 600 miles on a 20-gallon tank of gasoline. In March, 1950, the *Nash* company introduced the first modern compact car, and the nostalgic name of *Rambler* was revived for the new line.

The convenience and thrift of the little car was its own best publicity. It appealed to the "common sense" of the American people. Big cars were being assailed as "gas-guzzling dinosaurs," and cartoonists, newspaper editorial writers, university economists, and even songwriters joined in ridiculing the useless fins and ostentation of the big cars.

One famous humorist toasted the *Rambler* as "the greatest invention since the ice cube."

GREYHOUND

The *Greyhound* story has its beginning in the rugged Mesabi Iron Ore Range in Minnesota. There, in 1914, a young Swedish miner named Carl Eric Wickman opened an agency for the *Hupmobile* auto. Young Wickman failed to make a single sale, and rather than return to his job as a diamond drill operator, he used the seven-passenger *Hupmobile* to transport miners between the small towns of Hibbing and Alice. For this four-mile jaunt over treacherous and unpaved roads, he charged 15 cents, or 25 cents for a round trip. The first day's receipts netted $2.25.

The "jitney bus" proved to be popular with the miners, and was "stretched" to accommodate two additional seats, with extra passengers clinging to the running boards and fenders. Unable to take care of all the business coming his way, Wickman induced a blacksmith friend to go into partnership with him, and together they bought another *Hupmobile*. The new car was enlarged to seat ten passengers, and the two partners expanded their routes.

In 1915, these two pioneers offered the first long-distance trek —a ninety-mile stretch between Hibbing and Duluth. In fierce winter weather drivers were equipped with block and tackle and snow shovels, and their courageous passengers were provided with lap robes and hot bricks for their feet. By 1916 the partnership had grown to a five-member firm with five buses, each member serving as a director, an officer, and a bus driver.

Because of dusty road conditions in those early days, the buses were painted battleship gray. The addition of extra seats to the touring cars had given them an extremely long, slim look. One day an inn-keeper whose hotel was located along the route remarked to Carl Wickman that the buses looked "just like greyhound dogs streaking by." The name caught on, and Wickman adopted the slogan, *Ride the Greyhounds.*

Eventually, *Greyhound* was incorporated into the name of the company. The nickel-and-dime venture that began as a one-man, four-mile route in Minnesota fifty years ago is today the world's largest inter-city passenger carrier—with over six thousand buses chalking up more than half a billion miles every year.

CHEVROLET

One day, in the first decade of this century, behind the *Buick* plant which he headed in Flint, Michigan, William C. Durant, fabulous boy-wonder of the emerging automobile industry, raced two daring young Frenchmen in an automobile meet—Louis Chevrolet and his brother Arthur. On the dirt track, "with the wind whistling through his magnificent mustache" Louis Chevrolet came in first. To Louis' disgust, Durant then hired brother Arthur as his personal chauffeur because he had taken no crazy chances in the race.

Louis went on to fame and headlines as a daredevil racing driver, but, with Durant's backing, also designed an engine for a light car, and in 1911 directed the assembling of the *Classic Six*—a five passenger touring car. Because race drivers were heroes of the day and also because he felt the name Chevrolet "had a musical sound and the romance of foreign origin" Durant called his new car—and the company organized to make it—*Chevrolet*. The famous shaped name plate appeared in 1913 on the Baby Grand touring car and the Royal Mail roadster. Whence came the design for the name plate? From a scrap of wallpaper which world-traveler Durant had torn from the walls in a French hotel room years before. Showing it to friends he explained he thought it would make a good name plate for a car—that "it appeared to be marching off into infinity." And it appears he was right.

PHILLIPS 66

Many stories abound about the christening of *Phillips 66* gasoline. The Phillips Petroleum Company became so interested in these stories and their origins that it finally made a collection of them. Six of the most oft-repeated versions (all false) are:

(1) Frank and L. E. Phillips, brothers and founders of the company, had only 66 dollars left between them when they hit their first oil well. Immediately they decided that if ever they marketed gasoline they would call it 66. Fact: Although the Phillips brothers did have a run of nine dry holes before they struck their first gusher, they were not exactly broke when their first well came in. They started the company in 1917 as a producer of crude oil and natural gasoline with assets of 3 million dollars and 27 employees. (Today assets total more than a billion and a half dollars and there are 25,000 employees.)

(2) Frank Phillips, one of the founders, was 66 years old when he organized the company. Fact: He was actually 44.

(3) The first *Phillips* 66 gasoline was 66 octane. Fact: the manner of determining octane ratings was not adopted until five years after the name was selected.

(4) When *Phillips* started service station operations in Wisconsin, a state law required that the gravity of the gasoline be posted on the pumps. Most gasolines at the time had gravities in the low 60's, but *Phillips* offered a superior 66 gravity. Fact: *Phillips* didn't start marketing in Wisconsin until 1929. The 66 trademark was created in 1927.

(5) A *Phillips* official won the company's first refinery in a dice game when he rolled double sixes. Fact: The company's first refinery was purchased by the company in 1927.

(6) When the first *Phillips* station's opening day came to a close, the dealer noted he had sold 66 gallons of gasoline. "Boy!" he reputedly said, "66 is our lucky number." Fact: That first station sold 12,000 gallons of gasoline on opening day.

The real facts about the naming of *Phillips* 66 are, however, a matter of record, and it is certainly an interesting coincidence the way the number 66 kept popping up when the company was ready to market its first gasoline, and had everything prepared except a name!

The gasoline's fuel gravity rating was indeed close to 66, but company scientists objected to that tie-in. The company's refinery was near U.S. Highway 66, which had terminal points at Amarillo,

Rambler covered the countryside with more than 5,000 road signs giving directions and distances. Each sign was, of course, prominently inscribed with the word, "Rambler." Before this highly successful promotional gimmick a driver had to find his way from town to town by asking the nearest farmer.

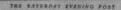

Above: A 1922 advertisement announcing the 1923 Chevrolet models.
Opposite: A 1904 Ford advertisement.

A good name is better than promises

THE FORD

has a reputation for reliability second to no motor car in the world. For the professional or business man who needs a machine for everyday use, **THE FORD** stands pro-eminent as "The Car of Satisfaction." Verified facts are better than "claims."

> **10 H. P. double opposed horizontal motor, cylinder head and water jacket in one piece (no packed joints).**
> **Planetary transmission in oil-tight, dust-proof case.**

The perfected construction of The Ford is the result of 13 years' actual experience in building gasoline automobiles. DON'T EXPERIMENT—JUST BUY A FORD.

Full particulars and catalogue for the asking.

FORD MOTOR CO.
DETROIT. MICH.

W. L. JUDSON.
FASTENING FOR SHOES.

No. 557,207.   Patented Mar. 31, 1896.

Fig.1.

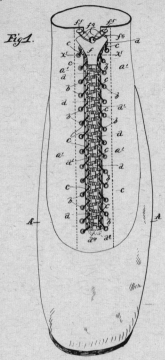

Witnesses.
E. F. Elmore
Frank D. Merchant,

Inventor.
Whitcomb L. Judson
By his Attorney,
Jas. P. Williamson.

The first patent for the incredibly complicated slide fastener, forerunner of the modern zipper, was issued in 1893. The above patent was issued for a refinement of the original invention.

W. L. JUDSON.
FASTENING FOR SHOES.

No. 557,207.   Patented Mar. 31, 1896.

Fig. 3.

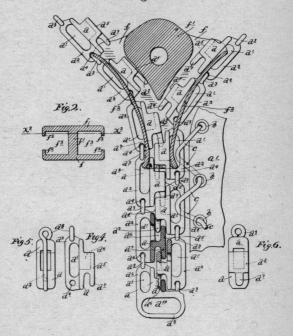

Fig. 2.

Fig. 5.   *Fig. 4.*

Fig. 6.

Witnesses.
E. F. Elmore
Frank D. Merchant.

Inventor.
Whitcomb L. Judson.
By his attorney,
Jas. F. Williamson

A detailed drawing of the "Fastening For Shoes" shown on opposite page.

From *Pioneer Press*, St. Paul, Minn.
Educational Sheet distributed by Minnesota State Board of Health.

Hair-raising illustrations like the one above were used to dramatize the danger of the public tin dipper. The early success of what is now Dixie Cup was closely linked to a growing awareness of the necessity for stricter sanitary measures. The railroads were among the first to crusade for the abolishment of the public drinking vessel.

Our Individual Cup
Dispenser—one of
the thousands in use
on leading railroads
PVBLIC CVP VENDOR CO.
NEW YORK

Community Plate introduced the first "pretty girl" advertising in 1910 when it commissioned one of the most famous commercial artists of the day, Coles Phillips, to do a series of full page advertisements in popular magazines.

Texas, and Chicago, Illinois, and which area was envisioned as the backbone of the *Phillips* marketing area. However, early tentative suggestions to combine the numerals 66 with Phillips as a name for the new gasoline met with a cool reception even though there was a current fad of combining numerals with a word to form a trade name.

Time was running out. A special executive committee session was called for the sole purpose of settling the question of a name. On the very eve of the meeting, a *Phillips* official was returning to headquarters in a company car being used to road test the new gasoline. "This car goes like 60 with our new gas," he remarked to the driver, who, glancing at the speedometer, said excitedly, "Sixty, nothing! We're doing 66!" At the conference the next day someone asked where this incident occurred. The reply was, "Near Tulsa —on Highway 66." That did it! Quickly a unanimous vote for *Phillip 66* was cast, and on November 19, 1927, it was introduced to the public at the company's first service station located in Wichita, Kansas.

And how about the forward slant of those sixes? Well, the most frequently repeated version is—they are meant to reflect the "fast starting" characteristics of the gasoline. Fact: The Phillips Company says that's one story they're just not going to debunk!

COOK'S TOUR

When your host invites you on a "Cook's tour," it may mean anything from an examination of his recently renovated attic to a detailed investigation of his yet unfinished basement. You may even vaguely associate the phrase with some sort of culinary briefing, but the oft-quoted "Cook's tour" actually has its roots in the world's oldest and largest travel organization.

Thomas Cook, an English printer by trade, and a temperance worker by conviction, was walking to a "dry" meeting to be held at Leicester. On the way he passed a billboard poster announcing that the Midlands County Railway had opened a rail extension between Loughborough and Leicester. It occurred to him that the steam engine could be profitably harnessed to the temperance cause, and he promptly persuaded the railroad company to substantially reduce its fare in return for his guarantee of five hundred passengers to travel the newly opened rail extension—which normally carried only one-tenth that number.

Cook made good his word, and on July 5, 1841, 570 teetotalers boarded an open rail carriage at Leicester Station—bound for a temperance conclave at Loughborough. Cost: fourteen cents for the round trip of forty-eight miles.

Thomas Cook's phenomenal travel empire had begun. Other societies soon solicited the travel impresario to arrange their excursions. He organized tours into the "wilds" of Scotland, and in 1851 brought 165,000 visitors to the Crystal Palace Exposition, a world's fair in London. In those days a visit to a foreign country was a major undertaking, and crowds of relatives would gather to see their brave travelers off amid many solemn farewells, admonitions and tears.

Cook's "tour escorts" led the adventure-minded little groups through strange places and gave a running commentary on *every* town, statue or scene. These briefings were so thorough and complete that the descriptions themselves became famous. Cook's fame reached such gigantic proportions during the early days of travel that to take any type of pleasure trip was the same as saying you were going on a "Cook's tour," and the phrase itself became a household word.

An alert and vigorous man to the end, Thomas Cook lived to the age of eighty-four, and attributed his longevity in equal proportions to "globe-trotting and temperance." But not even this venturesome, imaginative man could have foreseen that his first "Cook's tour" from Leicester to Loughborough would launch the fabulous billion-dollar travel industry we know today.

SHELL OIL COMPANY

The *Shell Oil* story began one hot summer day more than a hundred years ago in London, where Marcus Samuel owned a small novelty shop. Marcus' children were being given a holiday at the seashore, and they were fascinated with the beautiful shells they found on the beach. They amused themselves by fastening these shells to their empty lunch boxes and they proudly exhibited their handiwork to their father. Marcus was delighted with the pretty "shell boxes." Confident the idea would also catch the fancy of his customers, he made up a number of the boxes and labeled them from the various popular resorts where the shells were found. They were soon selling in stores all along the coast.

Ladies of that era were fond of knickknacks of every description, and for them Marcus imported fancy polished shells from other countries. The little curio shop acquired a wide reputation as "The Shell Shop," and Marcus' name became synonymous with conchology.

Profits soared when he found a commercial market for shells in the manufacture of mother-of-pearl, and by 1830 he had also built up a large international trade in Oriental curios and copra. When barreled kerosene was added to the growing cargo list, it brought rapid expansion, and the world-wide activities of "The Shell Shop" were consolidated under the name of Shell Transport and Trading Company.

From this the great *Shell Oil* Company evolved, and because some seashore shells once caught the fancy of a novelty dealer's children, the famous Shell emblem, the Pecten, is seen today all over the world on service stations, trucks, chemical plants—recognized by millions of people in every walk of life.

POTPOURRI

COMMUNITY PLATE

One of the most interesting stories in all brand name lore—that of *Community Plate* silverware—has its origin in the wake of a great tide of revivalism that swept America in the 1830's. Among the whole new crop of religious communities and cults that sprang up was one led by John Humphrey Noyes in Putney, Vermont. Noyes preached that the Second Coming of Christ occurred at the time of the destruction of Jerusalem in 70 A.D., and that man could therefore no longer pursue his old course of sin and repentance because he had already been redeemed. Consequently, he must strive for a state of perfection in his daily life, and this could best be achieved by eliminating any incentive for selfishness. "Family pride" motivated much of man's self-seeking, Noyes said, so personal property should be given over to the community for the common good. Any claim or rights over the lives of anyone else—including those of marriage and the individual rearing of children—must also be forfeit.

Seven years after their first meeting as a simple Bible Class in 1839, the little group organized the Putney Community to put John Noyes' doctrine into practice. They had prepared themselves for all the implications of communal living, but not for the intense hostility of the outraged citizens of Putney, who managed to break up their community within two years of its formation.

Meanwhile, on old Indian lands along Oneida Creek in central New York State, the families of a sawmill owner, Jonathan Burt, and a farmer, Joseph Ackley, had united into a communal association, and they invited John Noyes and his followers to join them, with Noyes as their leader.

Noyes accepted the invitation, and arrived with $100,000 and about 25 of his closest adherents. This marked the beginning of the Oneida Community, an experiment in communal living that was to last for thirty years.

The Community prospered from its beginning. In three years time there were 300 converts living there. They were mostly farmers and mechanics and by the end of 1849 they had moved into their first communal building which they built themselves from timber cut on their new farms. Later, a magnificent Mansion House, still a showplace of the Oneida company today, replaced it, but life inside was much the same as in that first frame dwelling.

Everyone, including the children, contributed to the communal life. Newborn babies stayed in their mothers' care until they were able to walk but from then on they were put into "The Children's House," a section of the great, rambling Mansion House given over entirely to the rearing of children and run by the men and women whom the Community judged best qualified. The children were taught that the whole Community was their "family." They still visited their parents individually once or twice a week but it was the family life of the Community as a whole that they accepted as the focal point of their lives.

One characteristic of Noyes' theory, then a radical idea, was the equality of women and men, and, insofar as possible, men and women shared alike in the work of barn and field, pantry and kitchen. One result of this arrangement was that the men, suddenly confronted with tedious household chores, invented many labor-saving devices. Forty years before such things came into general use, the Oneida Community laundry and kitchen were equipped with washing machines, dishwashers, a machine for paring apples, and another for washing vegetables.

Although they were aware of the inevitable variations in human abilities, the Oneida Community shared a fundamental belief in the dignity of all work and they regarded all classes of work as being equally honorable. A man who did his work well, whether he was a kitchen assistant or a factory superintendent, received the same recognition and respect. (John Noyes himself divided his day between the bag factory and the trap shop where he tended a common forge.) This was a logical attitude in a society where it was so apparent how directly the work of each person affected the welfare of the whole. Out of it grew an active sense of participation that proved one of the strongest factors in the success and harmony of the Community. Community affairs were managed through numerous committees and disciplinary measures were also the work of committees. A wayward member sat in complete silence while his good points as well as his bad ones were assessed. The backslider was then given the opportunity to defend himself, and criticize his accusers in turn. Because of this opportunity of its members to air their grievances the Community was singularly free from back-biting and scandal-mongering.

In the beginning, the Oneida group had expected to make their living entirely from the land but they found that agriculture alone would not support them, and they turned to packing and canning a part of their own crops for sale on the "outside." This venture proved so successful that the Community soon turned its efforts toward other commercial enterprises, including the manufacture of the *Newhouse* trap (named for the member who began it, Sewell Newhouse), and it became the standard in the United States and Canada, and then all over the world. By 1860 it was a $100,000 enterprise.

It was in 1877 that the Oneida Community embarked on the manufacture of tableware. It began through a branch Community that had been established at Wallingford, Connecticut, in 1852. The Wallingford group manufactured ungraded, tinned iron spoons in two patterns—Lily and Oval—and these two iron spoons were the direct ancestors of *Community Plate*.

As the scope of their commercial enterprises widened, it became necessary to hire "outside" labor for the shops and factories. The Community paid liberal wages, and there was no difficulty in recruiting people to work. As early as 1870 there were over two hundred "outsiders" on the payroll, and the influence of these people eventually contributed to the dissolution of the Community.

Another contributing factor to the dissolution of the Oneida Community was the fact that it sent its youngsters outside to college. Undoubtedly some of them returned with the first seeds of doubt about their religious beliefs, but, strangely enough, the Community was passionately interested in education (which it called "improvement") and Noyes himself encouraged the practice of sending boys and girls to the outside for their "improvement"— possibly because he foresaw the ultimate breaking up of the Community as a social experiment and he wanted its children to be prepared for life on the outside.

It was fortunate for the younger children who were born in the high tide of the Community's prosperity, that John Noyes had had this foresight because by the time they returned from college the Oneida Community had been dissolved and its assets distributed among its members as a joint-stock company.

The Oneida Community's conversion from a communal society to a joint-stock organization was inevitable, partly because of internal strife, accelerated by the influence of outside labor and outside education for its young, and partly because of outside pressure and growing criticism of the Community itself. When dissolution came it was a painful wrench for many of the older members who had spent the better part of their lives building the Oneida Community, but the property division and settlement was accomplished in a spirit of such fairness and unanimity that no voice was ever raised against it.

The joint company that emerged, Oneida Community Limited, was composed of the old Community's five manufacturing enterprises—canned fruit, traps, sewing silk, silverware, and chains— and had a capital of $600,000. Direction of the company was given to a board of nine men, seven of whom were John Noyes' closest and most trusted associates. After his death in 1886, however, the group began to disintegrate. Age and resistance to change took its toll, and the company found itself in serious financial straits.

The credit for its rescue and rebuilding belongs to a group of young men—headed by John Noyes' son, Pierrepont—who had been reared in the Children's House. At the time young Noyes returned to assume management of the foundering Oneida Community Company, he had already established himself as a wholesaler of silverware in New York City and was well on the way to personal success and wealth. In later years, Pierrepont Noyes said the decision he made to return to Oneida was made one day as he walked home through Central Park. He suddenly realized that the mere possession of wealth would never bring him happiness; that he did not really want to become just another rich man. At that time he was serving on the board of the Oneida Company and he had given much thought to the effect its failure would have on the older members of the Community who had been his father's friends and followers and who were now financially dependent on the company. By the end of the year, he and his wife (who had also been reared in the Children's House) decided that their lives belonged to the Oneida Company and its community.

When Pierrepont returned to Oneida, he and the closely-knit group of young men who surrounded him fought the Old Guard tooth and nail for control, and won. It was they who made the decision to concentrate the entire resources of the company on the manufacture and sale of *Community Plate* silverware, because of the five enterprises comprising the company, *Community Plate* alone had the potential for expansion and development they sought for the company.

The manufacture of all plated silver sold in America in those days was practically a monopoly, and in order to overcome it, Pierrepont decided to make a better plate than had ever been made before. The standard of the day was a 2-ounce plate, so Pierrepont introduced Oneida's "triple plus"—a 6-ounce plate with an overlay (an additional layer of pure silver on the points of greatest wear). Sales rose steadily, and within five years competitors were forced to follow Oneida's lead. In 1910 *Community Plate* introduced the first "pretty girl" advertising done in America with a series of full-page ads by artist Coles Phillips. Sales again spiraled and Pierrepont supplemented the series by initiating the use of photographs and endorsements by leading socialites and celebrities of the day.

Oneida Community Limited grew into an enterprise larger than its original directors ever dreamed of. Pierrepont Noyes remained at its helm for 27 years and then continued to live in retirement in the beautiful Mansion House.

In 1935 "Community" was dropped from the company name to prevent confusion in advertising. There was a sense of nostalgia and sadness among the older members at this change, but the old *Community Plate* name itself was retained, and it is today one of the two top-selling brands of silverplate ware on the market.

KODAK

Modern photography began in June, 1888, when George Eastman introduced a new kind of camera—the *Kodak*. It was a box
type camera, small and light, and loaded with a roll of stripping
paper long enough for a hundred exposures (transparent film was
introduced the following year). The price of the camera loaded,
and including a shoulder strap and case, was $25. After exposure
the camera was sent to Rochester, New York, where the exposed
strip was removed, developed and printed, and a new one inserted
at a charge of $10.

Before George Eastman's *Kodak*, taking pictures was not a popular hobby. The amateur photographic equipment that Eastman
himself began with was, as he later described it, "a packhorse load."
It consisted of all the paraphernalia of the wet plate days (so called
because plates were made of glass, coated with a gelatin emulsion,
and had to be exposed while they were still wet). The camera was
as big as a soap box and required a heavy tripod; the dark tent
had to be large enough to get into while spreading emulsion on the
glass plates before exposure, and later for developing the plates.
In addition, there were chemicals, glass tanks, a heavy plate holder;
and a jug of water. There was also a charge of $5 to teach the
novice how to use the equipment.

When Eastman bought his first camera he was 24 years old. His
life had been one of unusual hardship and struggle. Outright
poverty forced him to leave school at the age of 14 to help support
his widowed mother and two sisters, one of whom was crippled by
polio. In the classic Horatio Alger tradition, he worked as a mes-
senger boy for $3 a week in an insurance company where sweep-
ing the floors and emptying cuspidors were part of his duties. The
young boy was devoted to his mother and with grim determination
promised himself to relieve their desperate financial plight. He soon
found another job, also in an insurance company, which paid him
$5 a week. Through his own initiative he found time to help with
office work and at night began studying accounting. By his twentieth birthday, George Eastman had advanced himself to a position
of junior clerk in a Rochester bank. His salary was the munificent
sum of $800 a year.

After working at the bank for four years he felt he had at last earned a vacation. He wanted to go to Santo Domingo and it was the chance suggestion of a fellow employee that George should take pictures of his proposed trip that ultimately led to the modern era of photography.

For some unrecorded reason (probably the expense involved), George didn't make the trek to Santo Domingo but he did buy the camera, with the result that he became completely absorbed in photography. When he read about photographers in England using plates coated with a gelatin emulsion that remained sensitive after they were dry (in contrast to the wet plates which had to be exposed at once), he adapted a formula from one of the British journals and began experimenting with his own emulsions.

At first his efforts to simplify the complicated process of picture-taking was for his own use and personal enjoyment. Before long, however, he saw the great potential in making dry plates for sale to commercial photographers. Typically, he threw himself into the project with his whole heart. He worked at the bank in the daytime and at home in his mother's kitchen at night, mixing and cooking various emulsions. Years later, his mother reminisced of this period that George worked late into the night every day of the week until on Saturday night he would fall into an exhausted sleep until Monday morning, rousing only long enough to eat. Many times, she recalled, her son was so tired that instead of undressing for bed, he would sleep in his clothes on a blanket beside the kitchen stove.

Eastman himself described those first three years of his photographic experiments as the hardest and most harassing of a life that had never been easy. Memories of his early poverty and a deep devotion to his mother provided the incentive that kept him at his experiments, and finally, in April, 1880, using the money he had himself managed to save, George Eastman leased the third floor of a building on State Street in Rochester and went into the business of manufacturing dry plates. There were many difficulties and obstacles. Utter financial collapse was faced at least once when a quantity of dry plates went bad in the hands of dealers. It was only after intensive research and a frantic trip to England that Eastman was able to discover what had gone wrong, and make the plates good.

As soon as the strain of the new venture eased and progress was being made, Eastman again turned his attention to simplifying photography. He concentrated his efforts on replacing the heavy glass plates he was making (used chiefly by professionals for portraiture) with a lighter and more flexible material, and finally succeeded in adapting paper to carry the emulsion. At that time, the idea of its use by amateurs had not occurred to him. Advertisements in 1885 described the process as "a new sensitive film which it is believed will prove an economical and convenient substitute for glass dry plates both for outdoor and studio work."

"When we started out with our scheme of film photography," George Eastman explained, "we expected that everybody who used glass plates would take up films, but we found that the number which did so was relatively small, and in order to make a success we had to reach the general public." To "reach the general public," Eastman made an entirely new kind of camera for the new roll film and he christened it with a name which had never been used before—and one which he coined himself: Kodak. "I chose that name," Mr. Eastman said, "because I knew a trade name must be short, vigorous, incapable of being misspelled to an extent that will destroy its identity, and, in order to satisfy trademark laws, it must mean nothing.

"The letter K had been a favorite with me—it seemed a strong, incisive sort of letter. Therefore, the word I wanted had to start with K. Then it became a question of trying out a great number of combinations of letters that made words starting and ending with K. The word Kodak is the result."

Eastman had studied the dictionary in vain to find a name for the new camera, but today the dictionary contains the word he coined. The tradename was so successful that it was in danger of becoming a generic term. To combat this trend the company adopted the slogan, "Only Eastman makes the Kodak," and to further enhance its corporate identity the curled print trademark was added. Eastman continued his attempts to improve on the paper base in the film, and in 1889 the first Eastman transparent film in rolls was marketed. (This flexible, transparent film, plus apparatus built simultaneously by Thomas Edison in fortunate combination made motion pictures possible.)

In 1891, the amateur transparent film was further improved by spooling it so it could be loaded into the camera by daylight. The camera no longer had to be sent to Rochester to be filled: rolls of film could be bought anywhere.

The development of roll film photography produced a market very different from that which had existed previously. Until the coming of the *Kodak,* the photographer had to be a more or less skilled craftsman; he developed his own negatives and made his own prints, and had to have, therefore, some knowledge of the technical aspects of the subject. The manufacture of film became an industrial operation while thousands of small establishments sprang up to develop films and make prints for the photographer.

In simplifying photography, once a difficult and specialized art, so that anyone could take pictures with a handheld camera simply by pressing a button, George Eastman made photographers of us all. His contribution to photography rivals Gutenberg's invention of movable type as the most facile medium of communication for teaching and spreading knowledge. In medical research, the camera has become the "companion piece to the microscope." In science and industry it is the recording eye for observation and measurement. With the magic of photography the scientist explores and measures the light along the surface of the sun, or photographs atoms in steel or soft silk. Together with the telescope, the camera probes into the sky and reaches into outer space. It has become an instrument of justice, fingerprinting the criminal for absolute identification, and detecting forgeries and altered documents by infrared or ultraviolet plates. The familiar "movies" project art, entertainment and education to millions of people. Photography itself has emerged as an art form.

Paradoxically, there were very few photographs of George Eastman ever taken. He was a shy, reticent man, who, in spite of the accumulation of enormous wealth, remained a modest and unassuming person who could walk down the main street of his home town without being recognized. Many of his gifts to institutions were anonymous. One such gift was the $20 million he gave to Massachusetts Institute of Technology as "Mr. Smith." For several years the mysterious "Mr. Smith" caused quite a bit of speculation and was popularized in an M.I.T. song.

In later years he surrounded himself with the pleasures of life that had been denied him in his youth and middle age. Music and paintings and his great love for the out-of-doors became a significant part of his life. "What we do during our working hours determines what we have; what we do in our leisure hours determines what we are," he often said.

George Eastman also believed with all his heart that the "progress of the world depends almost entirely upon education," and this remarkable man did not wait until after his death to assign his great wealth to "making the world a better place to live." He gave it away during his own lifetime—100 million dollars—to art, education, scientific and medical institutions.

Inventor, technologist, patriotic citizen, philanthropist, George Eastman is one of the comparatively few men who qualify for greatness on the basis of outstanding, constructive and lasting achievements. At the time of his death in 1932, *The New York Times* editorialized: "Eastman was a stupendous factor in the education of the modern world . . . fostering music, endowing learning, supporting science in its researches and teaching . . . helping the lowliest in their struggles toward the light, making his own city a center of the arts and glorifying his own country in the eyes of the world."

In spite of his enormous wealth, however, he remained a man of simple tastes, who never lost his pleasure in working with tools. At his comfortable but unpretentious hunting lodge in North Carolina, he was happily engrossed one day in a menial plumbing task when a guest observed: "George, you're having fun, aren't you?" Replied the man who had been the largest single factor in making photography a science, "I'd rather wipe a lead joint well than do anything I know of."

He never lost the courage that had manifested itself even at the age of 14 when he took on the man-sized job of providing for his mother and sisters. It was still very much in evidence when, years later, on safari in Africa, he calmly filmed a huge rhinoceros as it charged at close range. His white hunter shot the animal at fifteen paces, and it fell five paces from the unflinching Eastman. When asked if he realized that his life had been in jeopardy, his reply was typical of the philosophy that had guided his hugely successful company, "Well, you have to trust in your organization."

MGM AND LEO THE LION

Of all the magical names and personalities that have "thundered across the motion picture screen," none has had greater impact—nor roared louder—than *Metro-Goldwyn-Mayer* and *Leo,* its trademark lion.

Leo owes his theatrical fame to a Polish immigrant who traveled to this country alone at the age of 11. By his thirtieth birthday, the immigrant was the prosperous owner of a successful glove business. His name was Samuel Goldfish—until he became entranced with show business and ultimately had his name changed to conform to that of a company he formed with Archibald and Edgar Selwyn—the Goldwyn Pictures Corporation. The name derived from the first syllable of Goldfish's name and the last syllable of Selwyn's. Judge Learned Hand personally granted Goldfish's request to have his name changed, and remarked: "A self-made man may prefer a self-made name."

When the Goldwyn Company was launched, Sam hired a New York advertising agency to promote both the company and its pictures. The job of dreaming up a suitable trademark was given to a young man in the agency named Howard Dietz. Howard was fresh out of Columbia University and still very much attached to his Alma Mater. One Saturday afternoon he was attending a Columbia football game and as the cheer leaders led the students in a vociferous rendition of their football song, "Roar, Lion, roar!" the team mascot (Leo the lion, naturally) bounded onto the field. Howard, his mind on his first big assignment for the agency, was inspired. What could be more appropriate than to have a lion, King of the Beasts, symbolize the great Goldwyn account. And animals were popular trademarks at the time. Pathé had its rooster, Selig's Bison Company had its buffalo and Metro had its bird—a parrot that tossed the name of the company onto the screen, letter by letter. The mighty lion would top them all.

Sam Goldwyn agreed with Howard; Morris Rosenbaum, a commercial artist, drew up the design and *Leo* the lion was born—born to become famous in his own right as one of the best-known animal trademarks ever devised.

Goldwyn's full-page advertisements were beginning to appear in the *Saturday Evening Post*—a bold innovation meant to appeal to a "discriminating public with taste." The ads proclaimed: "Pictures Built Upon the Strong Foundation of Intelligence and Refinement." Conspicuous in every ad was the regal *Leo,* reposing in a loop of film. In keeping with the arty tone the Goldwyn Company had adopted, Leo's creator, Dietz, came up with a motto in Latin: *Ars Gratia Artis*—"Art is Beholden to the Artists." Goldwyn had unquestionably struck a new note in publicizing films.

The man who brought about the merger that became *Metro-Goldwyn-Mayer* was Marcus Loew of the theatre chain, *Loew's, Inc.* Loew bought the Metro studio (the name of which derived from an abbreviation of "metropolitan") and saw the gigantic possibilities of a company that would unite the Metro and Goldwyn facilities, under the masterminding genius of Louis B. Mayer, who at that time had his own production company. Negotiations got underway in 1924. *Loew's, Inc.* acquired the Goldwyn Pictures Corporation through an exchange of stock and a new company, Metro-Goldwyn Pictures Corporation, was formed. There was only one dissenting voice in the whole deal: that of the aggressively independent Samuel Goldwyn. He withheld his approval and the Goldwyn Company was forced to buy in his shares for cash. The celebrated showman was no longer even a stockholder in the company that bore his chosen name.

Arrangements were worked out with Louis B. Mayer and his associates (one of whom was the immortal Thalberg) to direct production operations of the new Metro-Goldwyn Company. Mayer was given the option of having his pictures for the new studio bear the credit line. "Produced by Louis B. Mayer for the Metro-Goldwyn Corporation" or "Produced by *Metro-Goldwyn-Mayer*." Mayer chose the latter and that's how the familiar name came into being.

Leo retained his exalted position as the trademark for the new combine. The only problem with him was a unique one: there were just too many of him! It seemed that everytime an *M-G-M* official heard about a sleek new lion in town, he immediately issued an order to have it photographed to be substituted "eventually" for the original one, who by now, they reasoned, must be growing old and mangy. "Authentic" Leo's began to pile up. Which was the *real Leo,* asked a devoted and anxious public. To settle the controversy once and for all, *M-G-M* publicity came out with the heart-warming tale that as a reward for his distinguished and valued service, *Leo* was to be returned to his native land of Africa, and set free. This "heartwarming tale" backfired, and to the studio's consternation and alarm, it was swamped with a storm of protests from animal lovers all over the world. A lion reared in captivity, they said, as *Leo* had been, pampered and petted all its life, wouldn't have a chance for survival in the wild jungle. He would either starve to death or be murdered by his jungle relatives. Harassed press agents quickly revised the story. *Leo* would not be sent back to Africa after all; instead, he would be pensioned off to live out his days in the pleasant and peaceful surroundings of a palatial zoo. The truth was, no one at *M-G-M* had the remotest idea *which* Leo all the fuss was about.

By the late twenties the "talkies" era had arrived, and *Metro-Goldwyn-Mayer*'s first picture with sound effects was *White Shadows in the South Seas*. It had been filmed as a silent picture and then sent to the Victor Recording Company to have its musical score synchronized, and sound effects—such as waves breaking on the shore—dubbed in. There was a single word of dialogue: "Hello," and that too was dubbed in.

It was perhaps a clumsy attempt, but when it made its debut at the Astor Theatre in New York on July 31, 1928, it was a tremendous success and a new entertainment device was born.

White Shadows in the South Seas had another distinction, too. It was *Leo*'s "sound" debut, and he made the transition in fine form. The magnificent bass growl left nothing to be desired, either in volume or ferocity, and from that night on, his roar has been heard round the world.

DIXIE CUPS

The *Dixie Cup*—one of the best known and most affectionately regarded of all brand names—has a history as appealing as its name.

It all began in 1908 when young and enterprising Hugh Moore started a business to which he gave the rather imposing name of The American Water Supply Company of New England. The product he had to sell was *a drink of water*. He had developed a vending machine that for the price of one penny would dispense a cool drink of pure water in an individual paper cup (an awkward, two-piece construction with a flat bottom and rough brim).

This old penny vendor was a tall, white porcelain device divided into three parts. The upper part was for ice, the middle for waste water, and the lower part to hold discarded cups. Early descriptive literature was careful to point out that cups could not be restored to the machine; therefore, each purchaser was assured of a clean, new cup that became his very own property.

However, the water was the commodity being sold, and the cup only incidental. It was on this premise that the founder of the Anti-Saloon League vociferously endorsed the new-fangled contraption that dispensed a health-giving, soul-saving drink of water. He proclaimed that thousands of men were lured into saloons simply for a good drink of water but once inside were faced with "terrible temptation."

Several machines were set up (trolley line transfer corners being advertised as ideal locations for the new water vendors), and a few drinks of water were sold, but the ingenious young Hugh quickly saw the potentialities in the crudely fashioned, but sanitary, little paper cup itself, for these were the days of the old public tin dipper —seldom washed, never sterilized, and used indiscriminately by everyone, the diseased as well as the healthy. The knell of doom had already begun to sound for the dipper in the person of Dr. Samuel Crumbine, a young health officer fresh out of the cow town of Dodge City (where he'd spent most of his time extracting bullets from belligerent cowboys), and who was ardently crusading for a law to ban forever the public drinking vessel.

The stage was set for Hugh Moore and his paper drinking cups. But he lacked the capital to establish a business that could make enough paper cups to abolish the dipper. Determinedly, he and an associate, Lawrence Luellen, descended on New York to find the financial backing they so desperately needed. Their assets consisted mainly of an idea and a few hand-made samples. They had neither the production facilities nor the definite promise of a market to interest investors. Day after day they tramped the streets. Everyone they approached scoffed at the mere thought that paper cup manufacturing would ever become a successful industry, or that the old tin dipper was really a danger to anyone's health. There was more than a hint of resentment as prospect after prospect suggested that what had been good enough for Pa was good enough for them, and the old tin dipper had been just fine with Pa. Finally, when it appeared that theirs was indeed a lost cause, an investment banker with an over-active imagination came to the rescue. So horrified was he by Mr. Moore's hair-raising account of the possibility of a quick and agonizing death as the result of drinking from a public dipper, that he promptly invested $200,000 in the venture, incorporated as The Public Cup Vendor Company in 1909.

That same year Dixie received its first important support in combating the menace of the public drinking vessel: Kansas passed the first state law abolishing it after Dr. Crumbine had devoted five years to convincing the people of his state, and the state legislature, that "disease was communicated to well persons who drank from the same cup as did, for instance, tubercular persons." About the same time, Professor Alvin Davison of Lafayette College put some public drinking cups under the microscope and published a report of the germs of diseases known to be communicable found on the cups.

The publicity given Dr. Crumbine's campaign and to Dr. Davison's survey, caused state after state to pass laws prohibiting the use of a common drinking vessel in public places. Meanwhile, Hugh Moore and his associates were using the profits gained from the success of the penny vending machines to create and market the *free* dispenser with the paper cup itself now the product to be sold, as it soon became a matter of necessity to replace the communal tumbler in offices, schools and other places where the penny vendor was not practical.

By 1910 the name of the company had been changed to The Individual Drinking Cup Company, a natural selection since the earliest advertisements about the product referred to it as an "individual drinking cup." But despite the anti-dipper publicity and the glowing literature describing the Individual Drinking Cup, there was still a tremendous selling job to be done and Hugh was still being thrown unceremoniously out of prospective customers' offices. The general manager of a leading railroad company told him in an icy, barely controlled voice: "Look, son, I am 65 years old. I have drunk out of rusty tin dippers and out of my hands—unwashed—from a stream and I'm in good health. What's more, I'm trying to run a railroad and durned busy, and I'd appreciate it if you'd pick up your gadgets and get out of here!"

But as more and more states jumped on the legislative bandwagon, the railroads did see the advantage of the paper cup, and they, along with many consumer magazines, crusaded for it.

In 1912 Mr. Moore and his associates changed the name of their company, and their product, to *Health Kups*. Cup-making machines were improved and around 1915 the soda fountain, that gathering place of youth, began to see the benefit of using disposable paper cups. Convincing the soda fountain market was a slow process, however, and only those public spirited enough to pay extra to safeguard their customers' health bought them. One oldtimer recalls that the weekly wages of a dishwasher was less than the cost of 1000 paper cups for sodas. For a long time to come, sanitary paper cups would cost more than unsterilized drinking glasses, and a law requiring the sterilization of public eating and drinking vessels was then nowhere in sight.

In spite of the fact that the name, *Health Kups,* had been carefully selected, and even had the approval and blessing of the advertising genius of the age, the public remained cool and the name simply didn't "catch on." Then, in 1919, Hugh Moore, unhappy himself with the name that sounded so antiseptic and clinical, was inspired to change it to one that succeeded so well it became, and has remained ever since, a household word—*Dixie Cup*.

How did Hugh Moore happen to choose this name? His next door neighbor in the downtown loft building where he was producing his *Health Kups* was the Dixie Doll Company. One day after laboriously climbing the stairs to the loft, he stopped to chat with the doll maker. As they talked, Hugh recalled a story he had first heard as a boy in Kansas—how, over a hundred years ago, in the days when each individual bank could issue its own money, one particular bank in New Orleans had a great reputation among the Mississippi River traders for the strength of its currency. The $10 value notes had the word, *dix* (meaning "ten" in French) printed in big letters across the face of the bill. The riverboat men referred to these notes as "dixies," and were often heard to say they were "going down the river to pick up some dixies." Legend has it that the phrase, "Dixie Land" came to mean all the territory where the *dix* notes were held in such high esteem.

The word "Dixie" printed on his friend's door had reminded Hugh of the old Louisiana bank note story. Those "dixies" had, he mused, all the qualities he would like to have associated with his *Health Kups*. It was a short name. It looked well in print; it flipped off the tongue easily, and even had historical background. It was the perfect name. Would the doll maker mind if he used it? No, his friend did not mind, and from that moment, the name of *Dixie Cup* was destined to write its own legend and become one of the best-known of all brand names.

The first tremendous expansion came in 1923. The ice cream industry at that time sold only in bulk lots. It was seeking a way to increase ice cream consumption. *Dixie Cup* was appealed to for help, and went to work. It first produced a five-ounce *Dixie Cup* with a plain lid that was "pushed" into the cup. It was a dismal failure, quickly disintegrating after being filled with ice cream. *Dixie Cup* went back to work, and some obstacles were gradually overcome, but serious problems continued to rise. A large ice cream manufacturer purchased a special machine to fill *Dixie Cups* automatically and eliminate the costly, time-consuming process of filling them by hand. The experiment was another failure, resulting in crushed *Dixie Cups* and much wasted ice cream.

Dixie ingenuity and research then went to work in earnest, risking its hard-earned profits in a big gamble on this new market. In less than two years, an entirely satisfactory and successful, 2½ ounce *Dixie Cup* was produced for ice cream, thereby giving the ice cream industry its first and most powerful means of competing with bottled soft drinks and candy bars.

The "individual drinking cup"—an idea at which the public laughed heartily and was apathetic when not resistant—has undoubtedly saved many lives, and continues to safeguard public health; it has contributed to the wealth of the nation and extends leisure time and health protection in many homes.

Dixie Cup, today a division of The American Can Company, continues to expand. It has contributed numerous "firsts" to the industry, and it has developed multiple uses for hundreds of variants on its original product—but the one which many American youngsters (and most oldsters) still regard as synonymous with ice cream —is the all time favorite *Dixie Cup* for ice cream.

TALON ZIPPER

It seems incredible that the *idea* of the common zipper occurred to anyone in the first place. That is exactly what happened, however, and when the first patent for the forerunner of the zipper was granted, there was absolutely nothing in the patent office files even remotely resembling it.

The success and acceptance of the zipper was preceded by twenty years of hard work, bitter disappointment, technical and near financial failure. Its ultimate triumph was due to the faith, ingenuity and perseverance of three men: Whitcomb L. Judson, its versatile inventor; Colonel Lewis Walker, a civic-minded lawyer and businessman; and Gideon Sundback, a young Swedish electrical engineer.

The story begins with Whitcomb Judson and his fantastic creation of a "Clasp Locker or Unlocker for Shoes," for which he received a patent on August 29, 1893. Whether the invention was the result of a sudden inspiration or years of experimenting is, unfortunately, unknown. However, it seems likely that Judson thought of the device as he bent over the tedious task of lacing and unlacing his shoes, since the illustration accompanying his application for patent pictures the invention applied to shoes, although other articles it could be used on—such as gloves, leggings and corsets—are mentioned.

Very little is known about Whitcomb Judson, except that he was a prolific and talented inventor, receiving a total of 30 patents in his lifetime. In addition to the "clasp locker," and its later improvements, he was granted a patent for a machine with which to manufacture it. Other inventions for which he was awarded patents include internal combustion engines; variable speed transmissions and clutches for automobiles; a tread for traction wheels for use in desert or sandy countries; and a system to use compressed air as the motive power for street railways. In connection with the latter, a company was organized, The Judson Pneumatic Street Rail-

Way Company, and several experimental railways built in New York City and Washington. One of the stockholders in the company was Colonel Lewis Walker, and although it has been reported that Colonel Walker first saw Judson's "slide fastener" at the Chicago World's Fair in 1893, it seems far more likely that he became interested in it through his association with Judson in the street railways venture.

"Colonel" Walker was not really a military man—his title was honorary—he was a shrewd lawyer with great acumen for corporate organization and negotiation.

Colonel Walker was very much impressed with Judson's slide fastener. Even though it was a crude and complicated affair, he saw great possibilities in it, and in 1894 organized the Universal Fastener Company to manufacture and sell it. After two years of further experimentation, a slide fastener bearing the name *Universal* was launched.

The *Universal* was a metallic chain contraption made up of flat, curved hooks in the shape of battle-axes, and joined together by open links. Two of these chains could be brought together (closed) by progressively turning the hooks into the eyes with a slider. The pair of chains was laced into a shoe with ordinary shoe laces. Obviously, it was an extremely awkward feat, but nevertheless, Judson and the Colonel were enthusiastic and optimistic, and wore the *Universal* in their own shoes to publicize and promote it. For a while the fasteners were painstakingly made by hand, but finally at great expense a machine was custom-built to manufacture them. This machine is believed to be the model for which Judson received a patent in 1902. It was so complex and unsatisfactory that the company that built it had to employ two of its own engineers just to keep it operating. After a few years, it was abandoned completely. Meanwhile, the company headquarters had moved from Chicago to Elyria, Ohio, from there to Castasauqua, Pennsylvania, and then to Hoboken, New Jersey. These moves apparently represented the shifting financial affairs of the company.

In 1905 Judson designed a new fastener which was more adaptable to machine manufacture. Instead of being linked together in a chain, the fastening elements were simply clamped about the beaded edge of a fabric tape. Colonel Walker's enthusiasm, which had waned somewhat with the failure of the custom-built machine, waxed high again, and the company was reorganized as the Automatic Hook and Eye Company of Hoboken, New Jersey. The name was taken from the new fastener—the pins on one side being called "hooks" and the openings on the opposite side into which the pins fitted being called "eyes." Judson was an officer of the re-organized company and the Colonel a stockholder.

This was the first slide fastener to actually be marketed to any great extent. Someone (it isn't known who) came up with the name *C-Curity*, and the slogan, *A Pull and It's Done*. The fasteners were sold mostly for skirt plackets and trouser flies. The garment trade frowned heavily on the *C-Curity*, and most of the sales were made directly to the housewife by door-to-door salesmen. The new device was looked on as a novelty, and had some initial success. It sold for 35 cents, and was wrapped with a printed page setting forth elaborate directions for its application and use. An advertisement appearing in 1907 read:

> *A Pull and It's Done*
> *No More Open Skirts*
> *No Old Fashioned Hooks and Eyes or Fasteners*
> *Your Skirt is Always Securely and Neatly Fastened*
> *The C-CURITY Placket Fastener*
> *Ask the Girl!*

"Ask the Girl" proved to be an error, since the *C-Curity* was anything but secure. It had the disconcerting quirk of popping open when a girl sat down and at other times when she least expected it. Furthermore, if not used exactly right, it would catch and tear underclothing, and would, most assuredly, twist all out of shape if it were not removed from the dress or skirt before laundering.

But despite its faults and shortcomings and its limited market, the *C-Curity* was commercial and the company decided to assign an engineer full time to its development and improvement. Gideon Sundback was the young man selected for the job, and his work had a profound effect on the history of the slide fastener, and ultimately, the "zipper."

Gideon Sundback was born in Sweden in 1880, and was educated in Sweden and Germany as an electrical engineer. He served in the Swedish army and then came to this country in 1905 to work as an electrical engineer for Westinghouse Electric and Manufacturing Company in Pittsburgh. A year later, he joined the Automatic Hook and Eye Company as a draftsman and design engineer. He worked on production machinery before he was assigned exclusively to improving the *C-Curity* model. For the next several years his efforts were concentrated on eliminating the *C-Curity*'s tendency to spring open when flexed.

In 1908 Sundback produced an improved model of the *C-Curity*. It was intended primarily for dress plackets and was christened with the somewhat less than inspired name of *Plako*. The company's entire production was shifted to the new model. The garment industry again frowned, and salesmen again peddled the fastener from door to door, and to a few shopkeepers who bought it for resale. Like the *C-Curity*, the slight success *Plako* enjoyed was due to its novelty, and although there had been mechanical improvements the *Plako* was still far from satisfactory. Most of its sales were made in the theatre because of the necessity of quick costume changes.

House to house sales could not sustain the business, and the company teetered on the edge of bankruptcy. Most of the employees left, and the staff dwindled to only two people—Sundback and one clerk. Stockholders lost interest (except Colonel Walker who encouraged young Sundback to keep trying), and the company supplemented its small income by renting out the machine shop and engineering facilities for odd jobs to inventors and manufacturers. The small income derived from these activities enabled the company to stay in existence.

Gideon Sundback, with great tenacity and stubbornness, continued his experiments. He was determined to make a practical and a saleable fastener. The problems caused by the hooks and eyes inspired him to invent a new fastener without hooks and eyes. It was a radical departure from those previously made, and two patents were granted on the new fastener.

Samples were made up by hand, and it seemed the long search was finally over. Colonel Walker's fertile imagination was fired once again. New capital was raised, and in 1913 a new company, The Hookless Fastener Company, was formed. Colonel Walker took over the presidency—a position he held until his death at the age of 83 in 1938—and plunged wholeheartedly into the new company.

The real estate and plant in Hoboken were sold, and its equipment and personnel moved to the Colonel's cherished Meadville.

But even before production was underway, before the new machinery was completed, it was belatedly discovered that the new fastener, which had been labeled *Hookless No. 1*, was not practical because the corded edge used to replace the hooks wore out too quickly. The new company drifted while Sundback, stunned by the heart-breaking knowledge that the new fastener could not be marketed, returned doggedly to his experiments and started all over again—this time from the beginning. He studied every earlier attempt that had been made, and in 1914 invented, in all essential respects, the modern slide fastener. It was called *Hookless No. 2*, and in addition to the fastener, Sundback invented a machine that would satisfactorily produce it in large quantities. (During the following years, 78 patents were issued to Gideon Sundback relating to slide fasteners and the machinery for making them.)

The first sale of *Hookless No. 2* was made on October 28, 1914. It was for four fasteners at 25 cents each. While the Colonel and Gideon Sundback knew they had at last achieved the slide fastener they envisaged, others were slow to see its merits. Memories of the temperamental *C-Curity* and *Plako* still lingered to plague *Hookless No. 2*. Garment manufacturers steadfastly refused to accept the new slide fastener and tailors waged their own private war against it. The first break came in 1917 when a manufacturer in Brooklyn bought a quantity of them for use on sailors' money belts. That year a total of 24,000 slide fasteners were sold—most of them for the money belts.

The following year, the second break came with the sale of 10,000 *Hookless No. 2*'s to the Navy for use on flying suits. A misguided inventor had made a flying suit, using one of the slide fasteners, and submitted it to the Army for testing. When the test was over, all that had survived was *Hookless No. 2*. A naval officer had witnessed the test also, and when the Navy designed its own flying suit it specified the use of *Hookless No. 2*.

Glove manufacturers went all out for the new fastener, and then they were tried experimentally on tobacco pouches. The tobacco pouches were also a success, and through them *Hookless No. 2* came to the attention of the general public.

The real turning point came in 1923, when the B. F. Goodrich

Company introduced rubber galoshes featuring the *Hookless* slide fastener. *Zipper* was coined by an executive of the Goodrich Company when he was first shown the new boots. He "zipped" them up and down, and, delighted with the smooth operation, exclaimed, "Zip 'er up!"

Zipper was, of course, a natural for the slide fastener, and Goodrich's new galoshes became *Zipper Boots.* The name *Zipper* is a registered trademark owned by the B. F. Goodrich Company for boots, but in the lower-case spelling it has become a generic term for a slide fastener. The first order by Goodrich was in January of 1923 for 150,000 fasteners. With the great popularity of the *Zipper Boots,* the *Hookless Fastener* was finally on its way, and the following years saw tremendous growth and expansion of the company.

In 1928, the company adopted the name *Talon* for its fasteners. It was selected for both its pleasant sound and its connotation of claws or fingers, that grasp and hold securely. In 1937 the name of the company was also changed to *Talon.*

Today there are well over 150 distinct and separate uses for the zipper. In one major plant alone, *Talon* turns out approximately 700 miles of zipper tape every day. Its operations are international and it is the largest manufacturer of zippers in the world.

To the dedicated efforts of three remarkable men—Whitcomb Judson, who had the original idea, Gideon Sundback, who developed it, and Colonel Walker who unceasingly promoted it—we owe the most utilitarian device of our time.

SCOTCH TAPE

The Minnesota Mining and Manufacturing Company might be said to have been founded on a misconception. Its founders, prominent men of affairs, thought they were embarking on a venture to mine "corundum" (used in the manufacture of abrasives) in Minnesota's North Shore country. It took several years to get the operation underway and in the meantime, an inventor-scientist, Edward Goodrich Acheson, had discovered carborundum, an artificial abrasive of carbon and silicon which supplanted natural abrasives in many industrial factories and shops. However, even if Acheson had not appeared on the scene, 3M's (as Minnesota Mining and Manufacturing Company was known from the beginning) "corundum" wasn't corundum at all but a low grade anorthosite unfit for abrasives.

Strangely enough, no one discovered the fact for several years.

One of the stockholders came to the rescue when he induced a wealthy businessman to invest in the company and turn its activities from the mining of would-be corundum to the making of sandpaper. Accordingly, shortly after the turn of the century, 3M moved to Duluth and into a factory that had formerly been a flour mill, a site easily accessible for Lake Superior boats. Orders began to slowly trickle in—the first one recorded was to the South Bend Toy Company in the amount of $2; the second to Fort Madison Chair Company for $4; but the operation was at long last underway.

The birth of the *Scotch* brand came about through another mishap in 1926. At the time, 3M had evolved a two-inch wide masking tape for an automobile manufacturer who used it when painting two-tone automobiles to achieve a clean sharp edge where one color met another. The tape was expensive because of its width and the customer complained. Some bright young 3M fellow came up with the idea of limiting the adhesive coating on the tape to a quarter inch strip on each side rather than coating the entire two-inch width, the point being that by reducing the amount of adhesive, production costs would be lower, and the tape could be sold cheaper. Unfortunately, however, when the tape was not completely coated with adhesive it had a tendency to fall off. Annoyed auto painters complained, and when the 3M salesman called, he was told to "take this Scotch tape back to those bosses of yours and tell them to put adhesive all over it—not just on the edges."

The 3M company immediately did so, but when the salesman again called on the automobile manufacturer he was chidingly asked if he was still selling that "Scotch" tape. He wasn't, but the name stuck long after the error had been corrected and the tape restored to the auto manufacturer's good graces. When pressure-sensitive transparent cellophane tape was invented several years later, it too was given the *Scotch* trade name. Today there are an astonishing 300 varieties of the tape bearing the brand of the tartan.

The Minnesota Mining and Manufacturing Company is one of the great examples of the American free-enterprise system. From a one-room office in Duluth, an abrasive mine nearby, and a reputation as a "good little maker of sandpaper," 3M has expanded into a multi-million dollar industry, employing thousands of people, and marketing over forty separate product lines representing more than a thousand items.